UNIVERSITY OF NORTH CAROLINA AT CHAPEL HILL
DEPARTMENT OF ROMANCE LANGUAGES

NORTH CAROLINA STUDIES
IN THE ROMANCE LANGUAGES AND LITERATURES

Founder: URBAN TIGNER HOLMES
Editor: FRANK A. DOMÍNGUEZ

Distributed by:

UNIVERSITY OF NORTH CAROLINA PRESS
CHAPEL HILL
North Carolina 27515-2288
U.S.A.

NORTH CAROLINA STUDIES IN THE
ROMANCE LANGUAGES AND LITERATURES
Number 287

BUCOLIC METAPHORS:
HISTORY, SUBJECTIVITY, AND GENDER IN THE
EARLY MODERN SPANISH PASTORAL

BUCOLIC METAPHORS:
HISTORY, SUBJECTIVITY, AND GENDER IN THE EARLY MODERN SPANISH PASTORAL

BY

ROSILIE HERNÁNDEZ-PECORARO

CHAPEL HILL

NORTH CAROLINA STUDIES IN THE ROMANCE
LANGUAGES AND LITERATURES
U.N.C. DEPARTMENT OF ROMANCE LANGUAGES

2006

Library of Congress Cataloging-in-Publication Data

Hernández-Pecoraro, Rosilie
  Bucolic metaphors : history, ideology and gender in the early modern Spanish pastoral / by Rosilie Hernández-Pecoraro.
    p. cm. – (North Carolina studies in the Romance languages and literatures ; no. 287).
  Includes bibliographical references.
  ISBN 0-8078-9291-2 (alk. paper)
    1. Spanish fiction–Classical period, 1500-1700–History and criticism. 2. Pastoral fiction, Spanish–History and criticism. 3. Cervantes Saavedra, Miguel de, 1547-1616. Galatea. 4. Montemayor, Jorge de, 1520?-1561. Diana. 5. Women in literature. 6. Metaphor. I. Title.

PQ6147.P3H47 2006
863'.309321734–dc22   2006047152

Cover design: Heidi Perov

© 2006. Department of Romance Languages. The University of North Carolina at Chapel Hill.

ISBN 0-8078-9291-2

DEPÓSITO LEGAL: V. 5.273 - 2006

ARTES GRÁFICAS SOLER, S. L. - LA OLIVERETA, 28 - 46018 VALENCIA
www.graficas-soler.com

A Kevin, amigo y esposo

A Antonia Rosario, niña libre

CONTENTS

	Page
ACKNOWLEDGEMENTS	11
INTRODUCTION	13

CHAPTER 1: PASTORAL METAPHORS: HISTORY AS AN ABSENT CAUSE IN THE SPANISH PASTORAL NOVEL 29

    I. The Ideal vs. the Real: The Pastoral as Symbolic Act 30
    II. *Prados y Palacios*: History Narrativized in *La Diana* and *La Galatea* 44
    III. Historical Subtext and Gendered Subjects 58

CHAPTER 2: PASTORAL ESCAPES: IDEAL SUBJECTIVITY AND COMMUNITY IN MONTEMAYOR'S *LA DIANA* AND CERVANTES'S *LA GALATEA* ... 76

    I. Pastoral Love and the Construction of the Ideal Self 79
    II. Pastoral Communities: What's love got to do with it? 102
    III. Poetic Practice and the Pastoral Community: An Additional Note 121

CHAPTER 3: THE "OTHER" PASTORAL: ALTERNATIVE VERSIONS OF FEMALE SUBJECTIVITY IN *LA DIANA* AND *LA GALATEA* 130

    I. In the Beginning there was Garcilaso: The Second Eclogue and the Pastoral Novel 131
    II. Montemayor's *La Diana* and the Female Subject: Transgression and Reinscription 143
    III. *La Galatea*: The Pastoral Community Revisited 170
    IV. Cervantes Performs the Female Poetic Voice: *Enfadosas Suegras* and other Feminine Complaints in *La Galatea* 180

	Page

CHAPTER 4: THE METAPHOR UNDONE: CERVANTES'S UNMASKING OF THE PASTORAL 197

    I. *La casa de los celos y selvas de Ardenia*: The Pastoral Metaphor Disrupted 202
    II. *Don Quixote*: Parody, Female Agency, and the Undoing of the Pastoral Metaphor 210

WORKS CITED 247

ACKNOWLEDGEMENTS

THIS book could not have been written without the support of a number of individuals. I thank Anne J. Cruz for inspiring my passion for early modern Spanish literature and caringly directing this project in its initial phase as a doctoral dissertation. Since then she has been a mentor, a model colleague, and a faithful friend. She has also been discerning reader, a tough critic, and a tireless cheerleader. This is a debt that I can never fully repay. At the University of California, Irvine Ana Paula Ferreira and Juan Villegas graciously read chapters and gave me insights that to this day remain immensely useful. I would also like to thank my colleagues at California State University, Long Beach, University of Illinois at Urbana-Champaign, and University of Illinois at Chicago for encouraging my research. The diligence and optimism of my research assistant Montserrat Pérez-Toribio has been a true lifesaver. Finally, I am immensely grateful to my family, Hernández and Pecoraro, for their love and stanch faith in my ability to carry this project through.

The University of Illinois at Urbana-Champaign and the University of Illinois at Chicago provided me with valuable time to develop and finish this study. The University of Illinois at Chicago's Underrepresented Faculty Recruitment Grant and the Program for Cultural Cooperation between the Spanish Ministry of Culture and US Universities have materially supported the publication of this book.

The book includes revised and expanded versions of the following previously published essays: "Cervantes's *La Galatea*: Feminine Spaces, Subjects, and Communities." *Pacific Coast Philology*, XXXIII (1998): 15-30; and "The Absence of the Absence of Woman: Cervantes's *Don Quixote* and the Explosion of the Pastoral Tradition." *Cervantes*, XVIII.1 (1998): 24-45. I thank the editors for their permission to incorporate parts of the essays. I would also like to express my gratitude to Frank Domínguez for his initial interest in the manuscript and for caringly seeing it through to its publication.

I dedicate this book to my husband, Kevin, at times soundingboard, at times critic, at times editor, and thank him for his unwavering loyalty, a good measure of perspective, and a keen and always timely sense of humor. And to my daughter, Antonia Rosario, who happily came before the book.

INTRODUCTION

CHARACTERIZED by a profound exploration of the psychology of the lover and masterful mixing of prose and poetry, Spain's first pastoral novel captured the imagination of its time. Behind only *La Celestina* and the *Guzmán de Alfarache* in number of editions, *La Diana* was an instant best-seller.[1] The many imitators of Jorge de Montemayor stand as an important testimony to the genre's widespread appeal. As a form of diversion, the bucolic aesthetic was highly familiar to a court milieu where pastoral themes were integrated into most festivities and celebrations.[2] Moreover, specific references to court life and its members were anecdotally integrated into the plot lines, thinly disguised even if appropriately idealized. Nonetheless, the pastoral's popularity did not only depend on the court readers and their personal identification with specific characters or situations, given that the relevance of any anecdote was quickly lost for all except the most interested of readers. Fashionable as *libros de entretenimiento*, pastoral novels were especially well-liked by young adults, women readers, and *oyentes*.[3] But their

---

[1] The issue of the best-seller in Golden Age literature is a complicated one. As Keith Whinnom and Sara T. Nalle make clear, devotional literature far outsold fiction during the period. In addition, the ranking of the best-sellers above mentioned is offset if one considers the sale of the *Amadís* together with all its continuations by various writers. In this case, the *Amadís* series would be by far at the top of the list.

[2] According to Asunción Rallo, "Todo parece coincidir, sin embargo, en un mismo punto: la interrelación del bucolismo con el ámbito cortesano. La moda pastoril en la corte de Carlos V se reflejaba no sólo en la lírica de los poetas sino en las dramatizaciones, para celebraciones de fiestas tanto profanas como religiosas" ("Introducción," *La Diana* 29).

[3] See Nalle, Elizabeth Rhodes's "Skirting the Men," and Mariló Vigil.

popularity and influence upon the cultural imagination was not limited to this demographic. A notable increase in literacy among all social classes throughout the sixteenth century assisted these novels' mass dissemination and appeal. As Francisco López Estrada has ascertained, the pastoral novel became a vital element of the culture's collective experience: "El género de los libros de pastores representó para un número muy crecido de los súbditos de Felipe II, III y IV una experiencia literaria que, siendo en cada caso personal como siempre es la lectura, alcanzó por el número de repeticiones el rango de colectiva" 'The genre of pastoral novels became for a considerable number of Philip II, III, and IV's subjects a personal reading practice that because of its many repetitions increasingly reached the status of a collective experience' (*Los libros de pastores* 484; my translation). With an audience composed of both the elite and the popular classes, books such as *La Diana* became a common currency for Spanish early modern culture at large.

The pastoral's popularity points toward another interesting aspect of the genre, its potential as a conduct manual–amatory and social– for its readers. In the amatory realm, the pastoral exemplifies an array of relationships that provide idealized parameters for proper attitudes, expectations, and outcomes. Regarding social interactions, the pastoral's communal structure offers what Asunción Rallo describes as, "[un] manual de elegancia, pues ofrece fórmulas de comportamiento y conversación, en un múltiple muestrario de circunstancias" 'an elegance manual, for it offers proper formulas for conversation and comportment, in multiple settings and circumstances' ("Introducción," *La Diana* 32; my translation). Most writers of the era ventured at some point into the bucolic topography, courtiers and their ladies role-played as shepherds in masques and other court festivities, and the wider audience described its social encounters–amatory and fraternal–through the rhetoric of pastoral love. The 'instructive' function of the pastoral gains importance when we consider these texts mediation for their readership of the conflicts and contradictions that pervaded early modern Spanish historical experience.

As cultural artifacts Spanish pastoral novels echo the imaginary horizons of and ideological parameters enacted by early modern Spanish society on a vast scale. The pastoral novel's potential for filtering its current social discourses should be carefully considered, given that in Golden Age studies much of our present working canon enjoyed little circulation at the time. Devotional literature and hagiographies were the reading of choice throughout the sixteenth and seventeenth centuries, a fact made patent in the readers' testimonies and library inventories. The *libros de pastores*–together with the *libros de caballería*–thus clearly provided an alternative textual experience for society at large. The weightiness of the religious texts apparently was offset for the sixteenth-century reading public by the scenic and amatory ideality found in and fostered by the bucolic topography. If one type of literature was meant to direct the soul, the other cultivated those more worldly but integral aspects of human experience: love and a sense of adventure. In practice, religious and secular discourse often contaminate each other, especially when we think of the courtly love rhetoric used and heroic qualities embodied by religious figures; or, no less, when we consider the spiritual connotations upon which Neo-Platonism depended. Nonetheless, religious and idealizing secular literatures do, at least officially, maintain disparate objectives. This opposition often leads us to generally consider the pastoral novel primarily as a form of entertainment, and consequently as only partially and mostly superficially engaged with the social and historical issues of its time. In fact, this interpretative inclination is what usually upholds a description of pastoral literature as escapist. The implications of this critical position are many, but mostly it has, in my opinion, precluded a comprehensive consideration of the many varied and complex ways in which pastoral novels refer to the world beyond their bucolic borders. For this reason, I am interested in examining how Spanish pastoral texts, both directly and obliquely, sort out, respond to, and symbolize the latent anxieties and manifest ideologies of the period. In this study, I examine *La Diana* and three of Cervantes's works–his pastoral novel, *La Galatea*, his play *La casa de los celos*, and his seminal work, *Don Quixote*–to illuminate the relationship of the Spanish pastoral with the historical environment in which it was produced and consumed.

My aim is to expand the analysis of pastoral novels by placing emphasis precisely on the connections these *libros de pastores* maintain with the cultural conditions of sixteenth-century Spain. A number of fundamental questions are, thus, in order. What historical circumstances help shape the symbolism and psychology of the pastoral sojourn? How is this connection between text and its social-historical environment manifested in a highly idealized and abstracted bucolic topography? What social values and ideologies are promoted within what is supposed to be a simple and abstracted rural existence? And how does the relationship between text and socio-historical subtext compromise the ideality this genre struggles to produce? Rather than think of these texts as disengaged entertainment, I propose we read the pastoral as an imaginary literary space where many of the conditions and discourses that framed sixteenth-century Spanish experience are addressed in often circumscribed yet telling ways.

The pastoral mode has been extensively studied from its classical roots in Theocritus and Virgil, to its medieval, early modern and modern examples in the Western tradition. Yet an exact definition of the genre has been hard to achieve due to its varied and often contradictory manifestations and the diverse interpretations that each successive author has privileged within specific literary and historical contexts. As Paul Alpers makes clear, "Apart from the happy confusion of definitions, it is clear to no one, experts or novices, what works count as pastoral or–perhaps a form of the same question–whether pastoral is a historically delimited or permanent literary type" (8). In spite of such "confusion," the literary practice of pastoralism generally involves the representation of an idealized space in nature that situates itself in relation to the *polis* that lies beyond its limits. The symbolic and social relevance of the pastoral has been much contested, especially in Anglo-American criticism. For example, while William Empson sees the pastoral as representing complex human issues in a simple form so as to "give strength to see life clearly and so to adopt a fuller attitude to it" (19), Renato Poggioli views the genre as the representation of a psychological space where "the double longing for innocence and happiness is achieved through a retreat from the world" (1). Its Neoplatonic and Epicurean roots have been examined by Richard Cody and Thomas G. Rosenmeyer respectively, along with the ideological and ethical implications of both philosophies. More recently, Alpers has returned to an Empsonian understanding of the pastoral, proposing a reading of the genre as a 'representative anecdote,' a term borrowed from Kenneth Burke:

> But what connects pastoral works to each other, what makes them a literary "kind," is the way each deals, in its circumstances and for its reasons, with the representative anecdote of herdsmen

and their lives. To say that this is the representative anecdote of pastoral means that pastoral works are representations of shepherds (and, in post-classical literature, shepherdesses) who are felt to be representative of some other or all other men and/or women. But since all terms in this definition are subject to modification or reinterpretation, pastoral is historically diversified and transformed. (26)

The ability of pastoral texts to represent, filter, magnify, and reflect through an idealized lens diverse attitudes and tensions of the period in which they are produced is precisely what makes the genre both complex and fascinating. Annabel Patterson and Terry Gifford build upon and broaden this reading of the mode by emphasizing versatility of the 'anecdote,' its capacity to reflect, critique, and retreat from the ideological tensions that it negotiates. For these reasons, "Pastorals demand alert readings that are capable of making critical judgments about their inner tensions, their contextual functions, their multiple levels of contradictions. They are borderland spaces of activity which can be seen through a number of frames" (Gifford 12). This approach influences my examination of Spanish pastoral texts and the social conditions and ideological propositions they negotiated for an early modern audience.

A historically contextualized and discursive analysis of the pastoral mode finds one of its best known and finely articulated examples in Raymond Williams's *The Country and the City*. Williams bases his interpretation on the premise that pastoral texts manifest a "deep desire for stability, served to evade the actual and bitter contradictions of the time" (60).[4] For Williams, as for many critics that follow his work, the pastoral mode lends itself to the production of an ideologically compromised version of reality. As Patterson makes clear, "It is not what pastoral *is* that should matter to us [...]. [But] rather, to put the agency back where it belongs–how writers, artists, and intellectuals of all persuasions have *used* pastoral for a range of functions and intentions [...]" (7). Gifford similarly concludes:

---

[4] Gifford qualifies how, "For Williams this was an exploitation of the material attractiveness of the rural in order to cover the actual exploitation of the people who lived and worked in the rural landscape" (9). The investigation of the relationship between the idyll and history has also generally guided the work of William Empson, Peter V. Marinelli, Paul Alpers, Annabel Patterson, and Louis Adrian Montrose.

> [T]he pastoral can be a mode of political critique of present society, or it can be a dramatic form of unresolved dialogue about the tensions in that society, or it can be a retreat from politics into an apparently aesthetic landscape that is devoid of conflict and tension. It is this very versatility of the pastoral to both contain and appear to evade tensions and contradictions–between country and city, art and nature, the human and the non-human, our social and our inner selves, our masculine and our feminine selves–that made the form so durable and so fascinating. (11) [5]

By framing the pastoral as a historically bound literary expression, this approach requires that we take into account how this highly formulaic mode takes on and attends to the specific conditions surrounding both its production and consumption. It also asks that we decode and unveil the tensions contained within the bucolic fantasy. Despite its investment into a seamless idealization of nature, love, and rural life, pastoral texts cannot fully contain the contradictions of history. Perhaps Judith Haber has best surmised this problem when she expounds upon how from its origins the pastoral myth has been permeated by an anti-pastoral view of the world:

> In looking back at classical pastoral, however, I found not a stable origin from which later works deviated, but a mode that worked insistently against itself, problematizing both its own definition and stable definitions within its texts [...]. While the term "antipastoral" seemed, therefore, to be clearly reductive from one perspective, it also clearly answered to a fundamental self-contradictoriness within the genre–a contradictoriness that is frequently registered self-consciously in pastoral poems. (1)

The suggestion that the pastoral mode successfully reproduces a pure and undisturbed bucolic ideality is thus always negated. As a result, when we instead examine these texts' symbolic intentions, as well as the fissures and inconsistencies they concurrently manifest, we come closer to a deeper understanding of their historical and so-

---

[5] Gifford echoes Williams's earlier criticism when he states that, "So that even in these developments, of classical and other rural literature, which inaugurate tones and images of an ideal kind, there is almost invariably a tension with other kinds of experience: summer with winter; pleasure with loss; harvest with labour; singing with a journey; past or future with the present" (18).

cial significance. In the process it becomes possible to expose and examine those circumstances that the idyll is meant to negate.

Despite this set of analytical claims, Williams strangely sets aside early modern pastoral literature, claiming that it can tell us little or nothing about the society in which it is produced. While calling attention to the weight of history on eighteenth, nineteenth, and twentieth century pastoral literature, Williams largely tends to see the difficult negotiations of the bucolic retreat reduced to a purely aesthetic form by the court culture of the Renaissance, whereby "these living tensions are excised, until there is nothing countervailing, and selected images stand as themselves: not in a living but in an enameled world" (Gifford 18). The hyperidealized style and form characteristic of the Renaissance pastoral is taken to rule out a relevant connection to the early modern context in which these texts were produced and consumed. In short, despite Williams's contributions to the study of pastoral literature as political and ideological, the Renaissance pastoral is often categorized as existing in a pure aesthetic vacuum.

Generally speaking, this focus on the genre's aesthetic value has also served as a point of departure for the examination of pastoral novels in early modern Spanish criticism. Taking a rather extreme position on the matter, Menéndez Pelayo for example claims for the pastoral a radical and absolute disconnect from historical reality: "Ninguna razón histórica justificaba la aparición del género bucólico: era un puro diletantismo estético" 'No historical reason justifies the rebirth of the bucolic genre: it was pure aesthetic dilettantism' (2:185; my translation). Seminal studies such as Juan Bautista Avalle-Arce's *La novela pastoril española* and López Estrada's *Los libros de pastores en la literatura española* unwittingly perpetuate this assessment, by and large sidestepping the ways in which history and ideology seep into the formal and thematic fabric of texts such as *La Diana* and *La Galatea*. Or to be more exact, when the subject is broached by either author, the conclusions are limited to the occasional appearance of realistic elements in what are supposed to be exclusively idealized topographies. For example, Avalle-Arce offers as examples of historical circumstance in *La Galatea* the following: the shepherds eat regularly, some are university educated, the bucolic space is shared with noblemen and women from the court, and authentic Spanish geographical sites are mentioned (*Novela pastoril* 244). Given the limitations of these examples, for many contemporary Golden Age critics the pastoral novel still remains marginal to any study concerned with the social, economic, and cultural forces that framed early modern experience. This view of pastoral novels incorporates what Gifford, in regards to English pastoral literature, identifies as "a skeptical use of the term 'pastoral' as a pejorative, implying that the pastoral vision is too simplified" (2). Gifford prefaces this account of the genre by pointing out that, "the difference between the textual evidence and the economic reality would be judged too great by the criteria of social reality" (2). Likewise, Spanish pastoral novels have been commonly viewed, especially when compared to the various levels of realism found in the picaresque, the *novelas cortesanas*, and Cervantes's *Don Quixote* and *Novelas Ejemplares*, as a product of an overridingly escapist and aesthetic sensibility. Nonetheless, despite this general trend and as I discuss ahead, there have also been important reconsiderations of the pastoral among Spanish early modern scholars that offer a solid foundation and a point of departure for this book.

A rationale for a historicized reading of the genre is readily available when we take into account the way in which the classical pastoral was put to use in and by the Spanish court. Already by the late fifteenth century we see in Juan del Encina's eclogues a deliberate use of the bucolic fantasy to enhance his position within the house of the Duke of Alba.[6] The insertion of laudable characters that represent either Encina or pertinent members of Alba's court sets an important precedent for the numerous pastoral masques and other theatrical activities in the court of the Catholic kings and their successors. On the function of the pastoral in court life throughout the sixteenth and seventeenth centuries, Teresa Ferrer Valls asserts that,

> No hay más que recordar la utilización del disfraz pastoril por parte de los autores teatrales del primer Renacimiento como instrumento para reclamar todo tipo de beneficios a sus señores, recurso bien estudiado por el propio Salomon y todavía útil en manos de Lope, quien lo empleó para colocarse en sus comedias transmutado en el jardinero Fabio o en el rústico Belardo. (47)

> We have only to remember the use of the pastoral disguise by the theater authors of the first Renaissance as an instrument to reclaim all types of benefits from their lords, a recourse well em-

---

[6] See Ronald Surtz, especially pages 106-7.

ployed by Solomon and still useful for Lope, who used it to place himself in his comedies transmuting into Fabio the gardener or the rustic shepherd Belardo. (my translation)

The bucolic topography, from its very first manifestations in early Renaissance Spanish literature, proves to be a fertile ground upon which to plant the seeds and reap the fruit of personal and political advancement.

Beyond the genre's allowance for politically interested biographical representation and personal homage, the Spanish court and its authors appreciated the ideological range of the bucolic in its allegorization of significant historical and political events. Authors such as J.P. Wickersham Crawford, Ronald Surtz, and more recently and comprehensively Ferrer Valls have documented the extent to which the pastoral form played a part in the symbolic imagination of the court. As Crawford informs us, one of the earliest examples we have is Francisco de Madrid's *Égloga* written in 1494: "It deals with the invasion of Italy by Charles VIII and the consequent repudiation by Spain of the treaty of alliance with France. The interlocutors are three shepherds, two representing Charles and Ferdinand, and a third who tries to make peace" (57). This type of direct allusion to political and military events continues throughout the sixteenth and seventeenth centuries. Some well-documented examples include Martín de Herrera's *Égloga de unos pastores* which refers to the conquest of Orán, and Bachiller de la Pradilla's *Égloga real* which commemorates Charles V's arrival to Spain in 1517 (Surtz 42). Surtz describes the *Égloga real*'s ideological undertone as follows:

> In the first part [...], the Bachiller de la Pradilla mingles indirect praise of his own poetic ability with praise of Charles V. The second part consists of the representation of the homage paid to Charles by the *estados* of Spain. Charles had come to Valladolid in November 1517, and in December he had summoned the Cortes to convene in January of the following year. The play in question was thus performed between the calling of the *Cortes* and their first sessions [...]. Unless one accepts the improbable situation that Pradilla knew nothing of his countrymen's feelings toward their new monarch, the second part of the play is most certainly an example of wishful magic. (110)

In other words, the *Égloga real* is a blatant attempt to influence the *Cortes*'s reception of the new monarch. The pastoral mode, in fact, perfectly serves this political objective by placing within the harmonious confines of the idyll the auspicious reception of a foreign king by his reluctant subjects. Consequently, it should not seem far fetched to speak of the pastoral novel, the mode's most developed expression in early modern Spanish letters, as a genre whose entertainment value is matched by its capacity to negotiate and symbolize the social, political, and economic conflicts and contradictions that permeated Spanish early modern court life, and in many respects society at large.

Following this logic, a number of Spanish critics have taken notice of and closely examined the slippages, contradictions, and negotiations–generic, psychological, and historical–that pastoral novels display, thus creating an important precedent for my own investigations. From this alternative critical perspective, the pastoral is seen as producing a fictional space whose borders are porous and whose ideality is never hermetic. Barbara Mujica, for example, reads *La Diana* as ultimately adopting an anti-utopian stance that is most notably underscored by the figure of Diana as reluctant wife in a marriage of convenience: "She is the link with the real world, in which parental will and jealous husbands are factors to be coped with. Diana is a constant reminder that the pastoral dream is merely a figment of the imagination that corresponds to man's yearning for peace and order" (*Iberian Pastoral Characters* 141). Ruth El Saffar likewise finds in Cervantes's *La Galatea* an inherent tension and violence manifested in the trauma caused by love and the resultant distress of the shepherd-lover. In addition, El Saffar points out the sharp psychological split between male and female characters and the unexpected lack of community in Cervantes's bucolic world. In her reading, any utopian illusions are defeated by the inevitable contamination that the outside world brings to the bower–a development that El Saffar correctly concludes makes possible the pastoral parody in *Don Quixote* (*Beyond Fiction* 44-6). In focusing on the topic of death within Spanish pastoral texts Bruno Damiani and Mujica have together also contributed to this view of the idyll as a fantasy threatened in this case by the presence of sadness and desolation.[7] Indeed, I have

---

[7] See Damiani's articles, as well as Damiani and Mujica's coauthored book, *Et in Arcadia Ego*.

elsewhere examined the toll that violent death exerts upon this imaginary space.⁸

The subject of pastoral texts as historical documents has also been taken up by some early modern Spanish critics and their studies serve as a precedent for my own investigation. Damiani in his *La Diana of Montemayor as Social and Religious Teaching* has set forth a foundation for a historically and socially conscious analysis of the pastoral novel by emphasizing how *La Diana* "reveals an art form that combines pastoral elements with the everyday experiences of the common-sense world" (16). Among the many important points of connection that the critic finds between Montemayor's pastoral novel and its socio-historical context is its autochthonous Spanish setting, its reflection of human time, its occasional treatment of the shepherd's work, and its reflection of court practices and vogues, as well as of the social and religious values of its time. In a similar fashion, Pilar Fernández-Cañadas de Greenwood reads pastoral novels as a fictionalized version of the immediate social and literary concerns of the court milieu.⁹ In her *Unrecognized Precursors of Montemayor's "Diana,"* Elizabeth Rhodes traces more specifically the aspects of Montemayor's religious life and believes in the sources and composition of *La Diana*. Regarding *La Diana* from a markedly materialist perspective, Julio Baena has recently proposed a reading that depends on the contemporary rural economy. Regarding Cervantes's *La Galatea*, Geoffrey Stagg advances the theory of the split composition of the text by linking specific parts of the plot, as well as its literary sources, to the author's biography and historical experience before and after his travels to Italy and his years of captivity in Algiers. Carroll Johnson extends the scope of the relationship between text and history by examining *La Galatea* in the context of the annexation of Portugal in 1580. Although not formally examining *La Galatea*, Diana de Armas Wilson well establishes the way in which all of Cervantes's works are "stimulated by the geographical excitement of a new world" (*Cervantes, the Novel, and the New World* 3).¹⁰ With these studies in mind, Mary Malcolm

---

⁸ See Hernández-Pecoraro, "'Busco la muerte en mi daño, que ella es vida a mi dolencia': diversas manifestaciones de la muerte en *La Galatea*."

⁹ See especially her *Pastoral Poetics*.

¹⁰ Regarding *La Galatea*, De Armas Wilson calls attention to the "Song of Calíope" in Book 6 and its laudatory mention of Ercilla and his *Araucana*, as well as to Cervantes's possible personification of Ercilla himself in the character of the shepherd Lauso. See *Cervantes, the Novel, and the New World*, page 162.

Gaylord has recently argued for a historically aware reading of *La Galatea* stating that "although Galatea's shepherds do not, like Virgil's, talk politics, and though most never stray far from the bosky banks of the River Tagus, Cervantes uses his narrative and poetic means to bring cities, seas and nations beyond the borders of his fictional world into the heart of his pastoral" ("Cervantes' other fiction" 106).

Encouraged by this trend in Spanish pastoral criticism, I propose that we account for the ways in which pastoral texts simultaneously engage and deflect the broader social and historical conditions and contradictions that frame their production and reception. Certainly, I find immensely important the investigation of specific aspects of pastoral texts that can be linked to their author's biography and particular life experiences. Yet, from a broader perspective, this is a genre whose birth and development in Spain is set in the context of an aggressive international imperial policy, as well as an internal transformation in the demographic and economic organization of the city and the country. Harry Sieber has described the basis for the pastoral myth as "a desire to fill the gap between the reality of society (war, the ravages of time, hypocrisy) and the pastoral space which exists only in the minds and fictions of disillusioned "urban" men" (186-7). Rather than this "filling of a gap" between fantasy and reality, I would rather think of the pastoral as a mechanism through which the socio-historical environment, its experience and the ideologies that filter and order that experience for sixteenth and seventeenth-century subjects, is negotiated, represented, cleaned up, made palatable; or what Fredric Jameson has called a process of narrativization and symbolization, which I discuss at length in Chapter One of this book. The pastoral's ability to filter and obliquely depict and ideally reproduce the diverse attitudes and tensions of its time make the genre worth reexamining. As I demonstrate in later chapters, this process of symbolization is not hermetic or wholly satisfying. Yet, by focusing on the potential social and ideological functions of the pastoral novel, I hope to bring to the fore the assumptions and prescriptions that these novels represent for its early modern Spanish audience.

My interest on the pastoral novel, and specifically Montemayor's *La Diana* and Cervantes's *La Galatea*, is variously motivated. Widely popular throughout the Renaissance, the mode is prevalent in the poetry and court theater of the sixteenth century. Yet, it is only in the pastoral novel that the bucolic scene is developed and expanded in such a manner as to analyze fully the symbolic relationship between idyll and history. This is not to say that other Spanish pastoral texts, such as Garcilaso's First and Third Eclogues, do not share a similar symbolic and ideological function. Indeed, Garcilaso's *locus amoenus* brings to the shores of the Tagus an idealized version of the Spanish countryside that conforms to the social and economic expectations and necessities of the aristocracy and the ever-expanding *hidalgo* class. Moreover, Salicio's and Nemoroso's love for Galatea and Elisa promotes a vision of masculine virtue and female ideality that sanctions and elevates this same group's patriarchal values. Still, Garcilaso's First and Third Eclogues are narrowly composed in a Petrarchan fashion where pastoral life is strictly reduced to the immediate longing felt by desolate lovers and mythological figures. As such, this poetic form substantially limits my ability to explore in an extensive manner the social, economic, political, and cultural subtext to which the bucolic topography and its inhabitants in the novel symbolically refer. The pastoral novel, with its large number of characters and its frequent insertion of intercalated stories offers, by contrast, a wider and more complex spectrum of situations and references that point beyond the laments of the desolate lover and the characteristic idealizing conceptualization of the bower.

Montemayor's text thus proves to be an obvious choice. The first pastoral novel written in Spain, *La Diana* creates a formal model followed by all subsequent Spanish authors. It also determines the field of topics and sensibilities within which its imitators work. As a second and comparative example I analyze Cervantes's *La Galatea*. Published towards the end of the genre's creative peak in Spain, Cervantes's first novel can be considered the last substantial and true-to-form pastoral novel of the Spanish Renaissance. Unlike Lope de Vega who in his *Arcadia* takes Montemayor's model and transforms it into an unique and personal literary product—Avalle-Arce has curiously described it as a "pastoril-monstruo" (monstrous pastoral)—Cervantes generally follows *La Diana*'s more abstract and idealizing formal and thematic structure.[11] As I will demonstrate, *La*

---

[11] Avalle-Arce states: "Lope ha buscado siempre lo descomunal, y donde no lo ha encontrado lo ha creado. Así ocurrió cuando se enfrentó con la novela pastoril. El género había nacido en España con un perfecto equilibrio de partes [...]. Lope,

Galatea repeats and puts into focus many of the social connections and prescriptions that seep into *La Diana*. But it also significantly tests the symbolic limits of the pastoral fantasy, offering us a bridge between *La Diana*'s idealizing propositions and the deconstructive parody of the genre that appears in Cervantes's subsequent literary production. Following this evolution of the mode, I examine in some detail *La casa de los celos y selvas de Ardenia* and *Don Quixote*, two later Cervantine texts that ironically reproduce the pure ideality of the bucolic space in order to reveal and pick apart at pastoral ideology and the mode's symbolic function.

Throughout this study I read the pastoral as a genre well-suited to narrativize and symbolically resolve many of the social, economic, and cultural tensions and contradictions of the period. The Spanish empire, beleaguered by the demands of war, economic debacles, rebellions, and heresy, can be understood as a traumatic and unresolvable historical referent, resymbolized through the idealism of the pastoral metaphor. More precisely, I would argue that the myth of pastoral plenitude and harmony in Spanish early modern texts serves to address and reconfigure the various and very real problems suffered at all levels of Spanish society; including the depletion of agricultural and ranching resources, urban overpopulation and delinquency, the burden of constant military engagements, bankruptcy, and the unequal taxation of the poor. The unease provoked by blood purity statutes and the incongruity between women's actual political and economic roles and the patriarchal discourses that denied the reality of their agency are symbolized in the bucolic topography. Spanish pastoral texts can be read as a symbolic reformulation–admittedly not always even and often disrupted– of this socio-historical milieu. The texts put forward a coherent and comforting metaphor of social existence. The hidden referents of this metaphor are precisely the contradictions, failures, and fragmentation of the social order, or what Louis Althusser famously

---

con sus excesos, descentra la novela totalmente, y el único equilibrio que le queda es el que le confiere la firme intención, de siempre en él, de autobiografiarse en sus personajes. Nos hallamos ante una pastoril-monstruo, calificativo al que me obliga la desemejanza y descomunalidad de sus partes" 'Lope always tends towards excess and where he doesn't find it he creates it. The genre had been born in Spain displaying a perfect balance of its parts [...]. Lope, with his overindulgence, decenters the novel completely, and the only equilibrium left is that which is conferred by his firm intention to produce his own autobiography through his characters. We find ourselves with a monstrous pastoral novel, a qualifier to which I am obliged given the work's dissimilarity and immoderation in its parts' (166; my translation).

characterized as the function of cultural institutions and products and the ideologies reproduced and promulgated by them: "[I]t is not their real conditions of existence, their real world, that 'men' 'represent to themselves' in ideology, but above all it is their relation to those conditions of existence which is represented to them there" (164).[12] In texts such as *La Diana* and *La Galatea*, the pastoral reproduces and promotes aristocratic and patriarchal values.[13] The figures of the noble shepherd and his virtuous beloved are reassuring stand-ins for the lack of wholeness and harmony in real social experience. The diffused treatment of gender difference and sexual desire in the bower serves as an idealizing metaphor which functions as a symbolic resolution for the reader of the underlying social discord. In the process, the bucolic space privileges a vision of the world where the poor and destitute are conveniently largely substituted by a community of cultured poet-shepherds, and where the disruptive effects of female subjectivity within patriarchal society are recast in the image of a beautiful and inaccessible beloved.

In the second half of this study I examine the instability of the pastoral metaphor by identifying instances where bucolic ideality is subverted, where the idealizing metaphor fails to represent anew or fully repress the conflicts and contradictions of the historical subtext. I start this section with a limited discussion of Garcilaso's Second Eclogue, whose structural and thematic composition is often noted as a disappointment given its incoherent mix of the bucolic and the epic. To the contrary, I maintain that Garcilaso is here already, and as a preview to the First and Third Eclogues, pointing to the underbelly of the pastoral dream. I read the Second Eclogue as a suggestive departure for a study of the unstable relationship between the bucolic metaphor and its underlying referents as it is put into play in the pastoral novel. For example, a careful consideration of the relationship between the male shepherds makes apparent how *La Diana* and *La Galatea* inadvertently depict the disquieting persistence of class hierarchy and servitude within the equality of the bower. The main thrust of my argument in this section, however, focuses on the occasional yet significantly disruptive persistence of a femi-

---

[12] On the applicability of this proposition to the medieval and early modern period see Althusser, especially pages 150-2.

[13] Rachel Bromberg has noted, for example, that, "Diana [...] is to be taken as the story of a vision which illuminates common-sense experience by illustrating a set of values more or less accepted by the conservative social class" (72).

nine agency that is otherwise subsumed in the idealized and objectified figure of the shepherdess that the male lovers constantly recall. I explore the ways in which women pastoral characters both conform to and break with the gender prescriptions present in early modern aristocratic society. In *La Diana* and *La Galatea*, the female subject is thoroughly ignored by the male lovers and the accompanying narrative voice. Still, there are identifiable moments, slippages or gaps in the pastoral metaphor where feminine agency emerges as a contradictory element, destabilizing the idealized fantasy of the idyll.

The ramifications of these slippages come to full term in Cervantine pastoral texts of the late sixteenth and early seventeenth centuries. In the last chapter I offer an analysis of the play *La casa de los celos* and *Don Quixote* as examples of pastoral that explicitly expose, critique, and challenge the genre's ideological suppositions and aims. The economic competition and contentious female agency found in Cervantes's later texts impede a straightforward reproduction and dissemination of the pastoral metaphor. The desired symbolization, as a result, goes awry and gives in to parody, chaos, and death. Cervantes's treatment of the mode serves as a reflection on the irresolvable social and political conflicts and contradictions of early modern Spain, as they intensified in the late sixteenth and seventeenth centuries. As I see it, Cervantes grew suspicious of the pastoral fantasy and its idealization of a nation wrought by military defeat, political instability under Philip III and Philip IV, urban malaise, and rural poverty. Despite his origin as a pastoral author, Cervantes systematically uncovers the symbolic purpose of the bucolic metaphor with its interested reproduction of aristocratic values and patriarchal ideology. In the process, his texts put into question any future production or consumption of pastoral texts in which the mode's symbolic and ideological function is simply and thoroughly ignored. It is a testament to the power of the pastoral, nonetheless, that despite Cervantes's deconstruction of the pastoral metaphor, *La Diana* and its imitations remained extremely popular well into the eighteenth century.[14]

---

[14] Regarding the popularity of these novels into the eighteenth, Francisco López Estrada informs us that "[S]u lectura todavía proseguía en esta época entre una sociedad que seguía los gustos de los siglos precedentes. Y esto no como una imposición de la moda, más o menos dirigida por una corte señorial, sino como el efecto de una tendencia espontánea" 'The reading of pastoral novels continued at this time within a sector of society that still followed that tastes of previous centuries. Not as a fashion imposed by the court, but rather as a spontaneous tendency' (*Los libros de pastores* 478; my translation).

Chapter 1

PASTORAL METAPHORS: HISTORY AS AN ABSENT CAUSE
IN THE SPANISH PASTORAL NOVEL

THE pastoral myth offers a world of timeless prosperity, harmony, and peace. Nature, perpetually in the midst of a perfect spring day, meets every physical and material need. The temporal ideal of an age of gold, as manifested in the myths of Astraea and Saturn, is also a part of the equation. Always imagined as a time past, its remembrance recalls an era of innocence, prosperity, and benign rule when want, conflict, and violence were unknown. Only the pangs of love are felt, and then only to showcase the shepherd's virtue and constancy. By building upon these conventions, Renaissance pastoral texts portray a rural landscape where toil and poverty are replaced by a vision of the shepherd as an exemplar of the tastes and aesthetic preferences of an aristocratic audience. In early modern Spanish literature this model is most thoroughly developed in pastoral novels, where a bucolic Spain readily offers fresh springs, green hills, and the exquisite songs of lovers. As critics repeatedly note, the pastoral promises a fictional respite from daily life, a literary retreat where social discord and unmet needs are displaced.

As I will demonstrate, the pastoral mode is nonetheless allied to a web of social discourses that mediated the way people understood their lived experiences in early modern Spain. The idea of an agreeable nature where virtuous men and women labored and loved was a device often curiously deployed to frame what were very complicated and often thorny social, political, and economic situations throughout the emergence of the Spanish nation-state. The sixteenth-century Spanish pastoral novel, I contend, expands upon this practice submitting to the reader a parallel idealizing metaphor for those same historical conditions which it claims to excise from its pages. In an expanding empire laden by foreign wars, social change and occasional unrest, and ever-increasing economic pressures, the pastoral novel functions as an ideologically invested response to vexing issues that dominated the day.

I. THE IDEAL VS. THE REAL: THE PASTORAL AS SYMBOLIC ACT

A manifest nostalgia for a past Golden Age was a popular recourse in the social imaginary of early modern Spain.[1] This *topos* owes its currency to the scholastic and humanist interest in the recuperation and imitation of classical texts and themes. No less significantly, the idea of a past, parallel, or future Golden Age responds to the basic human need to imagine constantly the possibility of a better place than what is at the moment experienced, the often expressed certitude that the grass must have been, must be, or will be greener elsewhere. In Spain this idea was tacked on to political and social discourse. As José Antonio Maravall tells us,

> This dream [...] was alive in the sixteenth century and up through the time when Cervantes was writing. The strong influence on the Spanish Renaissance of [Vergil, Ovid, Seneca, and Boethius], in whom the concept of the *aetas aurea* is so prominent, and the constant reading and discussion of their works probably inspired sixteenth- and seventeenth-century Spanish writers to take up the theme and include it in their social and political thought. [...] [T]he theme of the Golden Age once again came to be a way of understanding the origins of historical development. (*Utopia and Counterutopia* 132-3)

Among the most prominent humanists and political and social thinkers for which the myth of the Golden Age was a part of their "inkwell" are Erasmus, Vives, Guevara, and Torquemada, among many others (Maravall, *Utopia and Counterutopia* 132-3). Making evident, thus, that the deployment of this *topos* in Spanish sixteenth-century intellectual culture went much beyond its simple application as a literary device.

---

[1] See Kamen's "Golden Age, Iron Age."

An originary utopian political narrative was employed to frame the passing of what by the mid 1500s many Spaniards were already calling a golden era under the Catholic Kings. This use of the pastoral myth in reference to Isabel and Ferdinand was not new, as manifested, for example, by Encina in his translation of Virgil's Eclogues, where he proposes the present Catholic reign as the institution of a new Golden Age: "[E]stas Bucólicas quise trasladar, trobadas en estilo pastoril, aplicándolas a los muy loables hechos de vuestro reynar según parece en el argumento de cada una" 'These Bucolics I wanted to translate, sung in the pastoral style, applying the laudable events of your tenure as kings to each of their arguments' (as quoted in Anderson 79; my translation).[2] Upset by Charles V's foreignness and costly imperial designs, many invoked the idea of this past utopia, elevating Isabel's piety and wisdom, as well the secure liberty that her reign provided, while disregarding an expansion of royal power and authoritarianism that presaged Charles V's own tenure.[3] For those who felt threatened by Charles V's allegedly cold personality or his style of government, the discursive idealization of the Catholic monarch's reign offered an exploitable contrast. As J.H. Elliott observes, the Castilian factions that opposed Charles V recalled this idealized past in a "gallant but hopeless attempt to prove [...] that, although everything was different, it could still be the same" (*Imperial Spain* 153). In other words, the idealization of the Catholic monarchs was a way of stopping the advent of modernity and the emergent nation-state as personified by the figure of Charles V. Regardless of the new set of historical and social conditions that transformed Spain's political and economic situation under the Hapsburg emperorship, those who opposed Charles V found refuge in an idealized past where most, if not all, of the contradictions of the earlier regime were conveniently suppressed.[4]

Yet, the rhetorical use of the *topos* of a Golden Age was not the exclusive domain of those who yearned for Isabel and Ferdinand.

---

[2] See Anderson for a detailed study of Encina's translation of the Virgilian "Bucolic Eclogues."

[3] See Elliott, *Imperial Spain*, page 153.

[4] The arguments against Charles V's right to rule were couched in a Castilian "nationalist" discourse that saw him as a foreign intruder who would work against the nation-building project heralded by his grandparents. See Elliott, *Imperial Spain*, Chapter 4.

Charles V's court saw itself as the seat of a vast, powerful, and rich empire that would dominate Europe and the Americas and spread and defend the Christian faith in the process, confirming its superiority and unlimited potential. The promise of world hegemony and the prosperity intermittently experienced by specific sectors of the population boosted the idea of Spain as an invincible empire in a present age of gold. As Maravall has well documented, "Carlos de Austria ve así el 'hecho de Imperio': a éste le competen unas obligaciones específicas no por su naturaleza, sino por su proyección universal: paz entre los príncipes cristianos, reforma de los abusos de la Iglesia, reducción de la herejía y guerra contra el turco" 'Charles V sees as such the work of the Empire: it has specific obligations not because of its nature as an empire, but because of its universalistic projection: peace among Christian princes, reform of the Church, reduction of heresy, and war against the Turk' (*Carlos V* 113; my translation). This idea of the universal Christian empire was in fact couched by writers such as Guevara and Alfonso de Valdés in a pastoral discourse that saw virtue and rational living of the shepherd as worthy attributes for the Emperor and his "flock":

> Un buen príncipe [...] bien sea rey de un gran reino o Emperador del pueblo cristiano, permite una existencia libre, igual y virtuosa, donde todos conservan la buena condición originaria del hipotético estado natural. Esta hipótesis de un estado social virtuoso que constituye el fin de la utopía humanista [...] se llama en la época la Edad dorada. (Maravall, *Carlos V* 225)[5]
>
> A good prince [...] whether the monarch of a great kingdom or Emperor of the Christian people, will permit a free, equal, and virtuous existence, where all conserve the benign condition hypothetically found in the original natural state. The hypothesis of a virtuous social state that constitutes the end of a humanist utopia [...] is called the Golden Age. (my translation)

The pastoral government would bring its people together, order would rule the day, and the good shepherd Emperor would lead at times of peace and at times of war with virtue and reason. Philip II's ascension to the throne was also framed by the rhetoric of the

---

[5] In his *Carlos V*, Maravall discusses at length the pastoral theory of government developed by Guevara and Valdés.

good shepherd, with his father as an idealized example for the young King to follow (Maravall, *Carlos V* 230).

However, as became increasingly evident, internal predicaments and external pressures interfered with this new *edad dorada*. Individual Spanish kingdoms refused to limit their sovereignty and curtail their particular political and material interests.[6] Unending military campaigns placed enormous demands on the country's population and economy. And uncontrollable inflationary forces and underdeveloped agricultural and commercial markets undercut economic prosperity.[7] With its coffers empty, the brunt of fiscal responsibility was repeatedly placed on those poverty-ridden sectors of society that could least afford, and that least benefited from, the crown's imperial designs. The monarchy first declared bankruptcy in 1557, making evident that the empire was vexed by its own political inconsistencies, military setbacks, and fiscal disarray. Unlike the literary idyll, the dream of a golden Spanish empire was–and would remain throughout the rest of the sixteenth and seventeenth centuries –on the defensive.

The conflict between pasture and arable land use–ranching versus farming–is an example of Spain's predicament that is especially relevant to the pastoral fantasy. The problem resided in whether to support a wool trade that met the needs of international markets and brought in much needed capital, to concentrate exclusively on national production and consumption of wool products, or instead to invest all resources in growing the foodstuffs needed to sustain

---

[6] Maravall describes the problem as such: "Sin duda, el Imperio de Carlos V no fué nunca, ni pudo serlo, una unidad orgánica. No tenía una estructura compacta, apoyada en una red institucional, ni podía tenerla. Después de la muerte de Gattinara no tuvo ni un canciller común. Fué, en principio, una yuxtaposición de reinos y principados en su mano, y Carlos quiso llegar a su fusión no por amalgama jurídica, sino por una idea cuya fuerza fuera capaz de mantenerlo en unión. Esa era la idea del Nuevo Imperio cristiano [...]" 'Without a doubt, Charles V's Empire never was, nor could it be, an organic unit. It did not have a compact structure, reliant on an institutional web, nor could it have it. After the death of Gattinara it did not even have a common chancellor. It was, in principle, a juxtaposition of kingdoms and principalities in his hands, and Charles wanted to reach their fusion not by juridical amalgam, but by the idea of a power whose strength would be able to maintain the union. This was the idea of the New Christian Empire [...]' (*Carlos V* 111; my translation).

[7] Kamen describes Spain as a colonial market, which served primarily European interests and depended on the institutionalization of "cycles of dependence" between Spain and foreign bankers and industries. See "The Decline of Spain: A Historical Myth," in *Crisis and Change*.

the population. This economic quandary also had a political dimension. The Mesta, a powerful guild that united the grazing operations throughout Old Castile and León, provided the Crown with an important source of taxable income and, in turn, demanded and obtained important privileges and concessions (Casey 48-9). The Honrado Concejo de la Mesta, spontaneously formed in Castile in the thirteenth century and given royal privileges by Alfonso X in 1273, had as its original mission the protection of the shepherds as they left in the winter their homes and farms in the north to the warmer climates in Extremadura, La Mancha, and Andalucía (Ruiz Martín 43). Yet, as the historian Felipe Ruiz Martín explains, the Mesta's ranks increasingly came to be dominated by interests foreign to its original goals (44-5). Notwithstanding the Mesta's influence and its constant lobbying for an open range between Castile and the lowlands of Andalusia and Extremadura, farmers, stationed herders (*estantes*), and other independents who wished to protect their grazing stakes increasingly partitioned the countryside. The issues surrounding this standoff were many and highly influenced by local power struggles, yet historians generally agree on a correlation between the growth of an arable economy and the decrease of grazing lands.[8] The development of this change from the fifteenth to the seventeenth century is traced by Ruiz Martín as follows. From the 1450s to about 1526 the migrating sheepherders coexisted peacefully with the considerably smaller number of *estante* ranchers. From 1527 to 1578 the proportion of *estantes* to *transhumantes* shifts. In turn, many of the stationary herds change hands from local villagers to rich landowners from the cities and major villages who consolidate numerous smaller flocks. These *señores de ganado* see a split between those who have their large herds travel from north to south and those who remain *estantes* in fertile riverbeds and flood plains. Major conflicts between these two groups increase in scope and intensity after 1579 through the seventeenth century:

> [L]a escisión y subsiguiente enfrentamiento entre las ciudades y villas que habían definitivamente triunfado conjuntamente de las

---

[8] Among the authors whose studies and collections of essays have informed my understanding of the Mesta and its history are Gonzalo Anes Álvarez, L.M. Bilbao and E. Fernández de Pinedo, Casey, Elliott, Pedro García Martín, Ángel García Sanz, Julius Klein, J. López-Salazar Pérez, and Ruiz Martín.

aldeas en el período anterior, se consuma, ya que de aquellas aglomeraciones se polarizaron unas como transhumantes y otras como riberiegas; ahora, enfrentadas unas con otras en medio de la regresión económica que abate a Castilla, chocan, y recíprocamente se desgastan [...]. La ganadería, como el campo y como el conjunto del país, pasa a ser patrimonio de los señores, algunos de viejo cuño, otros, los más, de nuevo cuño. (Ruiz Martín 45)

The separation and subsequent battle between the cities and the small rural towns, which definitively the villages had won in the previous period, is now sealed, since these agglomerations were polarized some as migratory and some as stationary; now, confronting each other in the midst of the economic regression that troubles Castile, they find themselves at a standstill and wear themselves out [...]. Ranching, like the rural areas and the rest of the country, as a result comes to be the patrimony of the nobility, some older but mostly new. (my translation)

The small scale shepherds, both *transhumantes* and *estantes*, whose herds were now largely controlled or outright owned by the *señores de ganado*, shared a similar fate. Overburdened by the *servicios* (taxes) owed to the Crown and their noble lords, the rural population grew ever poorer and unable to sustain either its flocks or its plots of land, forcing the dispossessed to relocate in large numbers to the towns and cities of Castile.[9] The only ones who benefited were the feudal lords and village potentates who further acquired and profited from the abandoned lands of the Spanish countryside.[10] Moreover, the fencing-off of land led to deforestation

---

[9] In fact, the demands placed on the rural population were even greater and more oppressive: "[T]here were increasing complaints after 1550 about peasant indebtedness and dispossession of peasantry from their lands by creditors from the towns. It was all too easy for a small peasant to run into debt as the result of a succession of poor harvests. Even in good times his profits were limited by the tasa del trigo; and at all times he was liable to be subjected to the attentions of the tax collector, the billeting officer, and the recruiting sergeant. [...] Faced with [these conditions], the unfortunate peasant was liable to take the line of least resistance and to abandon his village seeking shelter and safety with his family in the anonymous world of the town" (Elliott, *Imperial Spain* 294-5).

[10] Elliot states, "[R]eal power in the country lay in such few hands, that one or two individuals could effectively prevent the implementation of schemes that could have been of benefit to many. This was particularly true in the realm of agrarian development. Much of the soil of Castile belonged either to magnates, who had accumulated large estates through the workings of the entail system, or to the Church, which had accumulated them through mortmain. [...] [T]hese landowners appar-

and damage to the environment, hurting the very farmers and ranchers whom the increase in arable land was meant to benefit.[11] Rural existence, far from a golden promise of sustenance and hope, was a life of great hardship and constant disillusionment for the popular majority.

Migrating rural populations noticeably increased during the mid and late sixteenth century and put at risk the idea of the city as a golden *locus* of order, culture, and wealth. Although estimates vary, between 1526 and 1591 cities in Castile grew by at least 62 percent (Gelabert 184). Displaced and hungry, this new urban population hoped to find stable sources of income. Urban planners and civic leaders had initially envisioned the city in early modern Spain as a place of virtue, whose governance could serve as an example to its citizens. Parallel to the ideal of a golden pastoral retreat, the urban landscape promised redemption and shelter for those who entered a city's gates. Churches, plazas, and marketplaces promoted civic participation and offered the opportunity for positive social exchange. The city represented for these migrating masses prosperity and plenty, freedom from the hardship experienced in the countryside. Instead, what they found was, for the most part, unemployment, idleness, and high mortality rates. The perpetually stalled industrial sectors were unable to provide the jobs necessary to support a labor market glutted with low-skilled workers.[12] The situation was made even worse by multiple years of harvesting failures and famines, making adult vagrancy and pauperism the only "occupations" available to the urban masses. Charitable relief for the poor neither could effectively counter urban poverty nor could stave off the spreading sentiment that this segment of the popula-

---

ently showed no interest in irrigation projects, or in a more effective exploitation of the soil; and *bourgeois* landowners, who had acquired property from peasants, were either equally uninterested, or else lacked the resources to undertake improvements of their own. As a result, agriculture languished and the economy stagnated" (297). See also Casey, Chapter Five, "Feudal lords and village potentates."

[11] "When enclosures were for arable [...], they did more harm than good. The cutting down of trees, the setting fire to the undergrowth, the eventual abandonment of marginal land which earlier farmers, with good reason, had refused to plough, all led to a general deterioration of the environment both for the peasant and the shepherd" (Casey 50).

[12] As Cruz has explained, "Already by the latter half of the sixteenth century, [...] the chronic lack of employment both in agriculture and industry, heavy taxation, and the general rise in prices, [...] contributed to make the number of vagabonds in Spain the highest in Europe" (*Discourses of Poverty* 40).

tion represented a social disease.¹³ A rise in crime deepened the country's sense of gloom and impending chaos. Lacking the needed infrastructure and strained by the demands of the many that sought refuge in their walls, these urban centers became for the dispossessed one last stop in a life full of misery and despair. For the prosperous elite, living in any of the major Spanish cities meant both basking in the splendor of religious and political power, as well as feeling threatened by constant presence of the vagrant and the beggar. Even in smaller townships, the divisions between the few who held power and the many that lacked day-to-day sustenance could hardly go unnoticed. The ideal of the city–as a space of civic pride and material prosperity–became yet another endangered golden dream within early modern Spanish society.

The vision of an egalitarian Catholic society was also tested. The 1492 conquest of the kingdom of Granada announced an era of political and religious accord throughout the Iberian Peninsula. Yet, despite this glorious ideal of a unifying homogeneity, Spanish society found itself consumed by a climate of racial and religious suspicion. The wide variety of opinions concerning the Inquisitorial courts and the various ways they judged heretics for their sins, how the social stigma of having Jewish blood was or was not effectively negotiated, and how Moorish presence and labor was (de)valued in different parts of the peninsula, are complex and beyond the focus of this study. Nevertheless, it is undeniable that early modern Spain was fully engrossed with politics of identity and difference, and driven by an ideal of unity and sameness. Recalling an Edenic past, the Christian nation was to be populated by the loving children of the one true God. This inclusive vision could only be achieved through the identification and expurgation of those classified or feared as others. Spain was a nation obsessed by the inconsistency and difference that it continually perceived in its midst. On an individual level, this issue became entangled with the difficult business of fashioning oneself as an old Christian.¹⁴ Partially informed

---

¹³ For a discussion of the variety of discourses that dealt with poverty see Cruz, *Discourses of Poverty*, especially Chapter 1.

¹⁴ "It would be wrong [...] to assume that the Inquisition was the sole source of constraint in sixteenth-century Spain, or that it introduced entirely new features into Spanish life. Indeed, it may have taken such firm hold of Spanish society precisely because it gave official sanction to already existing attitudes and practices. Suspicion of those who deviated from the common norm was deeply rooted in a country

by comparisons to the fantasy of a past Golden Age, the ideal of a homogeneous and harmonious Christian land set a standard for Spanish national identity during this period. Unfortunately, it could only be secured by repressive mechanisms of Inquisitorial trials, general expulsions, and the illusive standard of blood purity.

Perhaps one of the most telling historical contradictions of sixteenth-century Spain was the sense of magnificence and wonder, joined by greed and lust for power, brought about by the discovery of the Indies. The New World was partially constructed by the Spanish imagination as a pristine land, a natural landscape uncorrupted by need or lack.[15] As Elliott informs us,

> The process of transposition began from the very moment that Columbus first set eyes on the Caribbean Islands. The various connotations of paradise and the Golden Age were present from the first. Innocence, simplicity, fertility and abundance–all of them qualities for which Renaissance Europe hankered, and which seemed so unattainable–made their appearance in the reports of Columbus and Vespucci, and were eagerly seized upon by their enthusiastic readers. (*The Old World and the New* 25)

The "image of golden, primeval happiness" was often cited among those writing in and about the Indies, both in literary and political treatises of the period (Maravall, *Utopia and Counterutopia* 133).[16] Yet this Edenic vision quickly clashed with the reality of lands exploited for treasure and damaged by war, disease, and death–a process that brought the Iron Age to American shores. As the debate between Bartolomé de las Casas and Juan Ginés de Sepúlveda famously exemplifies, the Indies–far from fulfilling its golden promise–became for Spain a site of imperial and

---

where deviation was itself more normal than elsewhere–and a man could be suspect for his race as well as for his faith. [...] Indeed, alongside the obsessive concern with purity of the faith there flourished a no less obsessive concern with purity of blood; [...] both had the effect of narrowing the extraordinarily wide range of Spanish life, and of forcing a rich and vital society into a straight-jacket of conformity" (Elliott, *Imperial Spain* 220). See also Casey, Chapter 7 "The Consolidation of an Aristocracy."

[15] See José Rabasa, especially his chapter "Dialogue as Conquest in the Cortés-Charles V Correspondence," Hayden White, and Margarita Zamora, especially her chapter "Voyage to Paradise."

[16] Maravall offers as examples the writings of Oviedo, Las Casas, Acosta, Inca Garcilaso, and Fray Martín de Murúa.

individual exploitation, of social turmoil, and of moral and religious incertitude.[17]

When considered from this political, economic, and social perspective, it becomes clear that the pastoral fantasy plays a much larger function than simply that of escapist entertainment. The fantasy that a golden past could be restored provided an imaginary standard relevant to the Spanish social and national discourse. The pastoral novel–the consummate literary manifestation of this golden standard of homogeneity and harmony–in turn asks to be read as a cultural product that mediates the disparity between these multiple Golden Age dreams and the underlying lived conditions of historical experience. In particular, Spanish pastoral novels seem to be a symbol of–by alluding to and simultaneously idealizing–the cultural circumstances of their authors and readers. As such, these novels function as a literary response to the conflicts and failures that permeated all aspects of the social fabric.

The critical position I adopt here is, in effect, a Jamesonian one, proposing that the pastoral can be understood as a "symbolic act" where "real social contradictions, insurmountable in their own terms, find a purely formal resolution in the aesthetic realm" (Jameson 79):[18]

> This interpretive model thus allows us a first specification of the relationship between ideology and cultural texts or artifacts [...]. [I]deology is not something which informs or invests symbolic production; rather the aesthetic act is itself ideological, and the production of aesthetic or novel form is to be seen as an ideological act in its own right, with the function of inventing imaginary or formal "solutions" to unresolvable social contradictions. (Jameson 79)

Jameson's argument relies on the proposition that history exists only insofar as its conditions can be made sense of, or represented, through the practice of narrativization. In a "revised formulation" of Althusser's formula for history as an "absent cause" he states: "[H]istory is *not* a text, not a narrative, master or otherwise, but

---

[17] For a discussion of Las Casas and Sepúlveda's debate see Lewis Hanke and Ángel Losada.

[18] Jameson here builds upon ideas drawn from Claude Lévi-Strauss's structuralist anthropology.

[...] an absent cause, it is inaccessible to us except in textual form, and [...] our approach to it and to the Real itself necessarily passes through its prior textualization, its narrativization in the political unconscious" (35).[19] Jameson's Marxist notion of history is clearly influenced by Jacques Lacan's understanding of language and the symbolic order as the dimension through which the lack of presence, truth, meaning, or finality which fragments the subject–the Real–is mediated.[20] Following this logic, the literary text, a cultural artifact dependent on its ability to construct intelligible stories, thus offers the perfect vehicle through which to symbolize–to narrativize or make sense of through language–the unresolvable contradictions and conflicts of history. Drawing on these propositions, it is my contention that pastoral novels are especially interesting as a Spanish early modern example of narrativization precisely because in their form and content the clash between the idea of a golden Spain and the underlying social contradiction and conflict is textually resolved. Contingency and impossibility are refigured as order, harmony, and plenitude. Through a recuperation and imitation of classical and Italian topics and conventions, the Spanish pastoral novel formally and thematically mediates through narrative language the inconsistencies and alienation that permeated the early modern Spanish social fabric. To read pastoral novels as symbolic acts is, therefore, to see their function as "inventing imaginary or formal 'solutions' to unresolvable social contradictions."

In following this theory of the relationship between text and historical subtext, I do not mean to suggest that the pastoral novel simply reflects or replicates historical experience. Rather, the bucolic landscape together with the social formations praised in these novels *creates* a surrogate reality, where the reader can virtually experience the dream of a Golden Age. The pastoral novel can be said to offer within fictional space what is inaccessible in unmediated historical experience: a social space typified by blissful sameness and uncontested harmony. These novels idealize existing social, political, and economic conditions, while intending to suppress their irresolvable contradictions–such as gender and class hierarchies, religious intol-

---

[19] For Jameson, as for Lacan, the Real is that which "resists symbolization absolutely" (35).

[20] Lacan fully develops his theory of the symbolic order during the 1950s in his Seminars II and IV.

erance, and the destruction of natural habitats.[21] It is in this way that the *libros de pastores* are directly engaged, formally and ideologically, with their historical subtext. While conflict and contradiction impaired the full materialization of an age of gold under the Catholic Kings and the Hapsburg succession, the pastoral novel can function for the reading public as an imaginary substitute where this national fantasy and its ideological suppositions and necessities are fulfilled. The bower may initially seem to be disconnected from Spain's social and political designs. And, without question, the contemporary reader was able to recognize the constructed ideality of the pastoral space. Still, these *libros de pastores* clearly validate and promote a variety of aristocratic and patriarchal values and ideologies that are essential to the stability of sixteenth-century Spanish symbolic order.[22] The pastoral novel advances a vision of Spain as a land of plenty exclusively inhabited by superior, noble, and talented courtly beings. As I will show in latter chapters, this act of narrativization is not always entirely fulfilled. Destabilizing disruptions–such as the persistence of violence, class hierarchies, and female agency–make their mark in the idyll and problematize the relation of early modern Spanish pastoral ideality to its conflictive and traumatic historical underside. Nonetheless, even if the pastoral's symbolic function appears at times frayed, the genre's principal effect is to transport the reader into a world where harmony, plenitude, virtue, and peace hold sway.

A suitable way to describe this symbolic process is to view the pastoral as metaphor. Metaphor, as Roman Jakobson reinterprets the trope, entails a transfer of meaning between normally unrelated domains, and can be perceived as incongruous or surprising.[23] The

---

[21] I would add that one of the most effective ways of representing specifically damaging aspects of the historical subtext is to simply ignore them, which, from an ideological perspective, explains the absence of concrete references to specific events or social and economic concerns in pastoral novels.

[22] The symbolic order can be defined as the social world of linguistic communication, intersubjective relations, knowledge of ideological conventions, and the acceptance of the law. The symbolic is made possible because of your acceptance of those laws and restrictions that control both your desire and the rules of communication. The symbolic, through language, is "the pact which links [...] subjects together in one action. The human action *par excellence* is originally founded on the existence of the world of the symbol, namely on laws and contracts" (Lacan, *Freud's Papers* 230).

[23] See Jakobson's "Two Aspects of Language and Two Types of Aphasic Disturbances."

metaphoric relationship is thus not dependent on the signifiers' similitude and comparability. More to the point, metaphor is apparently not compatible semantically with its context. I would propose that this Jakobsonian account of the unrelatedness and incompatibility of the terms or signifiers that participate in the metaphoric process allows for an interpretation of the Spanish pastoral as metaphor in its relation to the historical referent. To be more exact, the pastoral novel, both in its form and its ideological content, can be said to perform the role of metaphor for early modern Spanish culture: it both accounts and substitutes for the unresolvable trauma of lived experience. Despite their ideality, these texts emerge from and have as their referent the historical conditions to which they are conceptually and structurally opposed: urban malaise, rural poverty and destitution, and social fragmentation and alienation. As such, the bucolic ideal functions as a comforting metaphor that resignifies the underlying trauma of social existence. Of no less importance, the figuration of historical conflict and contradiction as pastoral harmony is guided by the dominant hegemony's ideological interests and social laws.

This interpretation may seem to imply that pastoral metaphor is perfectly constructed and devoid of any fissures in its structures or produced meanings. To the contrary, an examination of pastoral novels quickly reveals the multiple values that the idyll acquires when consumed in sixteenth and seventeenth-century Spain. Following Williams's distinctions between residual, dominant, and emergent ideologies, Jamesonian analysis allows for the struggle and negotiation of these competing ideological systems within a text.[24] As a result, it becomes necessary that we consider the ways in which the pastoral as symbolic act may inadvertently admit to ideological positions other than those of the dominant hegemony. Jameson addresses these issues through the following questions:

> [H]ow is it possible for a cultural text which fulfills a demonstrably ideological function, as a hegemonic work whose formal categories as well as its content secure the legitimation of this or that form of class domination—*how is it possible for such a text to embody a properly Utopian impulse, or to resonate a universal val-*

---

[24] See Williams's *Problems in Materialism and Culture: Selected Essays* and Jameson's "The Cultural Logic of Late Capitalism".

ue inconsistent with the narrower limits [...] which inform its more immediate ideological vocation? (288, my emphasis)

Jameson's question ("how is it possible?") is here posited as an affirmative reading strategy. It is not only possible but necessary to seek out the unpredictability of all ideological structures, those "values inconsistent with the narrower limits" of a text's conscious "ideological vocation." To this end, a reading practice should not only "unmask and demonstrate the ways in which a cultural artifact fulfills a specific ideological mission, in legitimating a given power structure, in perpetuating and reproducing the latter," but also must be equally committed to "project[ing] its simultaneously Utopian power" (291). The point here is that hegemonic ideology unwittingly can work against itself, undermining its manifest goals of privilege and domination. It is at these gaps that a text's *alternative* ideals–those that do not conform to the text's main ideological thrust–can and should be fleshed out.

A curious issue arises when considering Jameson's notion of Utopian power in relation to pastoral texts: they are generally understood by their readers as already utopian. In other words, one would have to seek for Jameson's Utopian power within the normative pastoral utopia.[25] This reading practice thus proposes that it is possible to debunk the pastoral utopian metaphor by privileging the fissures that reveal a non-conformist utopia, or alternative ideological values, within the bucolic topography. The analytical task as a result may appear contradictory: I propose we read against pastoral ideality in order to allow these novels' concealed utopian power to surface. My intention is not to construct an interminable word game. Yet, and as I will show in Chapters Three and Four, what Jameson's proposal enables me to do is to search the unconventional and often ignored aspect of these *libros de pastores*. Necessarily, this strategy highlights precisely those moments in which the idyll–in spite of its form and content–cannot fully symbolize the social and material subtext from which it emerges;

---

[25] In his conclusion to *The Political Unconscious* Jameson addresses the Utopian character of hegemonic ideology itself by reaching the conclusion that, "even hegemonic or ruling-class culture and ideology are Utopian, not in spite of their instrumental function to secure and perpetuate class privilege and power, but rather precisely because that function is also in and of itself the affirmation of collective solidarity" (291).

where the historical referent that the pastoral metaphor intends to name anew resists displacement, jeopardizing the efficacy of the pastoral as poetic trope and as a normative ideological act. It is in such textual gaps that other voices emerge, even if tentatively, and render problematic what in Jamesonian terms would be understood as the ideological vocation of the Spanish pastoral novel. More precisely, these gaps offer a glimpse of otherwise marginalized values and experiences that the pastoral metaphor seeks to cover over and symbolize.

But first, with this theoretical framework in mind, let us examine specific ways in which history is symbolized in Montemayor's *La Diana* and Cervantes's *La Galatea*.

II. *Prados y Palacios*: History Narrativized in *La Diana* and *La Galatea*

In the tradition of the Virgilian *Bucolics*, the pastoral mode depends on the fictional representation of a landscape where both characters and readers can find a soothing retreat in which no physical or material need is unmet. It is a space that restores and sustains the tired and the afflicted. In the amatory tradition, nature specifically functions as a point of reference to which the lover can compare and contrast his own deteriorating psychological state. This is all true for the Spanish pastoral novel, and confirmed in the first few lines of the seminal *La Diana*:

> Pues llegando el pastor a los verdes y deleitosos prados, que el caudaloso río Ezla con sus aguas va regando, le vino a la memoria el gran contentamiento de que en algún tiempo allí gozado había [...]. Consideraba aquel dichoso tiempo que por aquellos prados y hermosa ribera apacentaba su ganado [...]; y las horas que le sobraban gastaba el pastor en sólo gozar el suave olor de las doradas flores, al tiempo que la primavera, con las alegres nuevas del verano, se esparce por el universo [...]. (110)

> As the shepherd approached those green and pleasant meadows drained by the abundant River Ezla, he recalled the happiness he once knew there [...]. He reflected on that happy time when he fed his flock in the meadows along the beautiful river [...], while his leisure was spent savoring the sweet smell of golden

flowers at the time when spring spreads her glad tidings of summer through the universe [...]. (51)[26]

For the love-lorn shepherd Sireno, nature provides sustenance and, more importantly, acts as a perpetual source of *deleite* or pleasure, evoked through concepts such as *contentamiento, dicha, gozo,* and *alegría*. The flawlessness of the physical setting directly corresponds with the state of bliss enjoyed by the shepherd before his amatory disillusionment. Despite Sireno's present condition, the idyll remains eternal and provides an unchanging backdrop against which he may sing about his virtuous suffering and publicly establish his nobility. The lover–unencumbered by hunger, the need for shelter, or any other material contingency–is free to be a slave to love. I discuss in detail the formal and ideological implications of this apparent amatory paradox in the following chapters. For now, let us specifically examine the topography of the bower: what is let in and what is left out of its imaginary boundaries.[27]

The physical idealization of the bower is constructed in Montemayor's text–as later in Cervantes's *La Galatea*–through an evocation of the *alabanza de aldea, desprecio de corte* theme that immediately follows the above-cited description of the idyll:

> No se metía el pastor en la consideración de los malos o buenos sucesos de la fortuna, ni en la mudanza y variación de los tiempos, no le pasaba por el pensamiento la diligencia y codicias del ambicioso cortesano, ni la confianza y presunción de la dama celebrada por sólo el voto y parecer de sus apasionados; tampoco le daba pena la hinchazón y descuido del orgulloso privado: en el campo se crió, en el campo apacentaba su ganado, y así no salían del campo sus pensamientos [...]. (110-1)

> The shepherd never thought about the bad or good quirks of Fortune, nor of change or mutability. Nor did the cares and greed of the ambitious courtier cross his mind, nor the vanity and presumption of the lady celebrated only by the vows and

---

[26] All translations of *La Diana* come directly from RoseAnna M. Mueller's translation.

[27] Alpers, referring to a passage in Theocritus's *Idyll*, summarizes the general characteristics of the pastoral as follows: "idyllic landscape, landscape as a setting for song, an atmosphere of *otium*, a conscious attention to art and nature, herdsmen as singers, and in the account of the gifts, herdsmen as herdsmen" (22).

opinions of her suitors; neither did the arrogance and carelessness of the proud royal favorite trouble him. He was born in the country, in the country he fed his flock, and to the country his thoughts had been confined [...]. (51)

The importance of this passage to an analysis of the pastoral novel as symbolic act–of its function as an idealized metaphor for history–should be evident. First developed in the Horatian *Odes* and taken up in Renaissance Spain by authors such as Antonio de Guevara and Fray Luis de León, the theme stresses the tranquility and simplicity of civic life in the *aldea* when compared to the chaos and uncertainty of the city. Although the Virgilian pastoral tradition is not identical to the Horatian *topos*, they share a similar rural topography un-contaminated by the hostility and greed found in its counterpart favored for the solace it can offer humanity.[28] Montemayor's shepherd not only has every material and psychological need addressed in this land of plenty, but also is untouched by the lesser if indispensable human qualities that permeate the court: volatile fortunes, blind ambition, and pride. By referring to the city only to immediately negate the confusion of urban life, this *desprecio de corte* secures the function of the pastoral as a haven. Far from the turmoil of the urban chaos, the shepherd can tend contently to his herd and meditate on the beauty that surrounds him ("apacentaba su ganado, y así no salían del campo sus pensamientos").

All the same, there are a series of apparent ironies that underlie *La Diana*'s ideological use of the *aldea-corte* dichotomy. First, Montemayor most probably set *La Diana* on the shores of the Esla to commemorate the Dukes of Valencia de Don Juan who received Juana of Portugal and her entourage in their travels between Portugal and Castile.[29] In other words, an important function of an idyllic León is precisely to exalt the court and its privileged lifestyle. The

---

[28] An important difference between the two is that while the Virgilian bucolic tradition emphasizes the state of nature as bountiful and satisfying of the shepherd's needs, the Horatian theme focuses the simplicity and goodness of work and life in the countryside.

[29] Montemayor was Juana of Portugal's chamberlain during her regency in Portugal, and returned with her to Spain when she became a widow in 1554. For significant details regarding Montemayor's biography see Rhodes's *Unrecognized Precursors*, especially pages 20-50.

geographical location of the *locus amoenus* in *La Diana* generates an imaginary map of the Spanish countryside unfettered by any kind of contingency or need. No less ironic is that much of Montemayor's audience consists of those same *cortesanos* and *damas* that the passage seemingly maligns, and whose amatory fantasies, gender prescriptions, and aesthetic taste the shepherds so loyally reflect. For these reasons, although the *desprecio de corte* may seem to condemn life at court explicitly, most elite readers would not have felt threatened by this generalized and conventional denunciation of its vices. To the contrary, the audience's keen appreciation of the beauty and virtue found on the banks of the Esla makes them worthy of this literary and symbolic retreat. Together with the codified idealization of León as *locus amoenus*, the *aldea-corte* dichotomy overtly disregards (and represses) the social, economic, and environmental predicaments that did exist in and around the Spanish *aldea*. These instead are reassuringly neutralized for the benefit of an audience that either directly benefited from or preferred to ignore the local and national repercussions of this social condition. Instead, the audience enters a world both familiar and seductively abstract, a place the reader can both concretely locate within national boundaries while simultaneously imagining it anew through the pastoral fantasy. León, abstracted and purified, is in this manner conveniently transformed into a symbol for all of Spain, a metaphoric representation of the goodness and well-being of the people, nation, and, by extension, empire as a whole.

Equally significant to an analysis of the *aldea-corte* paradigm is the role of Felicia's palace in Books IV and V of *La Diana*. Despite the bower's portrayal as an unadulterated natural space, the pilgrimage to and sojourn in this luxurious palace is pivotal to this novel's narrative arch. The characters hope to elicit the witch's benign power and seek to restore their past amatory bliss. Felicia's "gran palacio" 'great palace' (256; 145) offers the reader instead another and parallel propitious fantasy to the *locus amoenus* through which to filter symbolically the historical subtext. Because the luxury of a court life is generally fashioned as contrary to the simplicity of the pastoral retreat, the palace's presence within the imaginary boundaries of the bower could be considered peculiar.[30] An ele-

---

[30] Cervantes, for example, in Chapter 6 of *Don Quixote*, disparaged Felicia's palace as anomalous in a pastoral novel. The curate states: "Y, pues comenzamos

ment often integral to other genres of amatory literature, such as the *novelas de caballería*,[31] the magical palace dazzles the reader with its magnificence and opens a space and time where transformation can take place. It also allows Montemayor and his readers to momentarily set aside the *aldea-corte* dichotomy, and indulge in an exquisite and laudatory representation of luxury. Even though the palace rivals nature, "más parecía obra de naturaleza que de arte" 'for it seemed more like a work of nature than a labor of human skill' (259; 146), Felicia's palace is not represented in *La Diana* as a jarring anomaly, an obtrusive *corte* in the middle of the *aldea*. Instead, the shepherds quickly acclimate to the "arte" and opulence therein found. The following is the pilgrims' first impression as told by the narrator when they are about to enter the palace:

> [T]oda la plaza era enlosada con losas de alabastro y mármol negro, a manera de jedrez. En medio della había una fuente de mármol jaspeado, sobre cuatro muy grandes leones de bronze. En medio de la fuente, estaba una columna de jaspe, sobre la cual cuatro ninfas de mármol blanco tenían sus asientos; los brazos tenían alzados en alto, y en las manos sendos vasos, hechos a la romana, de los cuales, por unas bocas de leones que en ellos había, echaban agua. La portada del palacio era de mármol serrado con todas las basas y chapiteles de las columnas dorados, y así mismo las vestiduras de las imágenes que en ello había. Toda la casa parecía hecha de reluciente jaspe con muchas almenas, y en ellas esculpidas algunas figuras de emperadores, matronas romanas y otras antiguallas semejantes. Eran todas las ventanas cada una de dos arcos; las cerraduras y clavazón de plata; todas las puertas, de cedro. La casa era cuadrada y a cada cantón había una alta y artificiosa torre. (258-9)

---

por *La Diana*, de Montemayor, soy de parecer que no se queme, sino que se le quite todo aquello que trata de la sabia Felicia y de la agua encantada y casi todos los versos mayores, y quédese en hora buena la prosa, y la honra de ser primero en semejantes libros" (118). [And as we're beginning with Montemayor's *Diana*, it's my opinion that it shouldn't be burned, but that the parts about the wise Felicia and the enchanted water should be cut, as well as nearly all the poems in Italian metre, and that the book should be welcome to keep its prose and the honour of being the first of its kind] (56-7). The potential irony in this passage should not be ignored. One must note that it is the priest who, predictably, censures Felicia's magic as well as the poetic interludes, the second element of which Cervantes used extensively in *La Galatea*.

[31] See Rallo, note 6, page 257.

> [T]he entire plaza was paved in a checkerboard pattern of alabaster and black marble. In the middle of it was a jasper fountain resting on four huge bronze lions. In the middle of the fountain was a jasper column, on top of which were seated four white marble nymphs. Their arms were uplifted, and in their hands they carried vases in the Roman style. On these were lions from whose mouths water flowed. The portal of the palace was of marble, the columns had bases and capitals of gold, as were the garments of the images on them. The entire palace was of shining jasper and had many battlements, on which were statues, some of Roman emperors and matrons and of other ancient personages. Each window had two arches, with silver locks and hinges; the doors were cedar. The palace was square, with a high and ornate tower in each corner. (146)

Possibly a reminder of the royal palace of Binche in Spanish Belgium (which Montemayor visited in his travels with Juana of Portugal), Felicia's palace is an image of the highest standards of court taste and luxury during this period. Commissioned by María of Hungary, sister of Charles V, and designed by Jacques de Broeucq, Binche was known for its architectural and artistic magnificence, as well as for its elaborate carnivals and other festivities, remembered with the popular phrase "Más bravas que las fiestas de Bins" ("more spectacular than the festivities at Bins").[32] As such, it provides the pastoral travelers, and the audience, a lavish rest stop where nature cedes its place and human design triumphs, placing an even greater distance between the real conditions of the agrarian topography and the fictional world of the text. Its presence in the bower offers a setting where the court audience–transported into the pastoral fantasy–can feel at home.

The descriptions of the palace are many, and the narrator takes obvious pleasure in offering lengthy and detailed explanations of the façade, inner rooms, and gardens. Complimenting the richness of the buildings and the grounds, there are also elaborate reports of Felismena's "natural" dress (266) (her courtly attire versus the "unnatural" shepherdess's dress), as well as of the fine glassware utilized to serve magic water (306). The symbolic aim behind this representation becomes even clearer if we think of Felicia's palace as a commemoration of the noble houses and country retreats that did

---

[32] See J. Subirats.

exist, but that here are stripped of the labor and the depletion of natural resources that sustained them. With roots in a medieval feudal past, the architecture of these residences was meant to separate and protect the affluent from the outside world, whether in the form of a foreign enemy or in the throngs of indigents that starved beyond their walls. In *La Diana* the fortress-like quality of Felicia's palace is demarcated by an "espeso bosque, y tan lleno de silvestres y espesos árboles, que a no ser de las tres ninfas guiados, no pudieran dejar de perderse en él" 'a dense wood, so full of thick and wild trees, had the three nymphs not guided them, they could not have helped but gotten lost' (255-6; 145). Following the logic of separation and seclusion, the "walled" palace can be read as an allusion to and a confirmation of class hierarchy and status. These social factors are typically excluded from the bower, but through Felicia's palace they find their way back into this pastoral novel, providing the audience a reassuring symbolic representation of wealth and privilege. The magnificence of the setting and the magical faculties of its inhabitants mesmerize and make welcome the shepherds and the readers, formally supporting an imaginary cessation of social and economic hierarchies.

Despite what convention may dictate, in *La Diana* this characteristic pastoral equality is not fully realized until the arrival at the palace. The text's social imaginary had up to this point in the novel maintained a veiled and deprecating division by negating the shepherds' admission into Felicia's courtly abode. In fact, we can justly argue that only Felismena's presence makes now possible their acceptance. It is she–as a representative of the court–who receives the better part of Felicia's attentions and affection. Accordingly, Felicia's very first words exclusively favor Felismena's comfort and consolation: "Para tan grande merecimiento como el vuestro [...] y tan extremada hermosura como naturaleza os ha concedido, todo lo que por vos se puede hacer es poco" 'Because you so deserve it," [...] "and because of the extraordinary beauty nature has granted you, all I could do for you would still not be enough' (258; 146). For the audience–and here one must also include the lower nobility and upwardly mobile *labradores ricos*–the palace thus denotes and promotes an ideal and ideologically charged model for aristocratic values.[33] Moreover, I would argue that Felicia's palace also could be

---

[33] Referring to the popularity of chivalric novels and their knack for adventure, fantasy, and romance Nalle reminds us how, "Many Castilians aspired to ennoble-

read as an illustration for a triumphant and hegemonic Spain, couched within the convention of an idyllic topography and detached from the human and material cost of acquiring and maintaining an empire. This interpretation becomes especially relevant when we consider that the palace of Binche was burned to the ground in 1554 (five years before *La Diana* was published) by the French who were vying for power in the Low Countries. The contrast between the trauma of history and the compelling vision of Felicia's magical castle highlights this text's desire to erase the conflict and destruction that are a part of the empire's reality. Felicia's palace emerges as a valuable metaphor that transports the reader from the messy referent of lived experience—lost wars, bankruptcy, and conflict-ridden class hierarchies—to an unblemished and reassuring fantasy of safeguarded luxury and comfort.

A similar type of ideologically driven representation of history is found in the various references to military figures during the visit to Felicia's palace. In the gardens, a statue of Mars stands glorious above a number of sculptures that represent classical and Spanish war heroes. Appropriately idealized men such as the Cid, Fernán González, Bernardo del Carpio, and Antonio de Fonseca trace Spanish might from the early stages of the Reconquest to the Catholic Kings, as well as pay tribute to the Vilanova family to whom *La Diana* is dedicated. An exaltation of these men may seem out of place in a pastoral novel. In Felicia's castle, however, it fits perfectly within a symbolic fantasy of Spain as a unified, powerful, and invincible Catholic nation-state. These heroes also recall a Golden Age of Spanish might that assuages any present doubts about Spain's hegemonic destiny. Finally, we must keep in mind that while the visit to Felicia's palace brings within the limits of the idyll a tribute to military aggression, any suggestion of violence and human suffering is diffused by the overall thematic focus on amity and love. In the midst of this garden of war heroes, the pilgrims dis-

---

ment and pure lineage, the first condition to be obtained in the royal courts, the second by certification from the Inquisition. The popularity of chivalric novels may simply reflect the fascination that noble status and values held for sixteenth-century Castilians. The inquisitorial evidence shows that [those] who owned chivalric novels were not hidalgos but rather farmers, small-town merchants of Jewish decent, and shopkeepers. The former two were groups that were but one patent of nobility and a certificate of pure blood away from entry into the hidalgo class" (88). I would argue that much of the same can be said regarding the popularity of pastoral novels.

cuss their conditions as lovers and the passage ends with Felicia happily resolving (or rather promising a resolution for) each of their amatory plights.

The symbolic function of the *locus amoenus*, the *aldea*, and the *corte* is–for the most part–effectively sustained in Cervantes's imitation of Montemayor. *La Galatea* is set, like its predecessor, in a wholly idealized yet recognizable geographical location, the shores of the Tagus. Following pastoral convention, Cervantes creates a world where any manifestation of need is intimately connected to the shepherd's love and where nature and feminine beauty form part of the same imaginary continuum. Here the narrator describes for the first time Galatea and her friend Florisa:

> Y después que las dos [Galatea y Florisa] dejaron ir a su albedrío a sus ganados a que de la verde hierba paciesen, convidadas de la claridad del agua de un arroyo que allí corría, determinaron de lavarse los hermosos rostros [...]. Comenzaron luego a coger diversas flores del verde prado con intención de hacer sendas guirnaldas con que recoger los desornados cabellos que sueltos por las espaldas traían. (209)

> After the two [Galatea and Florisa] had allowed their flocks to go at their will to graze on the green grass, they determined, invited by the clearness of the water of a stream flowing by, to wash their beautiful faces [...]. Straightway they began to gather diverse flowers from the green meadow with intent to make each a garland wherewith to bind up the disordered tresses that flowed freely over their shoulders. (33-4)[34]

This is a world where shepherds exclusively function as adoring lovers and where work, ambition, and hunger are displaced by poetry and friendship. A parallel narrative and ideological impetus is found in *La Diana*'s and *La Galatea*'s lengthy descriptions of cityscapes, related by visitors to the bower who in telling their stories of love and loss transport the narrative outside of the *locus amoenus*. In *La Diana*, for example, Felismena narrates her venture into the city dressed as a man in search of her lover. For Felismena

---

[34] All translations of *La Galatea* are largely based on H. Oelsner and A. B. Welford's translation. Upon occasion, I have slightly altered and modernized their work.

the city is a place of adventure, devoid of any sign of urban malaise. Even in *La Galatea*, where Cervantes engages in a much more realistic portrayal of the city as a place full of noise, confusion, and impending violence, all plot elements directly connect to the characters' disposition as friends and lovers. For instance, early in Silerio and Timbrio's tale, the friends survive an attack by Turkish pirates on the coast near Barcelona in which, "Poco le valía al sacerdote su santimonia, y al fraile su retraimiento, y al Viejo sus nevadas canas, y al mozo su juventud gallarda, y al pequeño niño su inocencia simple, que de todos llevaban el saco los descreídos perros" 'Little availed the priest his holiness, the friar his refuge, the old man his snowy hair, the boy his gallant youth, or the little child his simple innocence, for from all those unbelieving dogs carried off booty' (281; 78). Even so, when the friends do meet up again, the political implications and human toll of the Turkish threat is displaced in the mind of the friends to Timbrio's "sickness," his love for Nísida. Silerio states, "todo este placer mío se aguaba con el ver a Timbrio no tan bueno como yo quisiera, antes tan malo, y de una enfermedad tan extraña" 'but this my pleasure was all watered by seeing Timbrio not so well as I could wish, nay rather so ill, and with so strange a disease' (282; 79). The experience of violence and the threat to the empire's security is thus effectively disarmed and dissipated. Despite the *libros de pastores* conventional deployment of the country-city dichotomy, the cited examples clearly demonstrate how both the bower and the city can be used effectively as comforting symbolic versions of history: one where the peasantry is changed into courtly shepherds, where both the *prado* and the *palacio* are hyper-idealized and celebrated for their exquisiteness and wonder, and where the *corte* is inhabited by men and women guided not by greed or need, but by love. To summarize, the pastoral novel functions as a fictional locus where the contradictions and failures of both the city and country–political, military, environmental, and economic–are silenced in favor of a symbolic construct of Spain as an ideal land of plenty, virtue, and love.

Then again, as I previously suggested, *La Diana* and *La Galatea* contain moments where the symbolic undertaking is strained. Following the logic of the precept "et in Arcadia ego," critics have noted how the pastoral is never completely devoid of trauma.[35] I have

---

[35] See, for example, Damiani and Mujica.

elsewhere explored the ways in which the pastoral fantasy is threatened by specific acts of violence within its boundaries, for example in the murder of Carino in Book I of *La Galatea*.[36] The appearance of the lustful satyrs in *La Diana* is another obvious example of how unbridled desire can–even if momentarily–infiltrate the idyll in order to elevate the contrasting virtue of the shepherd-lovers. Yet, there are less conspicuous examples where the representation of history in these novels seems to falter in a manner significant for the purpose of this analysis.

One particularly intriguing example occurs when, during her stay in Felicia's palace, Felismena changes into a magnificent gown, showcasing herself as an ideal lady and worthy representative of the court's wealth and refinement. Among a number of jewels she is wearing is a necklace with a curious pendant "hecho a manera de culebra enroscada, que de la boca tenía colgada un águila que entre las uñas tenía un rubí" 'fashioned like a coiled snake with an eagle in its mouth holding a priceless ruby in its claws' (268; 151).[37] The image is disconcerting given that in traditional Christian iconography it is the serpent that finds itself defeated in the claws of the mighty eagle, a symbol for the triumph of good over evil, of virtue over vice.[38] Within a Spanish early modern context, this image is potentially even more charged given the identification of the Hapsburg dynasty with the eagle.[39] Is Felismena's pendant a veiled or

---

[36] See Hernández-Pecoraro.

[37] For a detailed interpretation of the significance of all of Felismena's jewels see Márquez Villanueva.

[38] For a description of the eagle's value as a symbol see Jack Tresidder.

[39] Sebastián de Covarrubias establishes two uses of the eagle by the Hapsburgs. First he refers to the two-headed eagle, a symbol of imperial power: "El águila con las dos cabezas significa el uno y otro Imperio, Oriental y Occidental; y éstos le pronosticaron a Alejandro Magno las dos águilas que aparecieron el día de su nacimiento, y han quedado incorporadas en las armas imperiales y en las de los Reyes de España, cuya potencia se ha extendido del Oriente al Poniente" 'The eagle with two heads means the two Empires together, the Oriental and the Occidental; this was a sign for Charlemagne that appeared on the day of his birth, and which has been incorporated in the imperial coat of arms as well as in the one for the Kings of Spain, whose potency has extended itself from east to west' (29; my translation). Later he adds, "El emperador Carlos Quinto batió en España una moneda cuyo reverso era el águila, con el rayo y el ramo de laurel debajo de los pies, y el mote *Cuique suum*; dando a entender que a los malos había de castigar y premiar a los buenos, destruir el vicio y coronar la virtud" 'The emperor Charles V instituted in Spain a coin which on the reverse side had the eagle, with lightning and the laurel at its feet, and the motto *Cuique suum*; for which he wanted understood that the bad had to be punished and the good rewarded, destroy vice and crown virtue' (31; my translation).

even an unconscious allusion to the political and economic troubles faced by the nation and the empire? Does it reflect the condition of a nation that even at its most powerful was vexed by constant war and bankruptcy? Perhaps, as Francisco Márquez Villanueva has suggested, the serpent is an *ouroboros*–a symbol of eternity–making its hold on the eagle a positive sign, signifying the everlasting glory of the Spanish empire and the house of Hapsburg. However, this positive reading of the pendant is problematized by the fact that the *ouroboros* motif requires the snake to appear to swallow its own tail. Because the eternal circle here is broken, the serpent may instead introduce a sense of finitude opposite to the *ouroboros*. If we also take into account the ruby held between the eagle's claws, the pendant's significance is further complicated. Generally speaking, rubies carry multiple meanings, including ardent love, vitality, royalty, and courage, all features that well-describe Felismena. In the mythological register, the ruby's association with blood acquires a double meaning. It is simultaneously linked to Ares and the bloodshed of war and to Cronos, who controlled passion.[40] Felismena herself represents both characteristics: at birth Venus denied her fruition in matters of love while Pallas offered her the gift of victory at arms.[41] In the Roman tradition, Ares and Cronos were respectively associated with Mars and Saturn; the ruby thus represents a paradoxical appetite for war *and* a peaceful age of gold.[42] A positive reading of the pendant may initially relate Felismena, and her unvarying passion for Felis, to Saturn. From a parallel perspective, the pendant thus could be seen as an allusion to a present Golden Age, with Saturn's ruby being held by the mighty Hapsburg eagle.

A negative interpretation of the pendant is also, and simultaneously, likely. Given the ruby's correlation with Ares, the eagle can stand for a bloodthirsty warrior, here wounded and defeated in the mouth of the serpent.[43] I am not suggesting that Felismena's pendant is an overt manifestation of Montemayor's or the reader's anxiety regarding the state of the Hapsburg Empire. Yet, Felismena's

---

[40] See Tresidder, page 173.
[41] Pallas is also Athena, the goddess of strategy and true courage.
[42] An alternative tradition in classical mythology rejects Cronos's tyranny and, like Saturn, makes him a benign ruler who presided over a blessed Golden Age. See Michael Grant and John Hazel, page 93.
[43] Ares, in contrast to Athena, was known for finding satisfaction only in battle and bloodshed. See Grant and Hazel, page 41.

own duplicity as a lover and a warrior opens up a space of indeterminacy in the text, which is in this episode further denoted by the ambivalent signification of the pendant. If the pendant can signify both Felismena's love and a "golden" Hapsburg empire, it also may bring to the fore the material and human cost brought about by constant military campaigns. Felismena's jewelry can thus be said to produce an ideological gap where the unresolved contradictions of a vast and powerful empire burdened by ever-expanding military commitments and mounting debts surreptitiously emerge, integrated within the rich attire of an idealized lady of the court.

Another example of uncertainty in both *La Diana* and *La Galatea* is the way in which material interests and class distinctions insidiously seep into the social fabric of the pastoral community. Despite a pastoral convention that claims freedom from economic concerns or class hierarchies, Diana, the shepherdess who is the focus of Sireno and Sylvano's love and after whom the text is named, is forced by her father to marry a man for his wealth. This is a decision that makes her personally miserable and consequently unavailable to her suitor Sireno: "Jamás tiene el rostro alegre, / siempre la cara inclinada, / los ojos por los rincones, / la habla triste y turbada, / ¿Cómo vivirá la triste / que se ve tan mal casada?" 'His face is never happy, / He always hangs his head, / His eyes in every corner, / His speech, sad and trouble. / How can a wretch / Who is so sadly married live?' (Lns. 37-42. 324; 180). Montemayor situates Diana within the tradition of the *mal maridada*, thereby offering the reader an easily recognizable literary referent for the character. Yet the conditions of her marriage can also be seen as indirectly marking the unforgiving material exigencies of rural existence and the real hardships and displacement that the rural peasantry did in fact endure. Diana's father, unable to sustain his family, sees no alternative but to marry his daughter to the rich but uncouth Delio.[44] For this

---

[44] When compared to Sireno and Sylvano, Delio is described as follows: "[A]unque es rico de los bienes de fortuna, no lo es de los de naturaleza, que en esto de la disposición ya ves cuán mal le va, pues de otras cosas de que los pastores nos preciamos como son tañer, cantar, luchar, jugar al cayado, bailar con las mozas los domingos, parece que Delio no ha nacido más que para mirallo" '[A]lthough rich in Fortune's riches, is not rich in Nature's, nor in his disposition. You see how bad it is, for of the skills we shepherds take pride in, such as playing, singing, wrestling, twirling our crooks, dancing with the maidens on Sunday, Delio was born to be but a spectator' (130; 63). This portrait of the bad husband is very telling since it reveals that Delio's flaw is his not sharing with the others the same pastoral aesthetic.

reason the father is vilified in the text. At the same time, it is undeniable that his need to marry off Diana introduces within this pastoral scene issues of economic desperation and helplessness that destabilize the symbolic aims of pastoral ideality.

This scenario is repeated and intensified in *La Galatea*. Galatea's father's unwillingness to listen to his daughter's pleas and his plan to marry her to a wealthy foreigner can be read as emblematic of an economy that exploits the weakest members of society—whether women or poor *labradores*. This social reality devolves at the end of *La Galatea* into the threat of violence and imperils the idyll's survival. The shepherds, unable to accept this chain of events, threaten to take up arms against Galatea's father and the Lusitanian suitor.

Equally as disturbing is the insistence in the first pages of *La Galatea* to establish a hierarchical distinction between the two main shepherds, Elicio as a *pastor fino* and Erastro as a *pastor rústico*.[45] Erastro's lowly condition is demarcated by the gruffness of his name, the herd he tends—goats rather than sheep—and the names he gives his dogs: León, Gavilán, Robusto, and Manchado.[46] Cervantes here is possibly recalling a more rustic medieval pastoral poetic tradition, which often contained both types. Nonetheless, the incorporation of this difference in *La Galatea* demonstrates the insidiousness of hierarchical class distinctions in the text's representation of the historical subtext. Even though Erastro's rusticity is attenuated by his love—the Virgilian topos *omnia vincit amor*—it nonetheless allows Elicio to disparage his fellow shepherd as an unworthy suitor for Galatea. Elicio eventually embraces Erastro's company and common love for Galatea, but not until he further demeans Erastro for his rusticity:

> No le daba a Elicio pena la competencia de Erastro, porque entendía del ingenio de Galatea que a cosas más altas la inclinaba; antes tenía lástima y envidia a Erastro: lástima, en ver que al fin amaba, y en parte donde era imposible coger el fruto de sus deseos; envidia, por parecerle que quizá no era tal su entendimiento que diese lugar al alma a que sintiese los desdenes o favores de Galatea, de suerte, o que los unos le acabasen, o los otros lo enloqueciesen. (172)

---

[45] For further discussion of this topic see Trambaioli.
[46] I refer you to Rallo's notes 22 and 28 on pages 171 and 173 respectively.

> To Elicio the rivalry of Erastro did not give pain, for he understood from the mind of Galatea that it inclined her to loftier things – rather did he have pity and envy for Erastro: pity in seeing that he did indeed love, and that in a quarter where it was impossible to gather the fruit of his desires; envy in that it seemed to him that perhaps his understanding was not such as to give room for his soul to feel the flouts of favours of Galatea in such a way that either the latter should overwhelm him, or the former drive him mad. (12-3)

Elicio's dismissal of his friend as poor and thus ignorant and unworthy, as well as the derogatory attitude communicated by his assertions, goes against the thrust of the pastoral metaphor, to create a harmonious history of Spanish social conflict. Instead, Erastro's position tacitly summons the inequities and prejudices that justified the oppression of the rural poor, and confirms a set of aristocratic values that are at the core of these novels.

III. HISTORICAL SUBTEXT AND GENDERED SUBJECTS

Much of the material and political difficulties in which Spain found itself are, as I have shown, ideally narrativized within the boundaries of the *locus amoenus*. But these issues are typically not what most capture our attention when we enter the pastoral fantasy. With texts such as *La Diana* and *La Galatea*, our reading experience understandably centers on the topic of love and the plight of shepherd. We encounter shepherds whose amatory devotion is motivated by a feminine ideal of unparalleled beauty, spiritual nobility, and corporal chastity. Yet, just as I have argued regarding the social and economic subtext, sexual hierarchies are masterfully idealized through the prism of pastoral love, which for the most part displaces the otherwise difficult business of gender relations in the social sphere. The audience–male and female–is offered instead a seductively docile representation of the standards that determined sexual roles during this period. Women are represented as forever young, delicate, and pure. In this capacity, they are treated as sublime beings that inspire and uplift their equally laudable counterparts. But the awe-inspiring likeness between lover and beloved is not as benign as it may first appear. Women characters remain objects to be adored, their individual desire and material corporality radically ignored in the amatory fantasy of their lovers. For sure many women inhabit pastoral novels and their voices and behaviors do not always conform to the feminine ideal therein created by the male community of lovers. But we must see these manifestations of agency and desire as notable yet temporary moments of instability and fragmentation of the pastoral metaphor. In other words, one could well argue that, despite the presence of these feminine voices in bower, from the lover's and the narrator's subjective perspective these shepherdesses disappear. They are physically present in the bower, but their individuality, agency, and desire is lost to the shepherd lover in a fog of abstracting devotion. The discourse of love in these texts only values the conceptual ideality these women are made to embody–and which reflects the good taste and nobility of the lover–rather than the specificity they otherwise possess. The result is that the unresolvable conflicts and contradictions intrinsic to gender relations also seemingly disappear from the idyll. The shepherds love the *idea* of woman, not the woman as such, and in the process the incongruity and inconsistency that draw up sexual social boundaries and prescriptions are conveniently ignored or repressed. Given the centrality of the amatory theme in the Spanish *libros de pastores* and the corresponding significance bestowed upon the experiences of the male characters, I would argue that idealized love acts as the primary metaphor that displaces and resolves all other sets of differences, conflicts, and contradictions.[47] In other words, if there is no manifest corrosive opposition between the male shepherd and his abstracted other, then all other tensions –whether political, social, religious, or economic–can also be easily obviated. The pastoral amatory fantasy, more than any other idealizing mechanism in these books, nurtures and secures these novels' aristocratic and patriarchal ideological vocation. This is a set of ideas which takes up much of the analysis done in subsequent chapters of this book.

For now, and in order to better understand the social subtext that the pastoral novel is metaphorically addressing, it is necessary that we look more closely at some of the actual conditions that framed women's lives during this period. Once again, I do not pre-

---

[47] In Jameson's terms, gender is the ideologeme, the key unit or material used to construct the representation/repression of history.

tend to offer an exhaustive account of the many and varied forces that shaped women's history in sixteenth-century Spain. Instead, I will briefly draw attention to some aspects of women's lives that I believe are relevant to an analysis of the ideological use or function of the pastoral metaphor, especially as it symbolically represents gender relations.

The gap between idealizing discourses and lived experience contributes to the complexity of early modern women's history in Spain. One of the more fascinating aspects of this history is the lack of correlation between what historians have increasingly documented was the actual participation of women in society and the officially demarcated roles and rights that were conferred upon them in legal and religious discourse. Antonio Domínguez Ortiz aptly summarizes the situation as follows:

> De esta forma se mezclaban en la condición femenina los factores positivos y los negativos, con un saldo muy difícil de establecer, porque estaba en relación con la situación ambigua de la mujer, desprovista de fuerza *legal*, pero con una apreciable dosis de poder *real*, en todos los ámbitos, incluso en el religioso [...]. Gracias a esas mismas dotes, las mujeres se introducen en el campo del poder político, rigen estados señoriales, rigen los destinos del propio estado castellano, participan en los descubrimientos y conquistas, demuestran que Isabel I no fue un mero azar histórico, sino un hecho que encajaba en la lógica de los tiempos. (160-1)

> In this manner positive and negative factors were mixed in the feminine condition, with a final balance being very difficult to establish, because it was related to the ambiguous situation of women, who lacked legal power, but possessed a considerable amount of real power, in all sectors of society, including the religious [...]. Thanks to those same qualities, women introduce themselves in the political arena, control seigniorial estates, even the destiny of the Castilian state, participate in discoveries and conquests, demonstrate that Isabela I was not a historical rarity, but a fact that belonged in the logic of the time. (my translation)

Historians and literary critics have thus accordingly delved into the lives of women whose access to power enabled their contributions to the religious, economic, and political spheres as laborers in a variety of marketplaces, heads of households, founders of convents, and political advisors and administrators at court. Whether we look at influential women at court such as Isabel of Portugal, Juana of Portugal, Empress María, Margaret of Austria, Margaret of the Cross, Isabel Clara Eugenia, the extended Mendoza women's clan, or religious and literary figures such as Saint Teresa of Ávila and Luisa de Carvajal, their deeds confirm the legitimacy of this long overdue revision of women's history in early modern Spain.[48]

Yet, power was not limited to those women who possessed sanctioned positions of authority. Women of all classes (single, married, widowed, poor, and rich) took an active role in the fiscal administration of the family estate.[49] Their influence and participation also became increasingly public in a society and economy that could not base its stability and prosperity solely on the activity of its men.[50] When men went away to foreign wars or to the New World, their wives managed their homes and businesses. When they died, widows inherited their monies, debts, and responsibilities.[51] Young women, if wealthy or titled, were sought after for the dowries and prestige they could bring into a marriage union.[52] For their part, underprivileged women and common *labradoras* helped take care

---

[48] See Anne Cruz's work on Luisa de Carvajal, Helen Nader, Kelli Rae Ringhofer, Magdalena Sánchez, and Alison Weber.

[49] Domínguez Ortiz characterizes the situation of women, including the *labradora*, in Spain during this period as follows: "La presencia, extensa y variada, de la mujer en diversos ámbitos profesionales no agotaba su capacidad económica, directa e indirecta. Nos hemos referido a la actividad de las viudas. En los padrones de la Edad Media, y también de la Moderna, se englobaban bajo tal rúbrica a todas las mujeres autónomas: auténticas viudas, mujeres separadas, mujeres cuyos maridos habían emigrado y solteras mayores de edad con casa propia. Todas ellas cabezas de hogar [...]" 'The presence, extensive and varied, of women in diverse professional settings did not limit their economic capacity, directly or indirectly. We have referred to the activities of widows. In the categories existent during the medieval and the modern period, all autonomous women were named as such: authentic widows, those separated from their husbands, those whose husbands had emigrated, and single older women with their own independent household. All of these women were heads of households [...]' (156; my translation). Mary Elizabeth Perry established many of the same parameters for the study of early modern women in Spain. See also Richard T. Vann.

[50] See Mercedes Borrero Fernández.

[51] It is estimated that due to high mortality rates among men, "nearly a fifth of the households in Castilian cities [...] might be in the care of widows" (Casey 122).

[52] Casey assesses women's economic power as follows: "Though the closure of the frontier led to a reshaping of inheritance law from the later Middle Ages, women continued to control much property–as heiresses in their own right, as recipients of dowry from their parents, as claimants on that dowry when widowed, together with one half of any 'gains' (*gananciales*) made during marriage" (200).

of their families through their labor. In rural and urban contexts, lower class women occupied an important place in everyday economic life: "[M]any [...] worked outside of the city walls where certain agricultural occupations were exclusively female. [...] Inside the city, certain retail occupations were filled only by women, who sold fruits, vegetables, fish, tripe, and dairy products. Regardless of marital status, those with little wealth worked" (Perry 16-7).[53] Their wealthier counterparts–the *labradoras ricas*–also were involved personally in the economic prosperity of their homes, buying, selling, or renting property, arranging marriages for their children, investing in commerce and forming their own commercial companies, or managing their husbands' business and investments.[54] In sum, women's participation in all spheres was essential to Spanish society's welfare.

The public presence of women pushed the limits of a patriarchal ideology that, as Fray Luis de León espoused in his *La perfecta casada*, preferably wished to curtail all liberty of movement: "[P]ara que se entienda que su andar ha de ser en su casa, y que ha de estar presente siempre en todos los rincones de ella; y que, porque ha de estar siempre allí presente, por eso no ha de andar fuera nunca; y que, porque sus pies son para rodear sus rincones, entienda que no los tienen para rodear los campos y las calles" 'According to this, the good wife must make up her mind that she is to walk about in her own house, and that its every nook and cranny is to be pervaded by her presence. And because she is always to be present at home, for that very reason she is never to walk abroad. Since her feet are to enable her to search into corners, clearly she is not to employ them in roaming about through streets and fields' (66; 73). Women laborers ventured into the streets and were exposed to all sorts of situations and exchanges. Prostitution and other "professions"–procuresses, potion makers, fortune-tellers, witches, and healers, to name some–flourished in a society and an economy that provided only limited prospects for the poor and the hungry. The urban landscape, crowded with a seemingly endless number of newcomers, travelers, and vagabonds, became an open

---

[53] Women in the cities and towns constituted a constant public presence as market vendors, bakers, and servants at inns, which in turn gave an impression of women having become "tougher." See Casey, Chapter 9, especially pages 204-5.

[54] See Perry, especially pages 14-6.

arena that challenged traditional notions of public decency and safety. According to the *arbitrista* Cristóbal Pérez de Herrera, "[T]here are in this kingdom more people than you can imagine who [...] live like pagans [...] most of them with unmarried partners [...] sleeping in doorways and barns" (cited in Casey 124). Concerned with the issue of women's deviancy, moralists such as Juan Luis Vives argued for a differentiation of decent Christian women from all others by covering their faces with a cloak when going out in public. But, as Anne J. Cruz has pointed out, "it was not long before prostitutes and other women of questionable virtue began to take advantage of the anonymity afforded by such a garment," an abuse that only ended with its prohibition in 1639 (*Discourses of Poverty* 139). Unable to tell the sinners from the saints, the social order was hard pressed to control the movement and exposure of women. The potential for confusion and corruptibility was perhaps best exemplified by the rise in popularity of the horse carriage among women of all classes during the sixteenth and seventeenth centuries:

> Se había puesto de moda entre las mujeres de toda condición conseguir que las llevasen en coche o disponer de coche propio para lucirse en los paseos de la villa, acudir los días festivos a los lugares más concurridos y desplazarse por las polvorientas calles madrileñas con mayor comodidad, disfrutando de un lujo que era propio del rango social más distinguido. (Bernardo J. García García 33)

> It was fashionable for women of all conditions to ride in carriages or to acquire carriages of their own in order to show off in the streets of their towns, go during festivities to the most sought out places, and venture in the dusty streets of Madrid with more comfort, enjoying a luxury that was deemed proper only for the upper echelons of society. (my translation)

García's account aptly shows the ability of the lower classes to gain access to a product formerly reserved for the rich. It simultaneously brings to light the desire and capacity of women to "lucirse" or take their place in the public arena, thereby threatening a social order dependent upon controlling the propriety and reputation of its women. In this type of environment, even the growing numbers of religious women–lay *beatas* and nuns–posed a threat, given the appeal of mysticism and the lack of power that priests held over these women's spiritual flights and visionary dreams. Magdalena de la Cruz, Lucrecia de León, and even Teresa de Ávila make evident the problems the Church hierarchy faced in light of an active and subjective feminine religious life.[55]

In response, moralists loudly voiced their concerns and increasingly sought to define the acceptable bounds of conduct for honorable Christian women. One could say they drew a portrait of the "golden" woman, not corrupted by the knowledge and agency afforded by the multiple and available social roles. Texts such as Vives's *Instrucción de la mujer cristiana* or León's *La perfecta casada* reveal the control that the Spanish patriarchy felt it needed to impose when faced with this historical reality. Ironically, as Vigil has pointed out, these idealized models for feminine perfection expose the actual patterns of behavior that women engaged in:

> [A] partir del siglo XVI, la mayoría de los moralistas optaron por dejar de lanzar improperios misóginos [populares durante el medioevo] y se dedicaron en gran medida a elaborar modelos de perfectas doncellas, perfectas casadas, perfectas viudas y perfectas monjas, para tratar de convencer a las mujeres de que se ajustaran a las normas de acción que correspondían a los papeles y estados en los que trataban de ser ubicadas por el poder masculino. *Estos escritos proporcionan bastantes datos sobre las desviaciones que surgían en la realidad* [...]. (17, my emphasis)

> Starting in the sixteenth century, the majority of moralists opted to leave behind their misogynist discourse [popular during the medieval period] and dedicated themselves to elaborating models for the perfect lady, perfect married woman, perfect widow and perfect nun, to try to convince women to adjust to the norms prescribed by the roles and states to which masculine power tried to tie them. *These writings offer data concerning the deviations that by contrast occurred in reality* [...]. (my translation and emphasis)

In other words, conduct manuals and other sources of instruction for women may be read against themselves, so that the prescriptions so adamantly defended and the idealized virtues proposed—silence, domesticity, and chastity—can be seen as veiling their oppo-

---

[55] See Richard Kagan and Alison Weber.

site: women's active and wide-ranging engagement in the private and public spheres. The didactic import of such manuals is in fact manifold, instructing fathers or husbands on the desirable characteristics that their daughters and wives should possess, all the while glossing over the economic and social contributions that women were required to make. Much like the Golden Age fantasy, these manuals offer an idealized definition of femininity that would resolve the contradictions between patriarchal discourse and women's actual experience.

Although radically different in tone and form, I find pastoral novels and conduct manuals very similar in their ideological aim: they address similar social anxieties and instruct their readers, both men and women, on proper gender roles. Indeed, the pastoral's use as an effective tool for the dissemination of a prescriptive model for feminine behavior gains more credibility when we consider these books' best selling status.[56] This function of the pastoral novel, I would argue, is especially relevant when we examine the figure of the shepherdess, whose ethereal perfection in the eyes of her lover denies her any active participation as equal partner in the relationship. Reflective of the ideal values of the court milieu where the pastoral mode first gained popularity, these novels provided narrow standards that the general audience–and especially those who aspired to become titled nobility–could imitate. In other words, despite the active and necessary participation of women in the social and the economic sphere, pastoral novels fed into a limiting vision of women as vessels of abstracted beauty attached to a highly restrictive expectation of demure invisibility. Like conduct manuals, these novels well served a society that increasingly depended on women's labor while also desiring to limit feminine agency.

La Diana saw at least twenty-six Spanish editions from its first publication in the late 1550's (Valencia, exact date unknown) to 1600, a publishing phenomenon widely attributed to women read-

---

[56] Regarding *La Diana*'s "best-seller" status among secular texts, Whinnom states: "Whichever set of figures one uses, *Celestina* was quite clearly the most successful piece of fiction in the entire Golden Age, eclipsed only if we allow *Amadís* to embrace its sequels. Second and third in the fiction class come *Guzmán de Alfarache* and Montemayor's *Diana*" (Whinnom 193). I speculate that Whinnom's "rankings" would change in the pastoral novel's favor if he considered *La Diana* and its "sequels" as one general unit.

ers and their preference for amatory literature.[57] In contrast to my contention that these novels served a prescriptive function, some critics consider their impact on the female audience as confirming two provocative assertions. First, pastoral novels, both structurally and thematically, are said to contain proto-feminist ideas which the female audience sought out. Second, it is argued that the increase in women's literacy resulted in their ability to exert pressure upon authorial choices and the marketplace.[58] Bruce Wardropper, for instance, claims that the idyll, interpreted as a "neutral background," grants women a sense of equality "that the social conventions of an urban setting would deny them" (129). Following Wardropper's lead, Elizabeth Rhodes focuses on the way in which pastoral texts set themselves apart from other Renaissance genres by avoiding aggressive masculine values (war, competition) in favor of an exploration of the "inner worth" and "inner experience" of the individual and of elements classified as "sexually subversive," such as the free intermingling of male and female characters and the candor with which characters express their desires ("Skirting the Men" 145-6).[59] Despite the intriguing nature of these propositions, there is cause for concern. To suggest there is an overt feminist posturing in these novels is also conspicuously to overlook the overriding formal and plot conventions established by *La Diana*. As the definition of female beauty and chastity glorified by shepherd-lovers demonstrates, the vision of womanhood in pastoral texts clearly addresses patriarchal values and expectations.[60] Moreover, shepherdesses and

---

[57] For a detailed list of known editions of Montemayor's text, see López Estrada's edition of *La Diana*.

[58] For example, Rhodes has argued that the genre's popularity was directly "influenced by a group of readers–women–whose presence directed the phenomenon" ("Skirting the Men" 131). Despite her assertion, Rhodes notes, "the intellectual level of Spanish women's involvement in literary endeavors still appears to have been far below that of their counterparts in other European countries" (ftn. 8. 135).

[59] One of the most controversial conclusions that can be reached from Rhodes's argument is that both humanism and religious reform in the sixteenth century can be considered movements that championed feminine values and the equality of women. Unfortunately, neither movement accomplished these goals, and perhaps can generally be said to have produced exactly the opposite results: reassert the "new" humanist man (not woman) and his intellectual, spiritual, social, and political being as the model to be privileged. For another feminist interpretation of Spanish pastoral texts see Begoña Souviron López's *La mujer en la ficción arcádica*.

[60] As Rhodes has not failed to acknowledge, "the female characters in *La Diana* and many of its continuations are subject to events dictated by men" (148).

their city companions are invariably young and inaccessible, traits that limit the possibilities for female character development and their interaction with their male counterparts. Contrary to historical experience, there are no positions of power for women to occupy. Instead, idealized beloveds exclusively portrayed as objects of abstract splendor and virtue deemed worthy of the adoration of their lovers. It is undeniable that–influenced by the medieval courtly love tradition–the shepherds' pleas are characterized by a servile and sacrificial tone. It is also a fact that these novels are structured around amatory relations and that the bower provides a space where male and female characters meet outside of the watchful eye of a chaperon or authority figure. Yet, these facts can hardly override the limited and limiting position that the female beloved occupies. It is important that we do not dismiss the type of gender ideology that ultimately prevails in the *libros de pastores*. And if, as a result, we see the pastoral novel as complicit with a larger symbolic and cultural project, then we need to admit to other, more probable explanations for the popularity these novels enjoyed among women. Unless we address these issues, we are bound to misread the pastoral's symbolic function within the period. Perhaps even more significantly, failure to tackle them would also lead us to overlook how these novels' patriarchal values are specifically, and at times surprisingly, challenged and disrupted.

It is important to consider how these books were meant to be read and what models of behavior female readers may have learned from them. Vigil has suggested a very perceptive historical interpretation of the relation between pastoral books (and other similar genres such as courtly love and chivalric novels) and their female audience. Instead of providing a fictional space where women readers saw a reflection of their own increasing agency within the social order, pastoral novels provided a sanctioned and subduing notion of love and female ideality. Women readers seem to have identified with the figure of the adored *doncella*, who possesses stunning good looks, carries herself with absolute poise and decorum, and is always attractively and demurely dressed (even if in pastoral garb). The damsel, in other words, is a perfect model of what patriarchal discourse has long advertised as proper for the female gender. Even detractors of *La Diana,* such as Malón de Chaide, tend to be bothered not by any images of unlimited female agency within the boundaries of the bower, but by what they see as the book's influencing of many young women to have expectations of being ministered to by their mates:

> ¿Cómo dirá el Pater Noster en las Horas, la que acaba de sepultar a Píramo y Tisbe en *Diana*? [...] Allí se aprenden las desenvolturas y las bachillerías; y náceles un deseo de ser servidas y recuestadas [...] y de ahí vienen a ruines y torpes imaginaciones, y de éstas a los conciertos, o desconciertos, con que se pierden a sí y afrentan las casas de sus padres y les dan desventurada vejez. (Malón de Chaide as cited in Vigil 67-8)

> How will she who has just buried Pyramus and Thisbe in the *Diana* say the Pater Noster? [...] There they learn self-assurance and witty behavior; and is born in them a desire to be served [...] and from that they come to ruinous thoughts, and from these to disconcerting acts with which they loose themselves and offend the homes of their parents and which results in an old age full of misfortune. (my translation)

These complaints against pastoral female characters have a lot to do with securing an appropriate balance of power between the lovers –with men always in command of the relationship–rather than with the threat of women as capable and independent subjects. Not without irony, Chaide's denunciation reveals a perhaps unconscious anxiety with women forgoing their practical duties in favor of a fantasy of love, damaging the material stability and prosperity of home and society. Women should submit to their husbands, not expect to be served by them. They should diligently work for the good and the benefit of their families, not expect life to be an endless succession of passionate encounters.

Following a similar logic, these same moralists indicted pastoral novels (and other amatory genres) for putting forward the idea that the pairing of individuals should be guided solely by love, free from parental supervision.[61] Even if seemingly contradictory, Church doctrine officially promoted the free will of the participants and the importance of love as the deciding factor in any union. Officially couples and their parents were to honor the sacrament and reject

---

[61] The two exceptions are Diana and Galatea, both of whom are given away by father's looking to profit from their marriage unions.

the idea of marriage as a pure material exchange. Despite this apparent endorsement of female agency both in amatory fiction as in Church doctrine, pastoral novels did not have the repercussions moralists so much feared. To the contrary, it seems that in general women readers were enticed not by a libertine tendency in pastoral society, but by the idea of being celebrated and adored by devoted lovers; of being, in other words, perfect and abstracted objects of desire. As Vigil has well argued,

> En la [literatura amatoria], la dama era presentada como un ser no-humano, como un estereotipo abstracto y genérico de feminidad que incluía la pasividad, la belleza y la objetualidad de un fetiche. Sin embargo, aquel modelo ejercía sobre ellas una gran atracción, y trataban de burlar las vigilancias familiares para ser "servidas" por caballeros, con el objetivo final de llegar a casarse. Su resistencia a la sociedad consistió en practicar un tipo de desviación que Mertón llama innovadora: ir más allá de los métodos considerados como legítimos por el sistema para lograr los fines que el mismo sistema marca. (91)

> In amatory literature, the lady is presented as a non-human being, as an abstract and generic stereotype of femininity that was characterized by passivity, beauty, and the objectification of a fetish. Nonetheless, that model had great attraction to female readers, and they tried to fool those who watched over them in order to be "served" by gentlemen, but always with the objective of an eventual marriage. Their resistance consisted in practicing a type of deviation that Mertón calls innovative: go beyond the methods considered legitimate by the system in order to achieve the same ends as the system requires. (my translation)

Amatory literature, and most definitively pastoral novels I will argue, actually promote a model of love that depended not on an equalizing relationship between men and women but rather on traditional and limiting notions of feminine beauty, chastity, and virtue.

In this manner, pastoral novels seduce the female audience into happily accepting an impossible ideal of female perfection and gendered relationships, hardly an empowering notion for women. What is so liberating or subversive about being a remote goddess-like figure that is served from afar? For male readers, the overall message is equally conformist: idealize women that will hardly be seen or dealt with, practice good manners, take up poetry, and spend a lot of time in the company of agreeable male friends. The bower is a place where love is celebrated. But, far from an engaged encounter between subjects, pastoral love requires men to focus on their own ennoblement and women to play the part of chaste–and preferably silent or absent–objects of desire. And in this manner the pastoral metaphor, I maintain, reconfigures the real and conflict-ridden experience of agency and self-determination made palpable in women's daily lives.

One example that perfectly illustrates the way in which women's history is represented–rid of any potential challenge to patriarchal discourse or social law–is the "Canto de Orfeo" in *La Diana*. Orpheus's song is a focal point in the visit to Felicia's castle both for the particular mode in which it is delivered–a statue magically comes to life and sings–as well as for cataloging many of the most important women of the Spanish nobility during the first half of the sixteenth century. Like Felicia's palace, Orpheus's choice of women seems largely out of place in a pastoral novel that by convention sees itself as opposite to the court, and especially to the superficiality of its court women whose "confianza y presumpción [es] celebrada por sólo el voto y parecer de sus apasionados" 'the vanity and presumption of the lady celebrated only by the vows and opinions of her suitors' (111; 51). Even so, Orpheus's song occupies a privileged position in Book IV, engaging for forty-three stanzas the undivided attention of all the pilgrim-shepherds. Most certainly, the author's own interest in praising the women and families to whom he owed favors or from whom he would request future protection is evident in the passage. Nevertheless, and especially if we take into account Montemayor's personal contact with women of the royal family, one could expect that this passage would also document the influence and authority that many of these women had in the affairs of the empire, Spain, and their families. The first two praised after a perfunctory tribute to the goddess Diana are a case in point. María of Hungary, Charles V's younger sister, was appointed regent of the Netherlands in 1531, a post that she held until 1556 (three years before the publication of *La Diana*).[62] Having

---

[62] María married King Louis of Hungary and Bohemia in 1522. The couple never had any children. Louis was killed at the battle of Mohács in 1526, five years before she assumed the regency of the Netherlands.

governed the Low Countries for over thirty years, she returned a widow and joined the now abdicated emperor and king at Cigales, where she died in 1558. Second in the "Canto" is Juana of Portugal, Charles V's daughter and Montemayor's most important protector, who returned to Spain a widow and soon after was named official regent during her father's and brother's (Philip II) absence between 1556 and 1559. The only woman ever officially to join the Jesuit order, Juana founded the Royal Discalced Convent in Madrid, which became an important secondary residence and religious retreat for the Hapsburg women, most prominently Empress María. Montemayor's contact with both women was significant. Born in Portugal and of Spanish decent, Montemayor first arrived at the Castilian court as part of the entourage of María Manuela of Portugal, Prince Philip II's first wife. By 1548 he seems to have been at the service of Charles V's eldest daughter, María, as a singer in the Royal Chapel. He traveled in 1549 to the Netherlands with Philip II, where he encountered at the palace of Binche María of Hungary. When Juana of Portugal returned to the Castilian court after the death of her husband, Montemayor once more found himself at the service of a member of the royal family. Juana's desire to surround herself with Portuguese servants and her interest in the arts placed Montemayor in a splendid position and he became her chamberlain for the duration of her regency.

Montemayor, therefore, was a first-hand witness to their influence within the Hapsburg court. In fact, according to Fernández de Retana's biography of Juana, Philip II narrowed down his candidates for the regency between precisely these two women, finally opting for his sister Juana, given his aunt's María's "carácter demasiado autoritario" 'very authoritarian temperament' (92; my translation). Nevertheless, the "Canto de Orfeo," rather than acknowledging their political deeds and agency, profusely utilizes a language of beauty, discretion, and grace, which belies any real power that these women exercised in their country's and family's affairs. True, the stanzas dedicated to María of Hungary and Juana of Portugal tout their royal standing as worthy of "el cetro, la corona y alta silla" 'the scepter, crown, / And mighty throne' (Ln. 36. 279; 155).[63] However, their standing is a source of personal power that

---

[63] As Orfeo points out, in Juana's case her rightful place as queen of Portugal was denied by her husband's sudden death.

in the "Canto" is curiously diminished by the song's emphasis on the fickleness of fortune, these women's regular absence from Spain, and their suffering as widows.

> Los ojos levantad mirando aquella
> qu'en la suprema sill'está sentada,
> el cetro y la corona junto a ella,
> *y d'otra parte la fortun'airada.*
> Ést'es la luz d'España y clar'estrella,
> *con cuy'absenci'está tan eclipsada;*
> su nombre, ¡oh ninfas!, es doña María,
> gran reina de Bohemia, d'Austria, Ungría.
> L'otra junto a ella es doña Juana
> de Portugal Princes', y de Castilla
> Infanta, *a quien quitó fortun'insana*
> el cetro, la corona y alta silla,
> *Y a quien la muerte fue tan inhumana*
> *qu'aun ell'así s'espanta y maravilla*
> *de ver cuán presto'nsangrentó sus manos,*
> en quien fu'espejo y luz de lusitanos.
> (Lns. 25-40. 278-9, my emphasis)

> Lift up your eyes, upon seeing her
> Who sits upon the highest throne,
> Her scepter and crown beside her
> *On her other side, angry Fortune.*
> She is the light of Spain, and her bright star
> *In whose absence she is eclipsed.*
> Her name, oh nymphs, is Doña María,
> Great Queen of Bohemia, Austria, and Hungary.
> The other, near her, is Doña Joana,
> Princess of Portugal and of Castile.
> *Angry Fortune stole* the scepter, crown,
> And mighty throne from this Infanta.
> *Death was so inhuman to her,*
> *That even he marvels and is awed*
> *To see how quickly he bloodied the hands*
> Of she one who was the mirror and light of the
> Lusitanians. (155, my emphasis)

The "cetro, corona y alta silla" are here melancholy symbols of a past or never realized power, removing each royal woman from any claim to authority and situating them as idealized victims of time, hardship, and death. It would be unwise to pretend that these facts of life did not in effect partially determine these women's destinies. The death of Juana's husband-prince, for example, resulted in her leaving Portugal and sacrificing much of the influence she would have exerted within the Portuguese court or upon her young son, Sebastian. At the same time, Juana's return to Spain afforded her an enviable position within the Spanish court, as well as in the religious community of Madrid. Orpheus's "praise" does not acknowledge Juana's role at court. Instead, she is transformed into the pure image of a suffering widow (focusing on her shock at her husband's early death), and taking no notice of her regency of the Spanish crown. Much of the same can be said for María of Hungary, a woman whose power in the Low Countries and whose close relationship with Charles V is in this passage completely obscured.

Rather than commemorate these women's particular achievements within the public arena, their stanzas serve two functions. First, they are clearly meant to remind the reader of Montemayor's own privileged connections to members of the Hapsburg court. Second, they reveal a veiled anxiety (most probably reflecting Montemayor's perception of his own situation as member of Juana's entourage) about the constantly changing web of relations and fortunes that dictate an individual's place at court. Moreover, when examined within the context of Orpheus's song as a whole, María and Juana's agency is even further buried in what becomes an interminable praise of suitable femininity–beautiful, discreet, and refined–couched in conventional Italianate amatory language:

> Cabella'stá un extremo no vicioso,
> mas en virtud muy alto y extremado,
> dispusición gentil, rostro hermoso,
> cabellos d'oro, cuello delicado;
> Mirar qu'alegra, movimiento airoso,
> juicio claro y nombre señalado,
> doñ'Ángela Fernando, a quien natura
> confom'al nombre, dio la hermosura.
> (Lns. 289-96. 291)

> Near her is a pure example
> Of virtue exalted and superlative
> A gentle disposition, a fair face,
> Hair of gold, delicate neck;

> A glance that gladdens, graceful movements,
> Clear judgment and distinguished name,
> Doña Angela Fernando, to whom nature
> True to her name, gave beauty. (162)

I count thirty-seven uses of the word *hermosa* in the "Canto" and at least as many of *gracia*, attributes which are predictably linked to the admiration these women provoke in all who see them and who turn them into objects of desire: "Su grande hermosura'menazando / está, y el fiero Amor el arco armado, / porque no pueda nadie n'aun miralla, / que no le rinda o mate sin batalla" 'Her great beauty threatens, / And fierce Love arms his bow, / For one cannot but look / And not be conquered nor be killed in battle' (Lns. 189-92. 286; 159-60). A logical extension of the pastoral's objectification of the shepherdess as an abstracted and idealized beloved, Orpheus's song efficiently advances *La Diana*'s implicit ideological vocation regarding gender and female objectification: "Mas cantaré con voz suave y pura, / la grande perfición, la graci'extraña, / el ser, valor, beldad sobre natura, / de las qu'hoy dan valor ilustr'a España" 'But I will sing with voice sweet and pure, / The great perfection, the extraordinary charm, / The valor and the special beauty / of those who illustriously grace Spain today' (Lns. 17-20. 278; 155). The "Canto de Orfeo" is a symbolic representation of women that diffuses any social, political, and economic agency, offering instead what we today would recognize as a Hollywood version of Spain as a land populated by blonde, wealthy, and gracefully silent icons. *La Diana* thus produces a fictional space where all women, even two powerful royal women, perfectly fit an emptied and unproblematic ideal as beautiful, chaste, and appropriately subdued.

These texts' symbolic representation of women supports a conservative reception from both the male and female readership. But even when considering this overall thrust of the pastoral fantasy, it is also pertinent that we allow for those specific moments in *La Diana* and *La Galatea* where the pastoral metaphor is disrupted and potentially undermined. My task, then, is double. In the following chapters I further examine these novels' prescriptive enunciation of gender and love as the symbolic resolution to all other conflicts and ambiguities, especially as it pertains to the successful construction of male subjectivity. Second, and no less important, I analyze the gaps where female agency seems to appear, compete with, and challenge these novels' overriding ideological vocation. What emerges from this analysis is the pastoral novel as a symbolic vehicle that creates, by means of gender ideality, an imaginary solution to unresolved historical contingency. As we shall also see, this genre is a fictional mechanism that at times also inevitably falters. And it is in those textual interstices where the "truth" of history and the place of women in that history can be said to emerge.

CHAPTER 2

PASTORAL ESCAPES: IDEAL SUBJECTIVITY AND
COMMUNITY IN MONTEMAYOR'S *LA DIANA*
AND CERVANTES'S *LA GALATEA*

> porque como el amor sea virtud,
> y la virtud siempre haga asiento en el mejor lugar,
> está claro que las personas de suerte serán muy mejor
> enamoradas que aquellas en quien ésta falta (*La Diana* 265).
>
> Since love is a virtue,
> and virtue always finds a place in the best places,
> it follows that those who are virtuous
> will always be more in love than those who are not (150).

So far I have argued for a reading of the pastoral novel that focuses on its discursive and ideological relationship with the historical context from which it emerges. Whether we think of the plenitude of the *locus amoenus* and its cultured shepherds, or of Felicia's palace and its extraordinary luxury, texts such as *La Diana* construct a world that confirms and promotes Spanish hegemony and aristocratic privilege and values, while suppressing the material and human costs expended. But this function of the pastoral is not limited to the symbolization of the larger forces that shaped social, political, and economic life in sixteenth-century Spain. Perhaps even more successfully, these *libros de pastores* put forward a coherent and comforting account of individual identity and psychology, or what we refer to in contemporary theory as subjectivity. Through the exalted emotional and moral state of the shepherd-lover, these narratives offer a carefully crafted account of pastoral subjects as whole beings. In tune with an early modern humanist and Christian sensibility, the figure of the shepherd confirms and promotes a vision of sixteenth century subjects–men–as ethically and spiritually superior.

As will become clear throughout this chapter, I draw a parallel between the pastoral's representation of the broad historical subtext and the construction of individual subjectivity. Like all social structures, the self is fraught with inconsistencies and threatened by fragmentation. The pastoral metaphor tackles this alienating and destructive aspect of the human condition. As virtuous and exquisite poets, shepherds put forward a sanitized profile for the reader, a reassuring illusion of eternal youth, physical beauty, and inner righteousness. True, the shepherd lover is often portrayed as a tormented soul, a being at odds with himself, torn between his previous self and his present sense of loveless abandonment. And the idyllic nature that surrounds the lover acts a cruel mirror for the lover's loss. Yet, as I will demonstrate in what follows, the lover's apparent falling apart does not lead to an impression of impending fragmentation or peril for the integrity of the self; of what would be, in other words, a dissolution of the self and by extension of the social order in which he exists. Rather it is perfectly fitted into an account of the male subject as a coherent righteous being, capable of great depth of feeling and of producing exquisite verse. I argue that it is precisely in this portrayal of the shepherd as a suffering lover that the pastoral fantasy offers its audience a version of social existence that represses the self's own persistent limitations. More to the point, these *libros de pastores* idealize the tenuous process through which each individual struggles to become a social subject. With the alienating effects of uncouth desire and violence effectively managed and erased, the reader can look at the figure of the shepherd-lover and contemplate a comforting reflection of his own, even if fictional, idealized self.

Pastoral ideality is largely channeled, as I have already suggested, through the image of the shepherd as a perfect lover who adores an equally virtuous and beautiful beloved. Nonetheless, this fantasy of gender relationships, presented as an uncontentious amatory equality, cannot fully disengage itself from its social subtext. Just as with hegemonic and aristocratic values, these novels implicitly promote a patriarchal bias that confirms the discourses and laws that organize sexual hierarchies. The pastoral metaphor claims to produce a world where love eliminates all differences between the shepherds, as well as between men and women. What is actually created, as I suggested in Chapter One, is an abstraction of women as eternal possessors of beauty and purity, and a veiling of female agency and desire. It is precisely through an idealizing metaphor of moral and spiritual parity between the lover and his beloved that the pastoral novel–as symbolic act–is most deceptive and prescriptive.

In what follows, I analyze in detail the figure of the pastoral lover as a model to be admired and imitated by male readers, as well as the gender ideology that this idealization depends upon and promotes. In examining the mechanisms that support the psychology of the shepherd and his extended community of lovers, I have found psychoanalytic theories on narcissism and group psychology particularly useful. Subjectivity, like history, is a structure beset by its own contradictions and failures, and in need of ideological symbolization. Whereas Jameson's perspective offers interesting connections between text and historical subtext, psychoanalysis allows for a more specific understanding of the conditions that shape pastoral characters as *gendered* social subjects. The debate stemming from Stephen Greenblatt's proposition that psychoanalysis is at once "the fulfillment and effacement of specifically Renaissance insights: psychoanalysis is, in more than one sense, the end of the Renaissance," is not far from one's mind when treating early modern texts through a psychoanalytic lens (210).[1] Questions regarding the early modern self as a product of material and cultural forces vis-à-vis the psychologically fragmented state of the modern subject lie at the center of Greenblatt's assertion. My purpose, however, is not to argue naively that Montemayor and Cervantes were psychoanalysts before their time or that early modern selfhood is wholly indistinguishable from ours. Nonetheless, it is my view that an examination of the ideological and imaginary structures that determine and support the shepherd's ideality finds profitable points of contact with a

---

[1] Most recently the debate centering on the alleged anachronism of psychoanalysis and its dispensing with historical accuracy in early modern studies has best been summarized and analyzed by Elizabeth Jane Bellamy in her review article "Desires and Disavowals: Speculations on the Aftermath of Stephen Greenblatt's 'Psychoanalysis and Culture'," where she ultimately questions whether "Greenblatt–as, after all, the author of the earlier Renaissance Self-Fashioning–finds the concept of early modern selves so utterly dispensable" (313). On the camp opposing Greenblatt's position, Carla Mazzio and Douglas Trevor have recently edited a compilation of essays titled *Historicism, Psychoanalysis, and Early Modern Culture* where authors including Ann Rosalind Jones and Peter Stallybrass, Jonathan Goldberg, and Marjorie Garber argue for and demonstrate the usefulness of psychoanalysis in a historically engaged examination of early modern texts.

psychoanalytic account of subject formation. Pastoral novels promote a version of identity that aims to at least keep at bay difference, fragmentation, and alienation. In this manner the idyll can be said to perform a specular function through which the reader is invited to imagine a faultless version of the self's and, by extension, of a community's social existence and laws. The pastoral's proposition is therefore double. First, as a literary form, it performs for the reader the function of a mirror that for the most part reflects a reassuring image of social harmony and prosperity. Second, within the amatory structure of the text this symbolic representation of history and subjectivity is largely effected through an abstraction of women as objects on which the shepherd and his community can reflect their own idealized wholeness as lovers and poets. It is in this way that bucolic love serves as a foundation to the ideology and values promoted by these novels.

1. Pastoral Love and the Construction of the Ideal Self

Both as a convention and in its literary manifestations, the pastoral depends on the physical and mental well-being of the shepherd as it parallels the bucolic topography. At the same time, the great paradox of pastoral love is that it is always impossible to attain. Because the beloved is dead, absent from the bower, unavailable, or uninterested, convention dictates that pastoral love is not consummated. As a result, the shepherd's life is constructed as a meditation upon his present frustrated passion and a sorrowful remembrance of a more fortunate past. An apparent tension is thus present between the ideal topography and innocence of the bower and the sense of desperate longing and at times utter desolation expressed in the songs of the lovers. This is a paradox of love that is inherent to the amatory pastoral tradition from Virgil on. Still, if we follow the argument heretofore presented, how does a genre so invested in the symbolic reconfiguration of the conflicts and contradictions of history benefit from the portrayal of a tortured, rejected, and desolate lover? The answer, I would propose, requires an analysis of the construction of identity and alterity in the pastoral novel, especially as it regards issues of gender and sexuality.

Although the convention of unrequited or impossible love is present in most Classical and Italian sources–from the Virgilian *Bu-*

colics to Dante's *Divine Comedy*, Petrarch's *Rime Sparse*, and Jacobo Sannazaro's *Arcadia*–it is especially visible in the figures of suffering and constant lovers in Spanish *amor cortés* literature.[2] Mainly a fifteenth century Castilian phenomenon, the *amor cortés* tradition first flourishes in Spain in the last quarter of the fourteenth century. Influenced by twelfth-century authors such as Andreas Capellanus, the Provencal poets, thirteenth-century Galician and French poetry, and Catalan poets such as Ausias March and Jordi de Sant Jordi, Spanish courtly love literature was fully developed by the first quarter of the sixteenth century. Other sources such as Ovid's *Ars Amatoria*, Hispano-Arabic poetry, the Bible, scholastic readings of classical literature, the *Roman de la Rose*, the *dolce stil nuovo* of Dante's *Vita nuova*, and the work of other Italian authors such as Petrarch and Boccaccio also notably inform the courtly Spanish tradition.[3] The combination of these literary sources, coupled with a relative relaxation of ethical and religious values in the fifteenth-century Castilian court, open the way for the immense popularity of the *Cancioneros* through the sixteenth century. In addition, the widespread distribution of the sentimental romances during the late fifteenth and early sixteenth century make their ideological and structural content especially relevant to the later Spanish Renaissance pastoral.[4]

Helen Cooper has argued that the Renaissance pastoral is a "different phenomenon from either *bergerie* or the Petrarchan eclogue, just as all three are different from the Virgilian bucolic" (100). Devoid of most "realistic" or rustic elements found in the *bergerie* or the *pastourelle*, pastoralism in Italy and Spain evolves into an idealized form where shepherds are accomplished poets, cohabitate with nymphs, and rarely preoccupy themselves with the burdens of rural existence. Renaissance pastoral characters come to embody both the simplicity of an idealized rural space and the nobility of character and artistic sensibilities of the idealized courtier.

---

[2] For a detailed account of the possible origins of courtly love, with an emphasis on the genre's Hispano-Arabic roots, see Roger Boase's *The Origin and Meaning of Courtly Love* and "Courtly Love in Spanish Literature."

[3] The influence of Dante and Petrarch on the Spanish courtly love tradition is facilitated and conditioned by their own adaptations of Provencal troubadour poetry. For a discussion of this element in Dante's *Vita nuova* and Petrarch's *Rime sparse* please see Robert M. Durling's introduction to *Petrarch's Lyric Poems*.

[4] For a more detailed account of the development of courtly love tradition in Spain see *Poesía Cancioneril*, by José María Azáceta.

The enigmatic political allegorization of Petrarch's eclogues (written in Latin and collected under the title *Bucolicum Carmen*) is abandoned. And while Virgil's *Bucolics* explicitly touch upon an array of subjects that include social, political, and private amatory concerns, the Renaissance pastoral in Spanish novels and Italian drama chooses to concentrate on the latter theme, building and intensifying its varied nuances, both structurally and aesthetically. In this Renaissance manifestation, the protagonist is a shepherd-poet who sings to commemorate his condition as a forlorn lover through cultivated and highly artistic verse.

Sannazaro's *Arcadia* is the principal example of this Renaissance transformation of the genre, offering an Arcadian world where the lover, his poetic artistry, and his relation to nature are the main focus.[5] Through his alternation of prose and verse (a form that had already appeared in Longus's *Daphnis and Chloe* and Boccaccio's *Ameto*), the Italian pastoralist incorporates and extensively develops all the main thematic elements that soon after become paradigmatic in sixteenth-century Spanish pastoral texts. Among them Solé-Leris cites,

> [The] idyllic nature descriptions (and especially beginning the first chapter with a *locus amoenus*); the rhythm of bucolic life [...]; songs by the shepherds, single or amoebaean [....], mainly about love, but striking sometimes a rustic or burlesque note; the telling of past love stories by individual characters (a device subsequently much expanded by Spanish pastoral writers as a means of varying pace and subject matter); speeches and debates about love, poetry and topics such as the praise of the Golden Age and denunciation of present times, the beauty and qualities of women, the secret properties of plants and stones, etc.; festivities and celebrations [...]; funeral rites; games and contests; magic, both black and white, and supernatural interventions by gods and nymphs of classical mythology. (22-3)

Sannazaro's identification of nature with the condition of the forlorn lover and the many paradoxes employed to illustrate the effects of love have been traced directly to Petrarchan influence.[6] As depicted in the *Canzoniere*, the Arcadian lover is tortured by the

---

[5] For examples in Sannazaro's text see the tales of Corydon, Damon and Alphésibóeus, and Gallus.

[6] See Alpers.

amatory experience, the conflict between passion and moral rectitude. But as Alpers reminds us, one of the *Arcadia*'s main purposes is to "mitigate the isolation and extremity of the Petrarchan lover experience by various rituals, most of them rituals of song" (115). The lover's condition is shared and thus alleviated by others who offer comfort, companionship, and distraction. The intense moral dilemma that causes Petrarch's plight in the *Canzoniere* is absent in the *Arcadia* and with it the isolation of the personal struggle. The lover's condition is attenuated by being a shared experience, depersonalized and universalized, as shown here by Sincero's account of the shepherds' reaction to Ergasto's plight:

> Ma poi che egli si tacque, e le risonante selve parimente si acquetarono, non fu alcuno de la pastorale turba, a cui bastasse il core di partirse quindi per ritornare ai lasciati giochi né che curasse di fornir i cominciate piaceri; anzi ognuno era si vinto da compassione, che, come meglio poteva o sapeva, si ingegnava di confortarlo, ammonirlo e riprenderlo del suo errore, insegnandoli di molti remedii, assai piu leggieri a dirli che a metterli in operazione. (*Arcadia* 10)

> But when he fell silent and likewise the echoing woods had grown quiet there was not a single one of that shepherd throng who had the heart to take leave of that spot to return to his abandoned games, or who cared to finish the pleasures already begun. Rather each one was so far overcome with pity that as best he could or as best he knew he attempted to comfort him, to admonish him, and to reprove him of his error, teaching him many remedies far more easily spoken than put into practice. (35)[7]

In addition, the songs that the inhabitants of *Arcadia* sing become cause for public celebration and praise of the lover's poetic craft. Sannazaro's lovers explicitly concern themselves with the form and artistic value of their representations. To love well is to poetically represent one's feeling in a manner that is aesthetically pleasing to all. In turn, commentary becomes integral to the lover's shared experience and the audience's response, as the following example illustrates:

---

[7] All English translations of Sannazaro's *Arcadia* are from Ralph Nash's edition *Arcadia & Piscatorial Eclogues*.

Piasque maravigliosamente a ciascuno il cantare di Galicio, ma per diverse maniere. Alcuni lodarono la giovenil voce piena de armonia inestimabile; altri il modo suavissimo e dolce, atto ad irretire qualunque animo stato fusse piu ad amore ribello; molti comendarono le rime leggiadre e tra'rustici pastori non usitate; e di quelli ancora vi furono, che con piu ammirazione estolsero la acutissima sagacita del suo avvedimento, il quale constretto di nominare il mese a'greggi et a'pastori dannoso, si come saggio evetatore di sinestro augurio in si lieto giorno, disse "il mese inanzi aprile." (25)

Galicio's song was marvelously pleasing to everyone, but in various ways. Some praised his youthful voice full of incalculable harmony; others his most sweet and gentle manner, well suited for ensnaring whatever natures were most rebel to love; many commended the versification, neatly turned and not in use among rustic shepherds; and of those there were some who with greater admiration extolled the penetrating wisdom of his perceptiveness, in that, being forced to name the month that is harmful to flocks and shepherds, he had called it as one who wisely avoids an unfortunate omen on so happy a day "the month of April." (49)

This concern for the aesthetic value of the lover's lament conditions the reception of the lover's state. For those who listen and evaluate, the sincerity of the lover's plight and the virtue of his suffering is measured through the effectiveness of his lyrical production. What for Petrarch was a private plight that in its literary manifestation would hopefully grant public fame, becomes in the Italian and Spanish pastoral tradition an immediate public concern, shared and quickly digested by an audience of equals. Each shepherd is regarded for his poetic talents as they reflect on the community as a whole, making the individual poetic manifestation a public enterprise to be lauded, remembered, and repeated by others. Conventions are thus continuously reproduced and expanded, generating a rhetorical currency that is easily exchanged and familiar to all in the pastoral community. In other words, to love in the *Arcadia* is to prove one's devotion through a poetic discourse acceptable in the public domain. The lover's worth, his 'sincerity' and virtue, are thus determined by the aesthetic value of his words and the community's reaction to and appropriation of both the form and content of the composition.

Sannazaro's *Arcadia* provides the literary precedent where the suffering lover can share his experience with a community of sympathetic listeners. But it must be noted that, although they are willing to indulge and console the victims of love's despair, the Arcadians are not exclusively a population of forlorn lovers. Even though the connection between suffering and love is prevalent in the text, some characters fulfill their desire, while others identify with amatory suffering but are not fully encumbered by it.[8] And while the inhabitants of Sannazaro's text are fully aware of the misery love can produce, they also explicitly manifest a concern with the task of poetic invention. Such is the case of Logisto and Elpino who practice the lyrical conventions of unfulfilled love as a form of rhetorical competition, not as a vehicle for the expression of personal anguish (*Arcadia*. Poesie 4. Eclogue 4. 27-31). Plot development, though mostly dependent on the concerns of Sincero as a forlorn lover, is also accomplished by other Arcadian activities such as the visit to the temple of Pales, which culminates in a prayer in which profit and other material concerns are the primary subject (*Arcadia*. Poesie 3). These aspects of the text distinguish it from *La Diana*, in which all the shepherds share an exclusive concern with their condition as unrequited lovers and where the plot revolves solely around that issue. Influenced by Garcilaso's exclusive treatment of the shepherd as lover, Montemayor condenses the pastoral experience into one that can only accommodate desolate lovers: "The Arcadian community–which in Virgil and Sannazaro could scarcely contain the passionate lover–has now [in *La Diana*] become a community of such lovers" (Alpers 351).

When one then looks at the Spanish pastoral model, the shepherd's suffering is further conceived as an extension of the bucolic ideal. As a point of departure the pastoral topography is characterized by a simplicity and purity that allows for an authenticity of feeling, both happy and sorrowful, which urban artificiality negates. As Maravall has well stated, "The 'pleasant solitude' of meadows, forests, and mountains is not harsh isolation but a delightful conversation among people who exist for each other, joined by wisdom and friendship" (*Utopia and Counterutopia* 139). Of no less importance is the profile of the shepherd as virtuous, indisputably chaste,

---

[8] Carino, for example, has found fulfillment in love, a happiness he attributes to good fortune (*Arcadia*. Poesie 8).

and unwaveringly constant. Lesser emotions, such as jealousy or anger, are exclusively manifested in his songs and not in any type of violent or harmful action. Untainted by lust and devoted to his beloved, the shepherd echoes the perfection of the idyll. In addition, the ideal nature of the lover finds its proper complement in the love object: the shepherd is perfect because he looks upon and adores a perfect other. The heightened beauty of the beloved, as well as her absence or her rejection, is pivotal to the lover's own ideality. Any alteration of or instability in her abstracted ideality would threaten the shepherd's identity as an admirable lover and inspired poet. The worth of the shepherd and his complementarity with the idyll are thus directly proportionate to the perfection of the love object. Perhaps ironically, her absence and refusal of his love structurally enable his ability to be a virtuous and constant lover. To be more exact, precisely because the shepherd does not have an evolving relationship with his beloved, he is able to imagine her and structure his own profound suffering and admirable constancy as he wishes. As made evident in the early modern Spanish pastoral novel, true bucolic bliss can only come from the rejection of the other and the resulting ennobling misery that the lover displays within the *locus amoenus*.

In Montemayor's *La Diana* the eponymous idealized female figure is a steady source of inspiration. Sireno and Sylvano, her two lovers, continually recall and recreate the figure of Diana in their lamentations and songs. Despite her alleged betrayal in having married another suitor, Diana is nonetheless constructed by her lovers as a flawless object worthy of their devotion. The text begins with a description of Sireno, who had known "freedom" in the pastoral countryside until "el crudo amor tomó aquella posesión de su libertad" 'until cruel Love took hold of his liberty' (111; 51). Of course, we must not lose sight of the fact that if he would continue to enjoy this liberty from love, he would have no role to play within this amatory topography. It is only as an abandoned yet constant lover that Sireno can stake out his place as *La Diana*'s central male figure. Roaming the *locus amoenus*, he is a slave to love, seeking solace in the places where he had seen Diana as he reconstructs her perfection through his songs: "Arrimose [Sireno] al pie de una haya, comenzó a tender sus ojos por la hermosa ribera hasta que llegó con ellos al lugar donde primero había visto la hermosura, gracia, honestidad de la pastora Diana, aquella en quien naturaleza sumó todas las perficiones que por muchas partes había repartido" 'He lay down at the foot of a beech and surveyed the bank of the beautiful river until he came to the spot where he first beheld the beauty, grace and virtue of the shepherdess Diana, she in whom nature gathered all perfection and bestowed it through her every part' (111; 51). Sireno's idealization of Diana thus invokes not her present condition as a married and inconstant woman, but his memory of her as chaste and loyal:

> Sylvano mío, un' afición rarísima,
> una beldad que ciega luego'n viéndola,
> un seso y discreción excelentísima,
>   Con una dulce habla, qu'en oyéndola,
> las duras peñas muev' enterneciéndolas,
> [...]
> vieras el claro sol envidiosísimo
> de sus cabellos, y ella 'llí peinándose.
>   (Lns. 34-8 / 47-8. 132)

> Dear Sylvano, a rare fondness,
> A beauty that blinds one upon seeing it.
> A most excellent wit and discretion.
> With a sweet voice, that upon hearing it,
> Hard stones are moved, becoming softened,
> [...]
> You could see the bright sun, envious
> Of her hair as she combed it. (64-5)

Diana's perfection and her "painful" absence make possible Sireno's claim as an exemplary lover.

Sylvano, Diana's other suitor, is almost an identical copy of Sireno; he too is a virtuous and constant lover. But while Sireno has the advantage of some past intimacy with Diana that he can then remember in his song, Sylvano's own recollections are based purely on casual contact and observation from afar. Even though he loves a woman whom he barely knows and has no hope of ever possessing, Sylvano constructs an imaginary relationship that gives meaning to his existence:

> Miré a Diana, y vi luego abreviárseme
> el placer y contento, 'n sólo viéndola,
> y a mi pesar la vida vi alargárseme.

PASTORAL ESCAPES: IDEAL SUBJECTIVITY AND COMMUNITY 87

> ¡Oh cuántas veces la hallé perdiéndola
> y cuántas veces la perdí hallándola!;
> ¿y yo callar, sufrir, morir sirviéndola?
> La vida perdía yo, cuando topándola
> miraba aquellos ojos, qu' airadísimos
> volvía contra mí luego 'n hablándola:
> Mas cuando los cabellos hermosísimos
> descogía y peinaba, no sintiéndome,
> se me volvían los males sabrosísimos
> (Lns. 71-85. 133-4)

> I saw Diana and saw drawing to a close
> Pleasure and contentment, seeing her,
> And to my sorrow I saw life grow long.
> Oh how many times I found her, losing her,
> And how many I lost her, finding her,
> And I silent, suffering, dying, serving her.
> I would die when I met her,
> I saw those eyes she turned
> Against me angrily when I spoke to her.
> But more so when she unbound
> Her lovely hair unaware of me,
> My suffering became delectable. (66)

Like Sireno, Sylvano masterfully transforms his defeat into victory and his unrequited admiration for "aquellos ojos" and "cabellos hermosísimos" into a reflection of his own perfection. His triumphant persistence elevates Sylvano and gives him license to comment on Sireno's sorrow: "[N]o porque ignorase la causa de su tristeza, mas porque le pareció que si él hubiera recebido el más pequeño favor que Sireno algún tiempo recibió de Diana, aquel contentamiento bastara para toda la vida tenelle" '[N]ot because he did not know the cause of his sorrow, but rather because he thought that if he himself had received the slightest favor that once Sireno had received from Diana, the happiness would have lasted him a lifetime' (119; 56). Constant in the face of Diana's rejection and absence, Sireno and Sylvano are defined and legitimized by their impossible love. They look upon her absent self and see in return an idealized version of themselves as lovers.[9] The reflexivity

---

[9] As José C. Pérez has noted, Diana's idealized image "desempeña el papel de un espejo en el que se reflejan los sentimientos de ambos" 'acts as a mirror in which both their feelings are reflected' (61; my translation).

between the emptied perfection of the other and the lover's worth is replicated by all the other shepherds in *La Diana*, as well as in the narrative voice, effectively denying a conscious recognition of a contending female subjectivity.[10]

In numerous instances the narrative voice, which fashions itself as an especially adept assessor of beauty and virtue, takes over the task of describing female characters. All shepherdesses are "hermosas" and "discretas" sustaining a vision of female identity emptied of any potentially disruptive singularity. One telling example is the narrator's idealized description of Belisa, a village shepherdess:

> Tenía una saya azul clara, un jubón de una tela tan delicada que mostraba la perfición y compás del blanco pecho, porque el sayuelo que del mismo color de la saya era, le tenía que aquel gracioso bulto se podía bien divisar. Tenía los cabellos que más rubios que el sol parecían, sueltos y sin orden alguna, mas nunca orden tanto adornó hermosura como la desorden que ellos tenían; y con el descuido del sueño, el blanco pie descalzo, fuera de la saya se le parecía, mas no tanto que a los ojos de los que lo miraban pareciese deshonesto. (228)

> She wore a pale blue blouse, a bodice of a fabric so fine it showed the perfection and measure of her white bosom, for the blouse was the same color as the bodice, and so loose that her charming shape could easily be discerned. She wore her fair hair, fairer than the sun, loose and in disorder. But not order ever adorned such beauty as the disorder it was in, and in the languidness of sleep, her white bare foot peeked from under her skirt, but not so that it seemed immodest to the eyes of those who beheld it. (127)

Admittedly, this depiction by the narrator potentially opens a more sexualized description of the object of desire. The description of Belisa's breast ("aquel gracioso bulto") and her naked foot are suggestive elements not found, for example, in the shepherds' chaste and codified recollection of Diana. Yet, even if a libidinal undercurrent could be identified in the narrator's voice, the association cre-

---

[10] Another perfect example is that of Danteo in Book VII and his own sacrificial adoration of the disdainful Duarda. Carroll B. Johnson makes an excellent point that although Danteo mirrors Sireno's and Sylvano's dedication to love and the poetic project that results from it, as a *pastor rústico,* he is not as idealized as his Spanish counterparts (33).

ated between physical and spiritual perfection quickly offsets and dissipates any tension between the carnal body and the abstracted ideal. The purity of her "blanco pecho," the order found in her disheveled hair, and the chasteness of her "blanco pie descalzo," create a Belisa, "cuya hermosura no menos admiración les puso que si la hermosa Diana vieran" 'whose beauty they admired no less than if they were seeing Diana herself before their eyes' (228; 127). Furthermore, the narrative voice clusters together all the female objects of desire thereby supporting a vision of these women as a single abstracted category.

Faithful to its famous predecessor, Cervantes's idyll is also populated by a pair of lovers who constantly lament their forlorn condition. Galatea is the motor of Elicio and Erastro's existence, and it is through their continual elaboration of her idealized and highly codified beauty that they assemble their own identities as virtuous and worthy.

> La blanca nieve y colorada rosa,
> que el verano no gasta, ni el invierno;
> el sol de dos luceros, do reposa
> el blando amor, y a do estará *in eterno*;
> la voz, cual la de Orfeo poderosa
> de suspender las furias del infierno,
> y otras cosas que vi quedando ciego,
> yesca me han hecho al invisible fuego.
> (Lns. 33-40. 177-8)

> The white snow of her cheek, the crimson rose
> Which neither summer wastes nor winter's cold,
> The sun's twain morning-stars, wherein repose
> Soft Love does find, the spot where time untold
> Shall guard the voice, strong to subdue our woes,
> As did hell's furies Orpheus' voice of old,
> The many charms I saw, though blind I ween,
> Have made me tinder for the fire unseen. (15)

Galatea's splendor is untarnished by any hardship, including the passage of time. Her voice is mythic and recalls Orpheus. Her chastity and discretion, which dictate that she will reject outright all her lovers' requests, are taken by Elicio as additional proof of her perfection, "[que] el valor de Galatea no da lugar a que de ella otra cosa se desee ni se espere" 'since Galatea's worth gives no opportunity for anything else to be desired or hoped of her' (264; 67-8). Elicio's only request is an acknowledgement of his condition by his fellow shepherds, a token that grants him his rightful place within the bower and insures his stature within the pastoral community. Elicio's sense of self feeds off of Galatea. She is a superb surface onto which he projects his identity and which offers back the sought after unified image. As the rustic shepherd who has even less hope of gaining Galatea's acceptance, Erastro imitates his fellow shepherd by attempting to adopt the discourse of the *'pastor fino'* so as to claim his place among the lovers. Despite his lesser talents as a poet, Erastro affirms Galatea's specular function by further codifying her already ethereal ideality:

> Dos hermosas manzanas coloradas,
> que tales me semejan dos mejillas;
> y el arco de dos cejas levantadas,
> que del Iris no llegó a sus maravillas;
> dos rayos, dos hileras extremadas
> de perlas entre grana; y si hay decillas,
> mil gracias que no tienen par ni cuento,
> niebla me han hecho al amoroso viento.
> (Lns. 41-9. 178)

> Twain apples rosy-red no tree can bear
> As those in Galatea's cheeks displayed;
> Iris herself could boast not bow so fair
> As the twain arched eye-brows of the maid,
> Two rays of light, two threads, beyond compare,
> Of pearls' twixt scarlet: –and if more be said–
> The peerless graces which in her I find
> A cloud have made me to the amorous wind. (15)

By identifying himself as Elicio's fellow lover, Erastro intends to diffuse his rusticity and alterity.[11] Through his simulation of Elicio's *"fino"* language Erastro engages in a discursive act of self-fashion-

---

[11] For López Estrada it is Cupid's mythical power that enables Erastro's transformation: "aquí se afirma el principio de *Omnia vincit Amor*, y así el rústico Erastro podrá hablar y cantar como los otros pastores, pues por su boca es Amor quien habla y canta" 'here is affirmed the inception of *Omnia vincit Amor*, and it is for this reason that the rustic Erastro can speak and sing like the other shepherds, for it is Love who speaks and sings through his mouth' ("Introducción" fnt. 22, 171; my translation).

ing that gives him entrance into this idealized pastoral community. We should keep in mind that if Galatea were ever to accede to love, Erastro's lower class standing would immediately disqualify him from contention. Although he would never be Galatea's chosen lover, he can act, talk, and sing like one nonetheless. And this upwardly mobile identification with Elicio is only possible by means of the erasure of Galatea as an agent of her own desire.

As an extension of Elicio and Erastro's figuration, Cervantes incorporates into his tale a considerable number of characters, all of whom share an identity as consummate lovers of absent and abstracted objects of desire. The narrative voice also adopts a prominent role in bolstering the shepherdess's function as a flattering mirror. For example, the narrator depicts Galatea and Florisa as rivals to the mythological Graces:

> Tan hermosas quedaron después de lavadas como antes lo estaban, excepto que, por haber llegado las manos con movimiento al rostro, quedaron sus mejillas encendidas y sonroseadas, de modo que un no sé qué de hermosura les acrecentaba, especialmente a Galatea, en quien se vieron juntas las tres Gracias, a quien los antiguos griegos pintaban desnudas para mostrar, entre otros efectos, que eran señoras de la belleza. (209)

> They remained as beautiful after washing as before, save that, through having rubbed their faces with their hands, their cheeks remained aflame and blushing-red, so that an indescribable beauty made them yet more fair, and especially Galatea. In her were seen united the three Graces whom the Greeks of old depicted naked to show (among other purposes) that they were mistresses of beauty. (33-4)

The reference to "las tres Gracias" is significant. From one perspective it would seem that Florisa and Galatea's "mejillas encendidas and sonroseadas" implicitly associate them with Aphrodite, the goddess of passionate love.[12] As in *La Diana*, the narrator ostensibly exhibits a more sexually charged interest in the shepherdesses. Yet, it is also true that the Graces were also popularly considered an ab-

---

[12] In Greek mythology the Graces either attended to or were associated with Aphrodite. For an extensive analysis of the potential meaning of Galatea and Florisa's "mejillas encendidas" (burning cheeks) see Frederick de Armas's "Ekphrasis and Eros".

stract personification of beauty, gentleness, and friendship. Their emblematic function is highlighted by the "griegos" penchant for capturing and reproducing in painting the nymphs' hyper-idealized form. This recollection of the nymphs thus bolsters the shepherds' specular abstraction of Galatea and Florisa. Like the Greeks before them, Elicio, Erastro, and the rest of the shepherds "paint" a vision of perfection upon the emptied canvass of these women's particular subjectivity.

As it quickly becomes clear in *La Diana* and *La Galatea*, the lover's praise of the desired woman is articulated not as a true recognition of her complexity but as an abstraction that holds no connection to her own particularity.[13] This process has several effects. First, there is a clear glorification of, and thus propaganda for, the idea of love as a codified practice. The beloved's absence precludes all the negotiations and compromises that her real presence would require. This, in turn, allows the lover to pursue his fantasy unabated, creating her, and his love for her, after his own liking. In addition, the one-sidedness of pastoral love frees the lover of all the possible conflicts that surface in any relationship, and especially in marriage. Love as imagined in the Spanish pastoral novel is the happiest kind of love, because it is devoid of the inevitable friction of human interaction. The shepherds' devotion to the beloved reflects upon them and enables the construction of their own identity as perfect lovers.

By defining pastoral love in this way, we can view the shepherd as narcissistic. Although a term now overdetermined by our culture's popular engagement with Freud, when we scrutinize Freud's theories of narcissism, along with Lacan's rearticulation of this logic in his propositions concerning specular idealization and subject formation, we encounter a provocative and useful account of love and its ideological aims. Psychoanalytic theories allow for an alternative

---

[13] The motives behind the pastoral lover's relationship with his beloved have been a topic of debate among critics. Joaquín Casalduero interprets this idealizing dynamic in Spanish pastoral texts as a sincere homage to women and as a desired return to a lost matriarchy. On the other end of the spectrum, some have instead emphasized the self-centered quality of the shepherd's desire and the manifest interest in idolizing the beloved. Bryant L. Creel specifically states that love in *La Diana* (and I would add in all Spanish pastoral literature), "recognizes no authority but its own ideality; it is a 'law unto itself,' independent even of the attainability of its object. It is its own object" (14).

examination of the motivations behind the construction of the self and the other. In pastoral novels, love, or more accurately the self-love manifested in the shepherd's amatory plight, functions as the chief mechanism through which lived conflict and contradiction –sexual and historical–are actively repressed.

Freud's account of the self focuses upon the fragmentation inevitably experienced in the process of entering social law or civilization. The fragmented subject is as a result always in need of a surrogate mechanism that compensates for the pre-Oedipal wholeness that has been lost. Freud's account of adult narcissism involves the internalization of an ideal ego that strives to reproduce an image of the self as a non-lacking, perfect being. This tenuous idealized self is constantly projected upon external objects of desire, reflecting back to the ego a false but much needed sense of flawlessness and belonging. In Freud's own words:

> This ideal ego is now the target of the self-love which was enjoyed in childhood by the actual ego. The subject's narcissism makes its appearance displaced on to this new ideal ego, which, like the infantile ego, finds itself possessed of every perfection that is of value. [Man] is not willing to forgo the narcissistic perfection of his childhood; and when, as he grows up, he is disturbed by the admonitions of others and by the awakening of his own critical judgment, so that he can no longer retain that perfection, he seeks to recover it in the new form of an ego ideal. What he projects before him as his ideal is the substitute for the lost narcissism of his childhood in which he was his own ideal. ("On Narcissism" 94)[14]

In short, the ego's discomforting fragmentation is, through the specular process, conveniently resolved, enabling the subject to fashion himself as a fully functional social being. As Freud concludes,

> The tendency which falsifies judgment in this respect is that of *idealization*. We see that the object is being treated in the same way as our own ego, so that when we are in love a considerable

---

[14] In "A Difficulty in the Path of Psycho-Analysis," Freud compares the narcissistic ego to an amoeba-like being: "The ego is a great reservoir from which the libido that is destined for objects flows out and into which it flows back from those objects [...]. As an illustration of this state of things we may think of an amoeba, whose viscous substance puts out pseudopodia [...]" (139).

amount of narcissistic libido overflows on to the object. It is even obvious, in many forms of love-choice, that the object serves as a substitute for some unattained ego ideal of our own. We love it on account of the perfection which we have striven to reach for our own ego, and which we should now like to procure in this roundabout way as a means of satisfying our narcissism. ("Group Psychology" 44-5)[15]

Lacan's account of narcissism shares with Freud's many of the same causes and effects. Linked more explicitly to the myth of Narcissus and his libidinal attraction to his own specular image, narcissism becomes charged by both an erotic and volatile dimension. The "drama" of subject formation, as defined in "The mirror stage," "manufactures for the subject, caught up in the lure of spatial identification, the succession of phantasies that extends from a fragmented body-image to a form of its totality [...]–and, lastly, to the assumption of the armor of an alienating identity" (4). The tension between what the subject sees in the mirror and his real state, between the apparent permanence of the image and the estrangement from the subject's origin that is produced, is always present, in need of constant negotiation, and only contingently settled throughout the subject's life. The passage into the social world does not in any way signify a resolution or erasure of the subject's conflicted initiation. In order to avoid a reaffirmation of his fragmentation, and the aggressive and self-destructive tendencies that, as in the myth of Narcissus, may arise, the subject reclaims the effects of the mirror stage, intent on continuously reconstituting a whole –even if fictional–subjectivity. This mechanism is most prominent in "love" relationships where the "self strives to see itself in the other" (Grosz 47). The beloved stands in as a specular image of wholeness and perfection. The subject finds solace in the intact ideal that he has projected on his object of desire.

The correspondences that can be drawn between this psychoanalytic perspective and my analysis of the pastoral are suggestive. In

---

[15] Elizabeth Grosz explains that love is, "[N]ot so much based on a valorization of *her* unique charms and attributes as much as in *his* position as lover. [...] The lover transfers narcissistic self-regard onto the love object and is thus able to love himself, as it were, in loving the other. While claiming to love the woman desperately, the [narcissistic] lover strives for recognition of his own active position. His own esteemed ego is complemented and its value proven if the love object attains perfection in his eyes" (127).

the pastoral novel the shepherd's ideal self rests upon a formal structure much like the narcissistic subject and the constructed image of perfect wholeness to which he resorts.[16] Love becomes an activity that, far from forcing the shepherd to "give of himself" to the beloved, actually allows his entrance into pastoral society, nurtures a sense of wholeness, and legitimizes his position as a subject and as a member of the extended sphere of lovers. For the reading audience, the shepherd provides a model of idealized subjectivity where the often uncertain outcome of narcissism is effectively symbolized.

Moreover, I understand the function of love as a means to repress lack and fragmentation, and this symbolic mechanism is parallel and complimentary to the genre's relationship with its historical subtext. If the pastoral novel is a cultural artifact that by and large redresses social conflict and contradiction, the shepherd's amatory fullness can be said to elicit similar effects on the individual historical subject. The difficulties of piecing together a secure subjectivity in an unstable world were central to the early modern Spanish experience. I have already addressed the complex web of social, economic, and religious pressures that structured the local and national experience. Nobility, honor, and *limpieza de sangre* were standards that the Spanish courtier was expected to embody but that often proved difficult to prove or preserve. In addition, the individual had to cultivate a coherent sense of self amidst competing and at times contradictory models and expectations. Humanist sensibility, for example, promoted a dialogical mode of thinking that ironically also undercut a person's ability to construct a stable identity. Tony Davies has drawn attention to the humanist scientific method's "anxiety for certainty and closure is constantly frustrated by the tantalizing provisionality of humanist debate. There is always something more to be said, and no speaker enjoys the privilege of the last word" (82). An unresolved duality and indeterminacy is also made patent in the ideal of arms and letters where aristocratic masculinity finds itself trying to simultaneously fill categories that even in a humanist worldview were not always easily reconcilable.

---

[16] The mechanism of narcissism is no doubt what Steven Hutchinson, in a discussion of the transitive verbs in *La Galatea*, proposes as the "work of cathexis, whereby desire becomes embodied, objectified, in other people and in things, taking the contours and properties of what they embody" (169).

As Cruz has shown in her commentary of Garcilaso's *Elegía II*, even the model warrior and poet makes patent his frustration at his inability to effectively sustain both pursuits:

> The oscillation between the muses and the business of war denotes the tensions he experiences when, as in his famous lapidary phrase, he takes up 'now the pen, now the sword.' But the poem registers the imbalance between the two categories: a mere hour is allotted to literary creativity dedicated to love, while he finds himself surrounded, as he laments in *Elegía I*, by 'an excess of wars, of dangers, and exile.' ("Arms versus Letters" 195-6)

Admittedly, I am here correlating a modern psychoanalytic conception of the subject's fragmented psychology with the problem of the conflicting categories available to the early modern individual. My point, nonetheless, is that neither the Freudian subject nor the early modern self can easily avoid the irresolvable tension between the ideal integrity to which they aspire and the uncertain reality–psychic, historical, and philosophical–within which they exist.

As expressed in modern psychoanalytic theories, the process of fulfilling the individual's lack is never completed. Desire never finds a state of full satisfaction or stasis. The specular idealization of the beloved addresses and aims to resolve precisely a perpetual threat of dissolution. And it is exactly because of this threat that the shepherd incessantly engages in the idealizing construction of the self through the other; a social, spiritual, and psychic necessity that to a large extent determines the repetitive thematic and plot structures of these narratives. Much in the same manner, we could argue that the pastoral novel, both in its form and its content, also acts as a comforting mirror upon which the early modern reader deflects his own and his society's fragmentation.

There is, nonetheless, a potential for inconsistency in this interpretation given that the lover's quest for fullness is posited in these narratives through constant suffering for an unrequited love. One could logically assume that the pain of rejection, rather than satisfy a need for wholeness, would be detrimental to the shepherd's psychic and subjective stability. Freud himself developed his theory on melancholia by examining the depletion that the ego suffers when the individual is rejected or otherwise loses the chosen object of desire.[17] Despite how opportune this category may seem, I would maintain that no such costly depletion of the ego occurs in the idyll. To the contrary, the lover's misery is, not without irony, a profitable endeavor. The greater the lover's distress, the more he confirms his perfect nature. The shepherd is most coherent, most "whole" when he is able to project successfully his ideal self as an absolutely happy–because tormented–lover, or what Felicia in *La Diana* qualifies as the privilege of "desamar a sí mismos" 'makes him lose his self-love' (298; 166). Montemayor's early description of Sireno demonstrates the key role that affliction plays in securing the lover's status: "Venía, pues, el triste Sireno los ojos hechos fuentes, el rostro mudado, y el corazón tan hecho a sufrir desventuras, que si la fortuna le quisiera dar algún contento, fuera menester buscar otro corazón nuevo para recebille" 'The sad Sireno, came, his eyes turned into fountains, his face changed, and his heart so used to suffering from misfortune that had Fortune wanted to make him happy, she should have had to look for a new heart' (111; 51). Similarly, in *La Galatea*'s opening segment Elicio proudly announces his righteous suffering in the face of Galatea's staunch chastity:

> Yo sí que al *fuego* me consumo y quemo,
> y al *lazo* pongo humilde la garganta,
> y a la *red* invisible poco temo,
> y el rigor de la *flecha* no me espanta.
> Por esto soy llegado a tal extremo,
> a tanto daño, a desventura tanta,
> que tengo por mi gloria y mi sosiego
> la *saeta*, la *red*, el *lazo*, el *fuego*.
>   (Lns. 25-32. 166)

> But lo, 'tis I who burn within the blaze,
> I waste away: before the net unseen
> I tremble not: my neck I humbly place
> Within the noose; and of his arrow keen
> I have no fear: thus to this last disgrace
> Have I been brought so great my fall has been
> That for my glory and my heart's desire
> The dart and net I count, the noose and fire. (9)

---

[17] See "Mourning and Melancholia."

Galatea recalls the goddess Diana as a hunter who threatens to destroy her lovers as prey. The lover, unable to protect himself against her fury, is left to suffer "la saeta, la red, el lazo, el fuego." A propos this declaration of apparent defeat, T. Anthony Perry perceptively warns: "It is clear [...] that such danger to the self is to be seen not as a misfortune but as a blessing" (229). The lover is in fact a willing victim whose nobility is directly proportional to the misery he endures in the hands of the cruel yet perfect huntress. The shepherd's distress therefore functions as a tool of empowerment; it is a perfect agony that fixes itself in the pastoral psychological landscape as a faultless subject position for the lover. At moments that are both candid and instructive, Montemayor's Sireno and Sylvano sing to Felicia, "los que sufren más, son los mejores" 'Because those who suffer most are best' (Ln. 10. 262; 147), while Cervantes's Elicio proclaims, "con mi dolor contento / [...] ¡Oh dura servidumbre, aunque gustosa" 'And in my grief find rest; / [...] Oh bitter bonds of Love, though fraught with pleasure!' (Lns. 2 /13. 259; 64). Rejection makes possible the lover's self-identification as a wounded and therefore fortunate and complete lover.

It is important to note that the shepherd's torment is also sustained by availing himself of his beloved's chastity: "[T]he virtuous are those who desire and love and yet have remained chaste in their emotions. That is to say, they have remained faithful to the object of their love even when fulfillment is impossible. They have renounced their own happiness" (T. Anthony Perry 229). I would again emphasize that this is a contented renunciation of happiness. The correlation between the beloved's chastity and the lover's positive self-regard is well established by Cervantes's Elicio, who feels great anxiety at the mere thought of Galatea falling for any of her many other suitors: "Quiero inferir de todo lo que he dicho, oh Erastro, que si tú quieres y amas la hermosura de tu deseo, sin pasar adelante a querer su virtud, su acrecentamiento de fama, su salud, su vida y bienes, entiende que no amas como debes, ni debes ser remunerado como quieres" 'I wish to imply from all I have said, oh Erastro, that if you love and worship Galatea's beauty with intent to enjoy it, and the goal of your desire stops at this point without passing on to love her virtue, her increase of fame, her welfare, her life and prosperity, know that you do not love as you ought, nor ought you to be rewarded as you wish' (341;

117).[18] Elicio's condemns Erastro's overt desire for Galatea and interprets it as a threat to his own ideal subjectivity. If Galatea were to surrender to Erastro she would no longer be a suitable specular surface upon which to construct a virtuous renunciation of sexual consummation. Even the possibility of a chaste marriage does not enter into the realm of possibilities for Elicio. He dreads any physical contact that would disturb the shepherdess's sole function as an abstracted specular object. Elicio thus stresses that he has lived for years wanting only "honesta correspondencia amorosa" 'by intercourse both honourable and loving' from Galatea, "contentándome sólo de mirar a Galatea y de ver que, si no me quería, no me aborrecía" 'contenting myself merely with looking at Galatea and with seeing that if she did not love me, she did not loathe me' (506; 216). With this statement he confirms his own chastity and the rewarding hardship that is attached to it. In turn, he reaffirms the profitability found in the specular configuration of unrequited love. Tirsi, a renowned shepherd-poet that comes to Elicio and Erastro's *aldea*, clearly echoes this position when he declares that love "no tiene otra paga ni otra satisfacción sino el mesmo amor, y él propio es su propia y verdadera paga" 'has no other reward nor satisfaction save love itself, and love itself is its own true reward' (444; 178). The lover, in the interest of promoting his own worth yearns for the conditions of his own rejection. Perry has connected a desire for fame in the pastoral with the lover's "willed impossibility" (231). I would add that this "willed impossibility" could also be seen from a psychoanalytic perspective as supporting a stable narcissistic subjectivity for both the characters and the readers, allowing them an idealized position undisturbed by contradiction or fragmentation and worthy of self-love and communal regard.

A succinct expression of these conditions appears in Tirsi's "defensa y alabanza del Amor" in *La Galatea*. Love (whether *honesto*,

---

[18] Erastro's admiration of Galatea's beauty and his admittance that his desire is born out of her physical perfection is what causes Elicio's sharp response: "Bien dices–dijo Erastro–, pero todavía no me podrás negar que, a no ser Galatea tan hermosa, no fuera tan deseada y, a no ser tan deseada, no fuera tan nuestra pena, pues toda ella nace del deseo" "You say well,' said Erastro; 'but yet you will not be able to deny to me, that if Galatea were not so fair, she would not be so desired, and if she were not so desired, our pain would not be so great, since it all springs from desire" (340; 116). Elicio offers his response and Erastro is never given the opportunity to further explain or justify his position. The incident is never mentioned again in the text.

provechoso or *deleitable*) is offered as a substitute for the constitutive lack of postlapsarian existence.[19]

> [L]uego que el atrevido primer padre nuestro pasó el divino mandamiento, y de señor quedó hecho siervo, y de libre esclavo, luego conosció la miseria en que había caído y la pobreza en que estaba [...] *Y de aquí nasce el amor* que tenemos a las cosas útiles a la vida humana, y tanto cuanto más alcanzamos dellas, tanto más no parece que *remediamos nuestra falta* [...]. Así que este primer movimiento (amor o deseo, como llamarlo quisieres) no puede nacer sino de buen principio, y aun de ellos es *el conocimiento de la belleza*, la cual, conocida por tal, casi parece imposible que de amar se deje. (437-8, my emphasis)[20]

> [A]s soon as our daring first parent transgressed the divine commandment, and from lord was made a servant, and from freeman a slave, straightway he knew the misery into which he had fallen, and the poverty in which he was. [...] *And hence springs the love* we have for things useful to human life; and the more we gain of them, *the more it seems to us we remedy our want*. [...] Hence this first motion, love or desire as you would call it, cannot arise except from a good beginning; and truly among good beginnings is *the knowledge of beauty*, which, once recognized as such, it seems well-nigh impossible to avoid loving. (173-4, my emphasis)

Tirsi's portrayal of love as a way to spiritual enlightenment is well within a Neoplatonic register, where the love of beauty enables the being to return to an original state of unity with God. It is this same philosophical foundation which contains the rhetoric of loss and substitution that infiltrates Tirsi's discourse. Through their treatment of love, philosophers such as Marsilio Ficino and León Hebreo explore the loss of perfection or wholeness that characterizes the human condition and that is remedied through an adoration of

---

[19] For a description of the Aristotelian and Hebraic sources that inform this segment of Cervantes's text, see footnotes 162, 163, and 164, pages 436-37, in López Estrada's edition of *La Galatea*.

[20] Although this segment of Tirsi's defense presents love as a utilitarian mechanism in which children are produced in order to perpetuate the human race, it could be argued that the idea of relieving our "falta" (fault or lack) permits the dual interpretation of children not only as biological products but also as specular images of our own past perfection. For a detailed analysis of this section of Tirsi's defense see Paiewonsky-Conde (71-81).

all that is beautiful.[21] In the *Symposium on Love*, for example, Ficino interprets Plato's opinion of the nature of man and his fall:

> *Men*, that is, the souls of men, *formerly*, that is, when they are created by God, *are whole*, they are provided with two lights, one innate and the other infused, in order that by the innate light they may perceive inferior and equal things, and by the infused, superior things. *They wished to equal God.* They turned themselves toward the innate light alone. Hence they were divided. They lost the infused splendor when they were turned toward the innate light alone, and they fell immediately into bodies. (73)

As Tirsi makes use of this discourse, man has fallen ("luego conoció la miseria en que había caído y la pobreza") and love ("el conoscimiento de la belleza") is the key to redemption in the face of a lost state of perfection. Despite a conventional understanding of the idyll as a space where no need is known, Tirsi's defense and its Neoplatonic referent operate from exactly the opposite premise. Even within the pastoral fantasy, man cannot entirely escape his need to "remediar su falta." The same issues of lack and alienation that we usually associate with the world beyond the bower's borders are present, but here as the motivating force for exalted love and pastoral ideality.

When we read the pastoral novel through this analytic lens, the logic of narcissism offers a fresh insight into the particular nature of the shepherd lover. Text and theory reveal a world that is fictional not merely because it is literary, but because it suggests the possibility of an ideal state where lack is in principal kept at bay. The appeal of this fantasy for the individual reader should not be underestimated and can in part account for the way in which the pastoral novel captured the reading public's imagination. Equally as suggestive, pastoral novels can be said to function as a narcissistic response to the political, economic, and social fragmentation that pervaded throughout the Spanish sixteenth century. In sum, pastoral novels provided its contemporary audience, both on a personal and on a broader social level, a temporary way out of the unstable nature of subjectivity.

---

[21] Due to Inca Garcilaso de la Vega's popular translation, León Hebreo's *Dialoghi d'amore* was often directly cited in pastoral novels.

II. Pastoral Communities: What's Love Got to Do With It?

Pastoral novels are characterized by a highly structured sense of community. The shepherd thrives on the public acknowledgement of his condition and the identification with others that arises from it. They share their fate as forlorn lovers, building on each other's experiences. And, unlike the epic or courtly tradition where the hero stands alone in his quest for victory and love, the pastoral novel fleshes out the dependence of the individual on his community.[22] As I will show, these communities add another level of ideality to the pastoral metaphor and its reshaping of social experience through fiction. It is through the formation of the bucolic community that the convention by and large succeeds in eliminating–or at least covering over–voices of dissent and signs of strife or inequality. Lovers, for example, share their admiration for the same beloved without destructive competition or animosity. Any host of potential turmoil is substituted by the collective composition of songs and poems. Even though these shepherds are united by the experience of lost or impossible love, it is their poetic practice (both the act of singing and listening to each other's songs) that makes possible and sustains their communal bond. Not surprisingly, thus, what we find in the pastoral novel is that though officially the shepherd longs for his beloved, his desire for his fellow poets is greater.

In pastoral novels male friendship is particularly vital to those characters who share the same beloved. Although therein could lie significant potential for conflict, competing lovers in *La Diana* and *La Galatea* find their rivals a source of solace and sympathy. In Montemayor's text the complementarity of another lover's plight is pivotal to Sireno and Sylvano, who see in each other a reflection of

---

[22] In his refutation of pastoral literature as "poesía de la soledad" (poetry of solitude), Karl Vossler well establishes the importance of community in these texts: "En el país de la Arcadia las soledades no son de fiar. No alcanzan más allá del sentimental desahogo para el nostálgico desamparo y siempre espía una ninfa desde la aliseda o detrás de un sauce, o sobreviene un pastor, cuando no es una multitud la que se llega al desconsolado intempestivamente y se informa con todo detalle de las causas de su dolor" 'In the country of Arcadia solitude is not to be trusted. They [the lovers] don't go any farther than an expression of longing sentiment, and always a nymph spies from a nearby meadow or from behind a tree, or a shepherd comes along, if not a multitude approaches the disconsolate lover and requests all the details of that which is causing him pain' (95; my translation).

their individual pain and a confirmation of its value. In their first formal encounter, they sit together, "abrazándose los dos con muchas lágrimas" 'they embraced and wept many tears' (119; 56). Sylvano erases any lingering animosity between them by expressing his identification with Sireno's suffering now that Diana has married and is absent from the immediate scene:

> Pensar debes Sireno que te quería yo mal porque Diana te quería bien, y que los favores que ella te hacía eran parte para que yo te desamase. Pues no era de tan bajos quilates mi fe, que no siguiese a mi señora, no sólo en quererla sino en querer todo lo que ella quisiese. Pesarme de tu fatiga no tienes por qué agradecérmelo, porque estoy tan hecho a pesares que aun de bienes míos me pesaría, cuanto más de males ajenos. (120)

> Did you ever think, Sireno, that I hated you because God [Diana] wished you well? And because she granted you favors, it might cause me to hate you? My faith was not of such base metal that I would love my lady and not also love all that she loved. That I grieve for your sorrow, you need not thank me for, because I feel so sorry for you, despite how sorry I feel for myself, because I feel sorrier for others' griefs. (56-7)

Sireno's response is no less sympathetic, acknowledging Sylvano's own predicament; whereas Diana loved and abandoned Sireno, she was unaware of Sylvano's devotion. This difference is key to their mutual identification. As Sylvano makes clear, he not only loves Diana, but also everything that she loves or once loved, including Sireno. He recounts that for so long he had watched Sireno and Diana together and how he had lived vicariously through their relationship. The climax of this scene occurs when Sylvano recites from memory verses that Sireno had once composed for and sung to Diana. The two lovers thus become one, indistinguishable in their expression of love. Their meeting ends accordingly with Sireno and Sylvano participating in an amoebaean song, alternatively relieving each other from their shared misery: "Ahora pastor–dijo Sireno–toma tu rabel e yo tomaré mi zampoña, que no hay mal que con la música no se pare, ni tristeza que con ella no se acreciente" "'Now shepherd", said Sireno, "take your rebec and I will take my pipes. Nothing so bad that music cannot dispel it, and no grief cannot be increased with it'" (130; 63).

Cervantes replicates the lovers' syncretistic union in the first pages of *La Galatea*, when Elicio and Erastro come together to share their passion and frustration. As pointed out in Chapter One, the initial class distinction in this pair is rapidly put in the background, transforming Erastro into Elicio's double. Their love for Galatea acts as a common cause, allowing both shepherds to cohabit and think of each other as a substitute for the absent beloved: "Con nadie la podría yo tener mejor [la siesta] que contigo, Elicio, si ya no fuese con aquella que está tan enrobrecida a mis demandas, cuan hecha encina a tus continos quejidos" "With no one,' replied Erastro, 'could I pass it better than with you, Elicio, unless indeed it were with her who is as stubborn to my appeals as she has proved herself a very oak to your unending complaints' (173; 13). In the conversation that closes their first exchange, Elicio recognizes Erastro's right to love Galatea and seals their friendship with an invitation to companionship:

> Y de aquí adelante no dejes por mi respeto de querer a Galatea [...]; antes te ruego, por lo que debes a la voluntad que te muestro, que no me niegues tu conversación y amistad, pues de la mía puedes estar tan seguro como te he certificado. Anden nuestros ganados juntos, pues andan nuestros pensamientos apareados. Tú, al son de tu zampoña, publicarás el contento o pena que el alegre o triste rostro de Galatea te causare; yo, al de mi rabel, [...] *te ayudaré a llevar la pesada carga de tus trabajos, dando noticia al Cielo de los míos*. Y, para señal de *nuestro buen propósito y verdadera amistad*, [...] acordemos nuestros instrumentos y demos principio al ejercicio que de aquí adelante hemos de tener. (175-6, my emphasis)

> [A]nd henceforward cease not on my account to love Galatea; [...]. But I pray you, by what you owe to the good-will I show you, that you should not deny me your conversation and friendship, since of mine you can be as sure as I have declared to you. Let our herds go united, since our thoughts go in unison. You to the sound of your pipe will declare the pleasure or the pain which Galatea's joyous or sorrowful countenance shall cause you, I to the sound of my rebec, [...] *will help you to carry the heavy load of your trouble, proclaiming mine to Heaven. And in token of our good intent and true friendship,* [...] let us tune our instruments and make a beginning of the practice which henceforth we are to follow. (14, my emphasis)

Their situations are finally perceived as identical. One shepherd's lament will help carry the other's emotional burden. As in Montemayor's text, these characters' experiences become one and their reunion ends with an amoebaean song in which they jointly declare their common condition as forlorn lovers.

In *La Diana,* Sireno and Sylvano form a community of two structurally supported by the figures of other shepherds whom they never meet, but who share their identification as lovers.[23] One of these figures is Danteo, the Portuguese shepherd who proclaims in the last book of *La Diana* the "positive" effects of suffering:

> A, pastora, se as lagrimas destos ollos e as mago as deste coracao, sao pouca parte para abrandar a dureza con que sou tratado! Nano quero de ti mais, senao que miña compañia por estes campos tenao seja importuna, ne os tristes versos que meu mal junto a esta fermosa ribeyra me faz cantar, te den ocasiao defadamento [...]. Pentea, fremosa pastora, os teus cabelos douro junto aquela cara fonte [...]. Se ysto te parece pouco amor, dize tu en que poderei mostrar o ben que te quero. (369)

> Ah, shepherdess, these eyes' tears and this heart's wounds are not enough to soften the harshness with which I am treated. I want nothing from you save that my company in these fields not be troublesome to you, and the sad verses my grief makes me sing beside this fair river bank not anger you [...]. Comb, fair shepherdess, that golden hair near that clear fountain [...]. If this seems a small token of my love, tell me how I can show you how I love you. (208-9)

Like his Spanish counterparts, Danteo idealizes Duarda's beauty and professes his desire to have his "sad verses" recognized, even if from afar, by his beloved. His chaste desire, sacrificial attitude, and virtuous nature identify him as a kindred soul to Sireno and Sylvano. As such, Danteo confirms Sireno and Sylvano's experience and becomes for the reader an imaginary extension of their pastoral community.[24] This community is always capable of growth; any

---

[23] The way in which female lovers, such as Selvagia, Felismena, and Belisa may or may not be part of this community is discussed in detail in Chapter Three.

[24] It is important to remember that by this point in Montemayor's text Sireno is no longer "in love" with Diana and Sylvano has moved on to a new idealized object, Selvagia. Therefore, it can be argued that Montemayor's somewhat erratic inclusion of the Portuguese shepherds in Book VII serves as reaffirmation of pastoral

shepherd who encounters Diana has no alternative but to join in their chaste adoration ("creo que no viviera que en Diana pusiera los ojos que osara desear otra cosa, sino verla y conversarla" 'I believe that no men alive could cast his eyes on Diana and wish for anything else but look upon her and to converse with her' [121; 57]) and resultant noble suffering. Her abstracted "perfection" provides an open invitation for other shepherds to enter the lovers' community and insures its growth and permanence.

In *La Galatea* the pastoral community is also structured around those who are taken by the title figure's beauty: "fue querida y con entrañable ahínco amada de muchos pastores y ganaderos que por las riberas del Tajo su ganado apacentaban" 'She was loved and desired with earnest passion by many shepherds and herdsmen, who tended their herds by the banks of the Tagus' (167-8; 10). Although they are never individually identified, this broad group of lovers is always implicitly present. Elicio's final protest against Galatea's arranged marriage is a fine example of the community's extended presence: "[Y] así la habré de poner en las manos de la razón y en las de todos los pastores que por estas riberas del Tajo apacientan sus ganados, los cuales no querrán consentir que se les arrebate y quite delante de sus ojos el sol que los alumbra, y la discreción que los admira, y la belleza que los incita y anima a mil honrosas competencias" 'I must place it in the hands of reason, and in those of all the shepherds that pasture their flocks on these banks of Tagus, who will not be willing to suffer that the sun that illumines them, the discretion that makes them marvel, the beauty that incites them and inspires them to a thousand honourable rivalries should be snatched and taken away from before their eyes' (513; 221). In addition to Galatea's admirers, Cervantes introduces a much wider range of forlorn lovers for whom a welcoming community is of utmost importance. The plot reflects this dynamic, with a steady grouping and regrouping of the lovers who attentively listen to each other's tales and songs. Even in moments of apparent solitude, other lovers are always near, furtively listening to their brother's laments. A case in point is Silerio, who despite retreating to the bower to become a solitary hermit, ends up repeatedly sharing his story with an eager crowd of listeners.[25]

---

love as constant and, again, wholly virtuous, even if these characteristics are transposed to newly introduced characters.

[25] Rhodes has proposed that, in spite of his assumed role as a hermit who is searching for a "higher source of authority" beyond love, Silerio embodies the "per-

La Galatea develops a sort of thesaurus of virtuous lovers who share the exact sentiments and whose stories, despite the particular circumstances of their protagonists, all follow very similar patterns of shared suffering and solace. All characters endure misfortune in love and all take comfort in singing together with other kindred souls. Among the many, we encounter Orompo, Marsilio, Crisio, and Orfenio who recite the text's central eclogue and exemplify the most common types of love: those who suffer the death of the beloved; those who are pained by rejection; those whose beloved is absent; and those who are plagued by jealousy, respectively. Arsindo has in his old age fallen for the too young Maurisa; yet his chaste desire for the girl eventually allows him to enter the pastoral community of lovers. As the suicidal lover, Galercio illustrates an overwhelming passion that serves the rest of the group as an exemplary but cautionary tale of love. Tirsi's case is perhaps the most telling when it comes to the need for participation in the pastoral community. Even though he is reciprocated by his lover, the shepherd leaves his beloved Filis behind, thereby forcing an unnecessary absence that allows his entrance to the community of desolate lover-poets. Tirsi's desire to associate with and be recognized by the shepherds as one of their exemplary figures (he is widely known and admired for his poetic talent) takes precedence over the consummation of his relationship. Another remarkable case is that of Lisandro, whose slaughter of his enemy Carino within the boundaries of the bower does not preclude Elicio from requesting his company. Despite the brutality of his act, Elicio hears Lisandro's lament and cannot resist asking him to share his sadness, assuring him of a sympathetic ear for his suffering:

> [P]ues por las palabras y quejas que esta noche te he oído, muestras bien claro la poca o ninguna [ventura] que tienes; pero no menos satisfarás mi deseo con decirme tus trabajos, que con de-

---

fect pastoral story," a symbol of the chaste, noble, and sacrificial lover ("Skirting the Men: Gender Roles is Sixteenth-century Pastoral Books" 356). In turn, Mary Gaylord sees in the figure of Silerio a character, "whose hermitage offers him temporary refuge from the chaos of human communication" (270). I would argue, more in tune with Rhodes's interpretation that Silerio's "perfect pastoralism" is based on his own self-definition as a virtuous lover. This is a position that dissipates his initial desire to find a "higher source of authority" and instead allows him to fully identify with his newfound friends. He not only suffers for love and idealizes Nísida's beauty and his own virtuous desire, but also constantly tells his story to the group of shepherds who admire his exemplary behavior.

clararme tus contentos. Y así la Fortuna te los dé en lo que deseas, que no me niegues lo que te suplico, si ya el no conocerme no lo impide, aunque, para asegurarte y moverte, *te hago saber que no tengo el alma tan contenta que no sienta en el punto que es razón las miserias que me contares*. Esto te digo, porque sé que no hay cosa más excusada y aun perdida que contar el miserable sus desdichas a quien tiene el pecho colmo de contentos. (187-8, my emphasis)

[S]ince from the words and plaints I this night have heard from you, you clearly show the little or none that you have. But you will no less satisfy my desire by telling me your troubles than by making known to me your joys. May fortune give you these in what you desire, so that you do not deny me what I beg of you, if indeed your not knowing me do not prevent it; although *I would have you know, so as to reassure and move you, that I have not a soul so happy as not to feel as much as it should the miseries you would recount to me*. This I tell you, for I know that nothing is more wasted, nay thrown away, than for an unhappy man to recount his woes to one whose heart is brimful with joys. (21, my emphasis)

Elicio's identification with the killer is telling. That he is willing to disregard Lisandro's murderous deed in favor of their shared experience of lost love, accentuates the ability of this community to repress or willfully ignore all conflictive elements in favor of an idealized communal identity.

When we try to establish the relationship between the lover and pastoral community Freud's insights again prove to be especially useful. Connecting the individual's self interest with his group identification, Freud defines a group as "a number of individuals who have put one and the same object in the place of the ego ideal and have consequently identified themselves with one another in their ego" ("Group Psychology" 48).[26] Members of a group share a common object whose "perfection" reflects upon all the participants. Group psychology can thus be understood as a form of collective narcissism that communally substitutes for and represses the whole

---

[26] Freud offers the army and the Church as telling examples of group psychology, groups that have a leader (the Commander-in-Chief or Christ) for whom all members share equal admiration and/or fear. Moreover, Freud proposes the possibility for leaderless groups, which substitute an object or idea for the "leader."

unit's fragmentation and alienation.[27] Like the narcissistic individual, when the group praises an ideal it is in fact attaching itself to those qualities and values that enable the members' own collective identity as worthy and whole. Through the figure of a "leader" (whether a commander-in-chief, Christ, or a beloved) transformed into the pure superiority of an "abstract idea," the group enters into a relationship of absolute "devotion," a "blind love," where no fault can be found ("Group Psychology" 45). By loving a common object, the community successfully creates and confirms the value and coherence of its shared ideal self.[28]

The premises that ground Freud's theory of group psychology are clearly evocative of the pastoral community as found in *La Diana* and *La Galatea*. They offer a profitable avenue through which to examine the group's dependency on love and the abstraction of women. In addition, this approach makes possible a new interpretation of the ideology behind bucolic male virtue and community, as well as the pastoral novel's prescriptive power in an early modern patriarchal context. Pastoral group identification is based on both the specular relation all members hold with the beloved and the common torment they endure for her–a state of misery, I reiterate, that feeds into the lovers' and community's ability to promote their own virtue.[29] The bonds shared between Sireno and Sylvano in *La Diana*, or between Elicio, Erastro and the extended group of fellow lovers in *La Galatea*, represent the positive effect that group formations have upon the more self-serving narcissistic tendencies of each

---

[27] Freud situates the first instance of identification in the resolution of the Oedipal drama, when the child understands and relates to his father's position vis-à-vis the mother as woman, wife, and object of desire.

[28] As Freud further explains, if *being in love* "is based on the simultaneous presence of directly sexual impulses and of sexual impulses that are inhibited in their aims, while the object draws a part of the subject's narcissistic ego-libido to itself," then group formation only multiplies this process and "adds identification with other individuals, which was perhaps originally made possible by their having the same relation to the object" ("Group Psychology" 74-5).

[29] Interestingly enough, Freud proposes that group psychology must also, even if paradoxically, be related to the "primal horde's" relationship with the cruel, all-demanding "primal father" ("Group Psychology" 57). Even though I have up to now emphasized the way in which the pastoral community projects a shared image of perfection upon the abstracted figure of the beloved, we should not disregard the fact that she is also a source of cruelty that the lover must endure in order to prove his worth and assure his place within the group. Like the primal father, the beloved is an image of perfection that is imagined as making constant and extreme demands.

individual member. Both for Freud and in the pastoral, group identification functions as the cornerstone of social existence and ethical life; comradeship and empathy are foundational to the lovers' idealized identity. The shepherds' grouping can also be understood as an idealized response to the strife and suspicion that plagued sixteenth-century Spanish society. If social existence during the period was strained by the political, economic, religious, and class tensions that proliferated at court and in society at large, the community of shepherds provides an idealized substitute that symbolically rearticulates actual historical conditions. Of equal importance is the way in which the pastoral community promotes an ideology of sameness. All members of this community love the same, suffer the same, and are virtuous in the same way, sanctioning a social model that discounts the acknowledgement or inclusion any difference or otherness. In other words, the pastoral community instructs readers to set as a standard a homogenous social framework in which any alternative voice or position is seen as anomalous and thus not worthy of full recognition.

A number of plot elements could be said to challenge the thematic and ideological import of bucolic homogeneity. In *La Galatea*, for example, Cervantes introduces a marriage between a shepherd and his beloved that would seem to disrupt the sameness of a community whose members are all forlorn lovers. *La Diana* ends with the promise of a series of marriage unions, which traditionally has been interpreted as either a sign of Montemayor's didacticism against the negative effects of passion or as a problematic ending within the pastoral convention of forlorn love.[30] Regardless of what critical position we take, it is important to note that none of these unions actually take place and that the lovers remain to the end within the community of righteous suffering shepherds. In the marital promises of Sylvano, Arsileo, and Filemón there is never

---

[30] The representation of marriage in *La Diana* is linked with the visit to Felicia's castle, the magic she performs on the visitors, and her decree: "Razón será, pastores y hermosa pastora, que os volváis a vuestros ganados, y tened entendido que a mi favor jamás os podrá faltar y el fin de vuestros amores será cuando por matrimonio cada uno se ajunte con quien desea" '"It is time, shepherds and fair shepherdesses, for you to return to your flocks with the understanding that my favor will never be lacking you and that your loves will end in matrimony, each joining his beloved' (310-1; 172). For a discussion of this topic see López Estrada's "Introduction," T. Anthony Perry pages 233-4, Avalle-Arce pages 89-91, and Rallo's "Introduction" pages 52-65.

any real connection, whether emotional or physical, established between the lover and the beloved. The emotional and physical compromises of marriage are never negotiated. Sexual libido is never spent, and marriage remains an abstract idea that never exerts any pressure on or causes any transformation in the makeup of the pastoral lover. As Pérez points out, "en lo que deberían ser puntos culminantes de la obra–el momento en que dos enamorados, después de superar mil impedimentos, obtienen la dicha que tanto han anhelado–los amantes apenas expresan emoción" 'In what should be the climax of the work–the moment in which the beloveds, after overcoming a thousand obstacles, obtain the happiness they have so longed for–the lovers barely express any emotion' (64; my translation). Instead, these shepherds staunchly sustain their identification with each other through a continuous abstraction of their objects of desire. They remain lovers who together sing the praises of their own virtuous devotion, and who at no point give up their rightful place within the group. The only consummated marriage is Diana's union with Delio in *La Diana*. Nonetheless, the practical implications of this conjugal bond are never addressed. Delio does not figure as a part of Sireno and Silvano's community (he never enters Sireno and Silvano's world) and Diana only appears, without her husband, after Book Five. In this manner, any potential threat to the formal structure of the pastoral community is disarmed. Neither does Sireno nor Sylvano ever have to consider a different type of identity or in any way adjust the parameters that define their group.

A similar treatment of marriage occurs in *La Galatea*. Daranio and Silveria's wedding ceremony occurs at the plot's center, creating an expectation that the theme of marriage will be fully developed in the second half of the narrative. Instead, as John T. Cull makes clear, what we find is a couple whose arranged marriage has been "primarily motivated by material interests," and who never speak or take an active role in the story (74).[31] Moreover, most of the action surrounding the wedding revolves around Mireno, Silveria's forlorn lover who laments his beloved's marriage to another. In addition, the epithalamia that follow the wedding are filled with ironic re-

---

[31] Referring to the likely impossibility that Cervantes actually planned to write a second part to *La Galatea*, John T. Cull states: "The pastoral romance can barely tolerate a single wedding, much less the multiple nuptials that a continuation would logically entail" (76).

marks and expressions of grief that address Mireno's disappointment, in sharp contrast to the celebration of marital bliss that typically characterizes this particular poetic form.[32] Consequently, this conjugal union creates the perfect conditions for the development of yet another shepherd's identification as a constant and noble lover. In another example from *La Galatea*, Rosaura and Grisaldo's marital promise is couched in a conventional discourse of chastity and spiritual virtue that permits the lovers to remain within the confines of the bower to the end of the narrative. No mention of the economic bonds or familial duties that this union would establish is ever considered. In the same manner, Silerio's and Timbrio's pledges to Blanca and Nísida are quickly passed over and their unions exist only as a promise to be realized in an untold future. Once these characters speak of marriage, little more is heard from or about them, as if they no longer are of interest to the rest of the shepherds or the narrative voice. Gaylord thus emphasizes how in *La Galatea*, "the weddings occupy the off-centered center, [while] the work does not give a prominent place to the consideration of marriage in itself" ("The Language of Limits and the Limits of Language" 257).[33] Although seemingly the logical conclusion to the desire proclaimed by the lovers, marital ties in fact would dissolve the chaste constancy that is essential to the shepherds' identity and the community's integrity. How can a shepherd identify with his fellow lovers and join in their devotion of a perfected and perfecting ob-

---

[32] See Deveny "The Pastoral and the Epithalamium of the Spanish Golden Age." Alban Forcione also makes clear that this epithalamium is "extraño, fuera de lugar, y ciertamente no aparece como el punto de reposo hacia el cual tendían la acción y la articulación temática" 'strange, out of place, and certainly does not appear as the point of respite towards which the action and the themes were moving' ("Cervantes en busca de una pastoral auténtica" 1025; my translation).

[33] Forcione adopts a similar interpretation of marriage in *La Galatea* when he argues that Daranio and Silveria's wedding is not only upstaged by Mireno's lament but also displaced by the Eclogue: "El episodio dedica una atención mínima a la boda y a las posibilidades del amor conyugal [...]. Y, lo que es más importante, la celebración ritual de la consumación que normalmente sería el clímax de la boda se ve desplazada por la 'contienda lastimera' de una larguísima égloga, que por más de veinticinco páginas glosa el tema de la frustración y examina analíticamente la naturaleza distintiva del sufrimiento del amante [...]." 'The episode dedicates minimum attention to the wedding and the possibilities offered by conjugal love [...]. More importantly, the ritual of consummation that would normally be the climax of a wedding is displaced by the laments of the eclogue, where for over twenty five pages the topic of frustration is glossed and the distinctive nature of the suffering of the lover is analyzed' ("Cervantes en busca de una pastoral auténtica" 1024; my translation)

ject if he must deal with the responsibilities that accompany marriage and childrearing?[34] The notion of marriage, remote and unrealized, ultimately nourishes the ideal of the virtuous pastoral subject without ever threatening its narcissistic coherency.

The *desamorado*, in his refusal to join in the laments of his friends, could also potentially introduce an alternative type of identification, one who would challenge the homogeneity of the idyll. If, as I have suggested, group identification depends on a common understanding of love as noble, constant, and sacrificial, shepherds who do not share these ideals can easily become a voice of dissent and a source of disorder and chaos. Instead, what the reader witnesses in both *La Diana* and *La Galatea* is a triumphant integration of the *desamorados* into the pastoral community–a key demonstration of the group's compulsory sameness.

In the last books of *La Diana* Sireno, after drinking from Felicia's magical water, is transformed and shakes off his affection for Diana.[35] Sylvano bemoans the loss of his friend's identity as lover and expresses pity for the now unfeeling Sireno:

> Todas las veces que te miro, amigo Sireno, me parece que ya no eres el que solías, mas antes creo que te has mudado, juntamente con los pensamientos. Por una parte casi tengo piedad de ti, y por otra no me pesa de verte tan descuidado de las desventuras de amor [...]. Porque me parece que estar un hombre sin querer ni ser querido es el más enfadoso estado que puede ser en la vida. (321)

> Whenever I look at you, friend Sireno, you seem different than you used to be, for I believe you yourself have changed, as well as your thoughts. On the one hand, I almost pity you, on the other hand, it grieves me to see you so free from the mishaps of love. [...] Because I believe to be a man who is not in love nor loved is the most disagreeable state in life. (178)

---

[34] This issue is discussed at length by Poggioli as a conflict between a desired erotic anarchism, married life, and the effects children would have upon the pastoral space. See his chapter "The Pastoral of Love" in *The Oaten Flute*.

[35] We must also point out that after the visit to Felicia's castle Sylvano has changed his object from Diana to Selvagia. Yet this change does not alter Sylvano's status as lover and his yearning to identify with others like him.

Contrary to what one would expect from amatory pastoral convention, the shepherd remains a *desamorado* for the duration of the text. However, as Elias L. Rivers correctly argues, "Sireno's final freedom from love leads to an empty nostalgia for something lost, but not to solitude as a positive value" ("Pastoral, Feminism, and Dialogue in Cervantes" 9). He continuously recalls his past as a worthy lover and insists in remaining a key figure within the pastoral community. Accordingly, Sireno constantly seeks the company of Sylvano: "A este tiempo bajaba Sireno de la aldea a la fuente de los alisos con grandísimo deseo de topar a Selvagia o a Sylvano; porque ninguna cosa por entonces le daba más contento que la conversación de los dos nuevos enamorados" 'At this time Sireno came down from the village to the spring by the alders hoping to meet Selvagia or Sylvano. Because nothing then made him happier than the new lovers' conversation' (348; 194). Not surprisingly, when Diana finally appears in Book Five, Sireno no longer loves her yet he continues to commemorate his devotion and constancy in the face of her betrayal: "Mas con todo eso, plega a Dios, hermosa Diana, que siempre te dé tanto contento, cuanto en algún tiempo me quitaste, que puesto caso que ya nuestros amores sean pasados, las reliquias que en el alma me han quedado, bastan para desearte yo todo el contentamiento posible" 'But aside from that, God grant you, fair Diana, as much happiness as you once took from me, because our love is now over, what remains of it in my soul is enough for me to wish you all possible happiness' (326; 181). Despite finding himself free from love, Sireno insists on holding on to his former identity by going back to the locations where he and Diana had once met, and where he can reminisce about the "happy state" of love:

> Y pasando por la memoria los amores de Diana, no dejaba de causalle soledad el tiempo que la había querido. No porque entonces le diese pena su amor, mas porque en todo tiempo la memoria de un *buen estado* causa soledad al que le ha perdido. Y antes que llegase a la fuente, en medio del verde prado [...] halló las ovejas de Diana, que solas [...] andaban paciendo [...]. Y como el pastor se parase a mirallas, imaginando el tiempo en que le habían dado más en que entender que las suyas propias [...]. *[C]osa que él no pudo ver sin lágrimas, acordándose que en compañía de la hermosa pastora Diana había repastado aquel rebaño.* (348-9, my emphasis)

And having forgotten Diana's love, the time he had loved her did not keep from causing him loneliness. Not because his love grieved him, but because the memory of *a happy state* causes loneliness to one who has lost it. And before he arrived at the spring, in the middle of the green meadow [...] he found Diana's sheep grazing among the trees alone, [...] And while the shepherd paused to look at them, thinking of the time when he had cared for them more than for his own [...]. *[A] thing he could not witness without tears, remembering that he had fed that flock in the company of the fair shepherdess Diana.* (194-5, my emphasis)

The memory of his love for Diana and his willingness to keep recalling this past "buen estado" enable Sireno to remain an active member of the lovers' fraternity. His nostalgic prolongation of his past into the present allows him to maintain his identification with Sylvano–so much so that they continue to sing songs of love in honor of Diana, even after she ceases to be their proclaimed object of desire (353-7). Sireno's self-awareness is therefore only marginally affected by his visit to Felicia's castle. He remains an *enamorado*, virtuous, whole, and supportive of the community of which he has been such an integral member.

Cervantes places the figure of the *desamorado* at the center of the amatory debates that anchor *La Galatea*. Lenio and Lauso make their presence known amongst the shepherds, playing key parts in debates throughout the text. Nonetheless, both characters willingly give up their much-touted liberty and happily integrate themselves into the group. Lauso is the first to fall in love, making his beloved so abstract that he never even feels a need to properly identify or describe. "Silena"–as he tentatively calls her–functions both as a narcissistic reflection of his self and as a means through which he can identify with all the other lovers. In fact, "Silena's" ambiguous identity becomes a point of conjecture in the plot, provoking the other lovers to ask who this woman is and why Lauso will not accurately name her. For all the readers or characters know, Silena could simply be an invention of Lauso's imagination, exhibiting the underlying structure of objectification and specularity in pastoral love. Ultimately, there is not much difference between a beloved such as Galatea and an abstract idea of a beloved like Silena, given that both exactly operate as reflective surfaces that support the lover's and the community's idealized integrity. Despite the apparently illusory nature of his beloved, Lauso succeeds in diffusing any negative impact caused by his former state as a *desamorado* and joins in pastoral song:

> Ya tengo nuevo ser, ya tengo vida,
> ya puedo cobrar nombre en todo el suelo
> de ilustre y clara fama conocida,
> que el limpio intento, el amoroso celo
> que encierra el pecho enamorado mío,
> alzarme puede al más subido cielo.
> [...]
> ¡Oh, más que la belleza misma bella,
> más que la propia discreción discreta,
> sol a mis ojos y a mi mar estrella!
> (Lns. 16-21 / 34-6. 399-400)

Now I new being have, now life possess,
Now I in all the earth can win a name
For lofty glory and renowned success.
For the pure purpose and the loving flame,
Which is enclosed within my loving side,
Can unto loftiest Heaven exalt my fame.
[...]
Oh thou that art more beauteous on thy throne
Than beauty's self, and more than wisdom wise,
Star to my sea, unto my eyes a sun! (154-5)

Much in the same manner, Lenio's apparently stalwart rejection of love is overcome eventually when he falls in love with Gelasia. Initially Lenio is described as a *pastor esquivo* and a bothersome anomaly within the community: "[E]l cual era un pastor en cuyo pecho jamás el amor pudo hacer morada; [...] y por esta tan extraña condición que tenía, era de los pastores de todas aquellas comarcas conocido, y de unos aborrecido y de otros estimado" '[A] shepherd in whose breast love could never take up his abode; [...] By reason of this strange disposition of his, he was known by all the shepherds in all those parts, and by some he was loathed, by others held in esteem' (230; 46). His eventual transformation is therefore particularly noteworthy, especially when considering that he earlier discredited the virtues of love in a debate with Tirsi. In that debate, Lenio proclaims that since love is a pointless pursuit for an always-fleeting object of desire, the lover's suffering is futile:[36]

> Extraña cosa es asimesmo seguir a quien me huye, alabar a quien me vitupera, dar voces a quien no me escucha, servir a una ingrata y esperar en quien jamás promete ni puede dar cosa que sea buena. ¡Oh amarga dulzura; oh, venenosa medicina de los amantes no sanos; oh, triste alegría; oh, flor amorosa que ningún fruto señalas si no es de tardo arrepentimiento! Estos son los efectos de este dios imaginado, estas son sus hazañas y maravillosas obras. (426-7)

> It is likewise a strange thing to follow one who shuns me, to praise one who reproaches me, to utter words to one who does not listen to me, to serve an ungrateful one, and to hope in one who never promises nor can give aught that is good. Oh bitter sweetness, oh poisonous medicine of sick lovers, oh sad joy, oh flower of love, that dost indicate no fruit, save that of tardy repentance! These are the effects of this fancied god, these are his deeds and wondrous works. (168-9)

There are two remarkable conclusions that can be drawn from Lenio's position. First, he seems to be fully aware of the fictionality of the notion of love. Cupid is "este dios imaginado," an artificer who fools the individual into believing that love is a state free of lack or alienation. Second, Lenio nevertheless wrongly identifies the effects produced by the lover's plight, taking his suffering at face value. More precisely, he does not understand that despite the falsity of love, it enables the subject to define himself even if only in an act of misrecognition, as a perfectly whole and noble lover.

Lenio's misinterpretation ultimately threatens his destruction, generating undue tension within pastoral society. His *desamor* places him in an untenable position that precludes him from partaking of the ideality afforded by the pastoral community. The lovelorn

---

[36] Forcione proposes: "En su anatomía del deseo amoroso, Lenio subraya el solipsismo y la violencia, la proliferación y la fragmentación infinitas, el movimiento fútil y obsesivo, la repetida frustración de quien quiera acercarse a la meta y objeto del amor" 'In his anatomy of desire, Lenio underlines the solipsism and violence, the proliferation and infinite fragmentation, the futile and obsessive movement, the repeated frustration of whomever wants to reach the goal and object of love' ("Cervantes en busca de una pastoral auténtica" 1020; my translation).

shepherds frequently mock his pretenses and see his rejection of love as utterly foolish. His warnings against the "trap" of love are therefore categorically rejected (304). A source of dissent within the group, his refusal of love is so offensive to the community on one occasion that Erastro threatens him with physical violence (235). Unable to sustain his position, Lenio finally allows himself to be captured by Gelasia's perfect beauty and chastity. He then adopts the position of the forlorn lover and is quickly reconciled with the community:

> Dulce Amor, ya me arrepiento
> de mis pasadas porfías;
> ya de hoy más confieso y siento
> que fue sobre burlerías
> levantado su cimiento.
> Ya el rebelde cuello erguido
> humilde pongo y rendido
> al yugo de tu obediencia;
> ya conozco la potencia
> de tu valor extendido.
> (Lns. 1-11. 535)

> Sweet Love, I repent me now
> Of my past presumptuous guilt,
> I feel henceforth and avow
> That on scoffing it was built,
> Reared aloft on mocking show;
> Now my proud self I abase
> And my rebel neck I place
> 'Neath thy yoke of slavery,
> Now I know the potency
> Of thy great far-spreading grace. (237)

In a complete reversal, Lenio triumphs as a lover. Imitating his fellow *enamorados*, he adopts a new desolate and virtuous identity that perfectly complements that of his community. Lenio's meekness when he again meets with Tirsi is indicative of the redeeming quality of the *desamorado*'s conversion: "sin más detenerse, se levantó y se fue a arrojar a sus pies, abrazándole estrechamente las rodillas y, sin dejar las lágrimas [...]." 'he arose without further delay and went to fling himself at his feet, closely embracing his knees, and said to him without ceasing his tears [...]' (537; 238). Emulating the rhetoric of Christian deliverance, Tirsi dutifully censures Lenio for his "error" and exalts the "restoration" to be found among his fellow lovers.

> La mayor culpa que hay en las culpas, Lenio amigo, es el estar pertinaces en ellas, porque es de condición de demonios el nunca arrepentirse de los yerros cometidos; [...] Y pues tú, Lenio, confiesas el error en que has estado y conoces agora las poderosas fuerzas del Amor, y entiendes de él que es señor universal de nuestros corazones, por este nuevo conocimiento y por el arrepentimiento que tienes, *puedes estar confiado a vivir seguro que el generoso y blando Amor te reducirá presto a sosegada y amorosa vida*; (537-38, my emphasis)

> The greatest fault there is in faults, friend Lenio, is to persist in them, for it is the disposition of devils never to repent of errors committed, [...]. And since you, Lenio, confess the error in which you have been and now know the mighty forces of Love, and understand of him that he is the universal lord of our hearts, by reason of this new knowledge and of the repentance you feel, *you can be confident and live assured that gentle and kindly Love will soon restore you to a calm and loving life;* (239, my emphasis)

Love offers Lenio an antidote to the anxiety of unmediated social existence. Lenio's entrance into the pastoral fold keeps at bay any sense of fragmentation or difference within the group. No less importantly, his conversion frees the community from having to question its own assumptions. Lenio's case, as it were, functions as a perfect lesson on how to successfully and happily reproduce a stable subject position, and secure one's place within a homogeneous symbolic and social community.

Apparently fascinated by the narrative and thematic gaps caused by the figure of the *desamorado*, Cervantes has Lauso revert his position when he falls out of love with "Silena." Her haughtiness transforms her into an object of scorn and an unworthy mirror for Lauso's narcissism. Despite Lauso's reversion, Tirsi doubts his friend will be able to completely disavow love and its promise of specular completeness: "No sé si té de el parabién, amigo Lauso, del bien en tan breves horas alcanzado, porque temo que no debe de ser tan firme y seguro como tú te imaginas" 'I know not, friend

Lauso, if I should congratulate you on the bliss attained in such brief hours, for I fear that it cannot be as firm and sure as you imagine' (527; 231). Cervantes tellingly places Lenio's fall and integration into the community of lovers immediately after Lauso's reversal, structurally undermining Lauso's sudden *desamoramiento*.[37] Inevitably, the reader is left with the impression that all the shepherds, including Lauso and Lenio, are happily incorporated into the community of *enamorados*. In this club, the most significant member benefit is the illusion of wholeness that collective narcissism provides: All its members are–have been or will again be–perfect, constant lovers.

The community's cohesiveness is ostensibly tested once more in the final pages of *La Galatea* when the shepherds pledge to save Galatea from an arranged marriage by whatever means necessary. Made vulnerable by the loss of their collective ideal object of desire, the group has no choice but to react aggressively: "[T]odos llevaban intención de que, si las razones de Tirsi no movían a [Aurelio], de usar en su lugar la fuerza y no consentir que Galatea al forastero se entregase" '[A]nd all were minded, if the reasonings of Thyrsis did not move Aurelio to act reasonably in what they asked him, to use force instead of reason, nor to consent that Galatea should yield herself to the foreign shepherd' (628; 317). Yet the alternative is even more destructive: Erastro and his community could find themselves without a proper vehicle through which to structure their own specular identification and cohesiveness. The threat of force rightfully can be interpreted as a break from pastoral convention. But if read through the logic of group psychology, the community's actions provide a sound finality to what is presented otherwise as a text to be continued. The unity of the group, as well as its perfected self-image, must prevail. And in Cervantes's text this coherence is preserved, ironically but effectively, by way of the shepherds' readiness to forcefully defend what is theirs.

---

[37] Marcella Trambaioli rightly points out how Lenio, "trueca su papel con el de Lauso" 'exchanges his place with that of Lauso' (48; my translation).

III. Poetic Practice and the Pastoral Community: An Additional Note

Up to this point I have argued for a specific psychological and ideological reading of the mechanisms that sustain the pastoral lover and his community. But what has been for the most part left out of my discussion is the central role that aesthetic practice plays in this process. Shepherds continuously compose poetic laments, constructing and mediating their experience largely through verse. Critics have rightly paid much attention to the variety of poetic forms in these narratives, locating them within the larger literary history of Renaissance Spain.[38] My intent instead is to examine the specific role that poetic practice plays in the construction of the civilized pastoral self as a virtuous and refined lover, as well as in the role that this practice may play in these texts' wider symbolic function.

Gaylord has noted that talk about love, not love itself, dominates every aspect of Renaissance pastoralism ("The Language of Limits and the Limits of Language" 254). The shepherds' idealized identity–as well as that of the beloved–is entirely dependent on rhetorical acuity. Passion, never actively realized, finds its sole expression in carefully constructed laments. The city dwellers that join the shepherds in the bower tell intricate stories of love and adventure that recall romances and Byzantine literary models. Nonetheless, even these world-weary characters immediately upon entering the bower adopt the idealizing discursive positions of the native shepherds. Because language is given privilege over action, pastoral love has been interpreted as detached from real experience; that is something not truly felt but only contemplated.[39] Gaylord expands upon this interpretation by remarking upon the inability of language to communicate true love or any other truth:

> First, language cannot tell the truth; it fails absolutely as a mimetic mirror in the domain of feeling. Second, language *should not* tell the truth; its mask necessarily, rightfully, conceals. Finally, the paradoxical result: despite language's lamentable inadequacy, the greatest misery comes from finding one's self beyond its civi-

---

[38] See Avalle-Arce and López Estrada.
[39] See Perry, especially page 227.

lizing power [...]. Charged with saying the most that language can say, verse nonetheless presents itself as a problematical vehicle of communication. ("The Language of Limits and the Limits of Language" 261)[40]

The continual effort of the pastoral lovers to represent themselves and their 'love' through recourse to a vast repertoire of poetic forms, thus implicitly confirms "the inevitable exteriority of all discourse to the vision of truth or of self that it pursues" (Gaylord, "The Language of Limits and the Limits of Language" 265). Jonathan Cull attempts to salvage love's standing in the pastoral novel by making a distinction between shepherds who do "feel" and those who simply "adopt a pose" and "yearn to be dispassionately passionate" through their poetic compositions (70), with those who experience love beyond and above a formal rhetorical filter. But I would argue that this difference is ultimately impossible to maintain given the stylistic and plot conventions that these books follow. Shepherd-poets tend to blend together easily. Names frequently sound alike and their stories follow similar patterns. Furthermore, as I have shown in the previous section, the shepherds adopt a homogeneous pose proper to the narcissistic imperative of the group. True, some of the poetic expressions in these novels are more stylized than others. For example, the eclogue in *La Galatea* (338-72) is intentionally composed and performed for the benefit of an audience. It is meant to aesthetically describe "la naturaleza distintiva del amante" 'the distinctive nature of the lover' in a deliberate manner (Forcione, "Cervantes en busca de una pastoral auténtica" 1024; my translation). Yet the same can be said of all instances where lovers, both in the solitude of the *locus amoenus* and in the comfort of a group represent their experience through the filter of poetic language. As Polydora (one of Felicia's nymphs) remarks in Montemayor's text, "Bien está todo pero yo sé muy bien que por la mayor parte los que aman tienen más de palabras que de pasiones" 'I know very well that, for the most part, those in love manifest

---

[40] Lacan sees this impossibility of 'true' communication in language first emerging in the misrecognition (*méconnaissance*) of narcissistic identification, where the ego engages in a "systematic refusal to acknowledge reality" [*méconnaissance systématique de la réalite*] ("Some Reflections on the Ego" 12). Also see "The Mirror Stage" and "The Split Between the Eye and the Gaze" in *The Four Fundamental Concepts of Psycho-Analysis*.

more words than passion' (300; 167). It is only through the "dispassionate passion" of poetic representation that pastoral subjects are able to attain and deploy effectively their identity. Just as the beloved facilitates the shepherd's self-fashioning as an ideal lover, poetic idealization enables his existence as a consummate poet. This abstracting and idealizing quality of poetic language acts as the perfect vehicle for the enactment of a narcissistic subject position. In the same fashion, poetry performs the function of a shared mirror through which the group can construct itself as unified and nonlacking. Because it represses the basest and alienating forces that underlie psychic and social experience, pastoral poetry is the ultimate medium through which a perfected self-image–individual and collective–can be produced.

In *La Diana*, poetry functions as a core activity for the group from the opening scene. After acknowledging themselves as worthy lovers of Diana, Sireno and Sylvano seal their identificatory bond with a song: "No estaba ocioso Sireno al tiempo que Sylvano estos versos cantaba, que con sospiros respondía a los últimos acentos de sus palabras, y con lágrimas solemnizaba lo que dellas entendía" 'Sireno was not idle while Sylvano sang this song, for he responded to the last words with sighs and solemnized what he heard with tears' (119; 56). The scene is rehearsed at various points in the plot, most saliently at Felicia's castle when they sing together in defense of all *enamorados*: "No's menos desdichado/ aquel que jamás tuvo mal d'amores/ qu'el más enamorado/ faltándole favores,/ pues los que sufren más, son los mejores" 'Nor is he who never suffered / From love less fortunate / Than he who is most in love, / But is not granted favors, / Because those who suffer most are best' (Lns. 6-10. 262; 147). What better way to express love's affliction than by constantly recalling it in the form of a shared poetic lament? Within a psychological and ideological analysis of the pastoral novel, the most interesting aspect of these shepherds' songs is the ritualistic character that they acquire. Quickly exceeding the particular referent (i.e. their love for Diana), the ceremonial and reiterative pattern of these songs formally and thematically enable the community's sense of self. After Sireno and Sylvano drink Felicia's water and are freed of their amatory bondage, we could legitimately expect their collective poetic practice to end. After all, Sireno becomes a *desamorado* and Sylvano falls for Selvagia. To the contrary, as previously noted, Sireno and

Sylvano remain close companions and, in probably one of the most telling episodes in the text, continue to compose love poems expressing a sentiment that, if we follow the plot, they no longer feel for the eponymous Diana: "*hagamos cuenta* que estamos los dos de la manera que esta pastora nos traía al tiempo que por este prado esparcíamos nuestras quejas" '*Let us pretend* the two of us are as we were [when] the meadow resounded with our complaints for this shepherdess' (353; 197, my emphasis). Otherwise unable to sustain their identities as lovers, poets, and companions, Sireno and Sylvano embrace amatory poetic language–even if emptied of its referent–as an exclusive and appropriate vehicle for self-fashioning. Given the rupture between word and meaning, this final song to Diana is key to our understanding of the ideological role that poetry occupies within the pastoral space. It clearly demonstrates how all along poetic conceit– not truly felt emotion–is the foundation of the relationship between the shepherd and his beloved. The shepherds and their community are sustained not by love, but by their poetic practice. Sireno and Sylvano sing not because they are earnestly devoted to Diana, but because the reproduction of poetic language gives order to their individual and collective experience as ideal lovers.[41] The positive effects are substantial: this abstracting poetic practice insures the individual shepherd and his community's psychological coherence precisely by avoiding any real engagement with the fragmented state of his own subjectivity, or that of his ideal beloved.

In *La Galatea*, the utility of poetic language for communal identification is even more apparent. Songs performed by groups abound. The shepherds constantly display their lyrical skill with the intent of sharing their common experiences. Like that of Sireno and Sylvano, Elicio and Erastro's first encounter draws to a close with an affirmation of their collective lot in an amoebaean song. By Book VI the poetic consonance of the community has been so well perfected that Elicio, Marsilio, Erastro, Crisio, and Damón spontaneously compose verses around the same theme, responding to each other's improvisations. The narrator highlights the facility with which the lovers follow each other's compositions, creating a multi-authored poetic product realized as a single expression of love:

---

[41] From a purely literary perspective, these poetic compositions are a conscious intent to insert the text within an amatory poetic tradition, from Petrarch's *Rime Sparse*, to the *cancioneros*, to the *poesía italianizante* of Boscán and Garcilaso.

Parecióle a Marsilio que lo que Elicio había cantado tan a su propósito hacía, que quiso seguirle en el mesmo concepto; y así, sin esperar [...] comenzó a cantar. (594)
[...]
[Y] luego Erastro, dando su zampoña, sin más detenerse, de esta manera comenzó a cantar. (595)
[...]
Calló Erastro, y luego el ausente Crisio, al son de los mesmos instrumentos, de esta suerte comenzó a cantar. (596)
[...]
A todos pareció bien la orden que los pastores en sus canciones guardaban, y con deseo atendían a que Tirsi o Damón comenzasen; mas presto se le cumplió Damón, pues, en acabando Crisio, al son de su mesmo rabel, cantó de esta manera. (597-8)

It seemed to Marsilio that what Elicio had been singing accorded with his mood so well that he wished to follow him in the same idea, and so, without waiting for anyone else to take the lead in it, [...] he began to sing thus: (291)
[...]
[A]nd straightaway Erastro, handing over his pipe, without further delaying began to sing thus: (292)
[...]
Erastro became silent, and straightaway the absent Crisio, to the sound of the same instruments, began to sing in this fashion: (293)
[...]
All approved of the order the shepherds were keeping in their songs, and with desire they were waiting for Thyrsis or Damon to begin; but at once Damon satisfied them, for, as Crisio finished, to the sound of his own rebec, he sang thus: (294)

The Eclogue performed after Daranio and Silveria's wedding is the most important example of the function of poetic language in *La Galatea*. The four poems read as a catalogue of the identificatory models available to the community: the mourner, the jealous, the one who suffers his beloved's absence, and the rejected. It is conceived as a contest designed to compare and rate the degree of torment among these lovers. Even though at the end of the competition "el celoso Orfenio" (the zealous Orfenio) is the victor, the Eclogue's main effect is to enable the singers common bond: "Eran todos amigos y de una mesma aldea, y la pasión de uno el otro no la ignoraba, antes en dolorosa competencia muchas veces se habían juntado a encarecer cada cual la causa de su tormento, procurando cada uno mostrar como mejor podía que su dolor a cualquier otro se aventajaba [...]" 'They were all friends and from the same village; each was not ignorant of the other's love, but, on the contrary, in mournful rivalry they had oftimes come together, each to extol the cause of his torment, seeking each one to show, as best he could, that his grief exceeded every other, counting it the highest glory to be superior in pain' (337-8; 115). For the rest of the community the four lovers reproduce aesthetic patterns that are consistent with its own poetic practice. As we have seen in *La Diana*, *La Galatea*'s Eclogue showcases the ritualistic character of pastoral poetry. It also well demonstrates its ability to substitute for real engagement with the more confusing and less savory qualities of love, identity, and social interaction. Lacan proposes that in all socio-symbolic systems language hides the contradictory and fragmented nature of subjectivity. Likewise in pastoral novels, poetry stands as the most important and efficient means of sustaining community. Cervantes's Elicio is well aware of this when he equates Tirsi's fame as a poet with his worth as a lover and as a friend: "Bien conforma tu agradable semblante, nombrado Tirsi, con lo que de tu valor y discreción en las cercanas y apartadas tierras la parlera fama pregona; y así, a mí, a quien tus escritos han admirado e inclinado a desear conocerte y servirte, puedes de hoy más tener y tratar como verdadero amigo" 'Your pleasing countenance, renowned Thyrsis, agrees well with what loud fame in lands near and far proclaims of your worth and discretion; and so, seeing that your writings have filled me with wonder and led me to desire to know you and serve you, you can henceforward count and treat me as a true friend' (261; 65-6). In ways analogous to the Neoplatonic correspondence between inner and outer beauty, a shepherd's lyrical abilities are seen as corresponding directly to his inner virtue. As Cervantes's narrator points out, "tenían todos tal ingenio (o, por mejor decir, tal dolor padecían) que, como quiera que le significasen, mostraban ser el mayor que imaginar se podía" 'and all had such wit, or, to express it better, suffered such grief, that, however they might indicate it, they showed it was the greatest that could be imagined' (338; 115). Without poetic language there would be no medium for idealized identification among the lovers. Through it the shepherds successfully avoid the alienation brought about by unmediated social existence, and which the pastoral as symbolic representation intends to repress. The desire for a non-fragmented state is channeled into aesthetically pleasing forms and converted into a group venture that makes pastoral society possible.[42]

Following the logic of this description, the pastoral poetic practice could be seen as an example of Freudian sublimation. Spanish pastoral novels depend on the abstraction of love and the beloved, precluding any possibility for realized sexual contact, or the spending of accumulated libidinal energy. Freud defined sublimation as a process by which the subject redirects unspent libidinal energy "towards an aim other than, and remote from, that of sexual satisfaction" ("On Narcissism" 94).[43] Although the emphasis here might seem to be on Freud's ever-present preoccupation with sexual behavior, the theory of sublimation is above all concerned with the mechanisms that create socially viable and productive subjects, which in turn make possible stable and coherent civil societies: "Sublimation of instinct is an especially conspicuous feature of cultural development; it is what makes it possible for higher psychical activities, scientific, artistic or ideological, to play such an important part in civilized life" ("Civilization and its Discontents" 44). Although Freud does not directly relate this process to group formation, only through sublimation can a community flourish, as is well demonstrated in the idyll. The pastoral community profitably sublimates all disruptive desires, producing a world where the practice of love as art structures the subject's position and participation within the social realm.

Given the reading I have made of *La Diana* and *La Galatea*, we can reach some important conclusions regarding these texts' ideological aim. The shepherd and his fellow poets symbolize for the reader an idealized paradigm for civilization. The model promoted is one that privileges poetic production over any other type of instinct or behavior. The reading audience is persuaded to redirect all baser instinct or impulses in favor of an aesthetic ideal: men are

---

[42] Poetic skill is something that can be cultivated. In *La Galatea* this expectation is made explicit in the debate between Tirsi and Lenio (*enamorado* versus *desamorado*), both of whom are chosen for this debate because they have attended the university and possess "un alto grado retórico" (high rhetorical status). See also Estrada and López García-Berdoy's edition of *La Galatea*, endnote 92, page 416.

[43] Freud writes of the "artist's joy in creating" or the "scientist's [joy] in solving problems or discovering truths" as satisfactions that seem "higher and finer" ("Civilization and its Discontents" 26).

imagined as consummate poets with women as their corresponding abstracted sources of inspiration. Not without significance, this sublimatory model also avoids issues of class, race, religious strife, and gender inequality, forfeiting any direct engagement with the conflicts and contradiction of lived history. It encourages the reader to reproduce a set of idealized aristocratic and patriarchal values that can be sustained only if the real conditions of Spanish early modern history are ignored.

Pastoral novels offer an escape into a world where love not war, poetry not arms, define social experience. These *libros de pastores* consequently offer the promise that human beings are made to love and to sing poems, and that society can flourish in peace and harmony—a message that must have been of great comfort to a wide audience that surely experienced the conflict of lived history in much different terms.

Nonetheless, the sublimatory effect of the pastoral metaphor is always already undermined by its inability to completely repress all the disruptive elements that remain in the historical referent. The Spanish idyll is no exception. Even a fictional ideal civilization cannot wholly rid itself of its discontents. The tenuous character of the pastoral fantasy is made evident in moments such as the surfacing of the lustful satyrs in *La Diana* and with Lisandro's murderous act in Book I of *La Galatea*. These are extreme and thus, more easily contained examples of the potential corruptibility of the bower. Perhaps more insidious, as I have discussed in the previous chapter, are the material concerns and class divisions that obliquely persist within pastoral society. Diana's and Galatea's marriages of convenience are cases in point. The difference in class status between Sireno and Sylvano, and Elicio and Erastro, although quickly dismissed as unimportant by the narrator and the characters, is a symptom of the underlying hierarchies that endure in the community.

Despite the civilizing ideal that these narratives convincingly enact, the contested foundation upon which pastoral ideality is constructed cannot be avoided. Spanish pastoral novels exemplify the problem that plagues all symbolic formations, both real and fictional: all societies, even those imagined as idyllic, are ultimately unable to fully sublimate or repress all contradiction, difference, or alternative desire. In the pastoral novel, repression and its failure are most evident in the corrosive abstraction of women as subjects. This is a matter that I have discussed in this chapter in relation to the construction of the male pastoral subject as an ideal lover. It is now pertinent to examine where this process fails. *La Diana* and *La Galatea* uncomfortably include a number of women characters who, counter to their status as ideal objects of desire, insist in manifesting their positions as desiring subjects. It is only proper that we take a look at how and under what conditions those other female subjects come forth and ask to be heard. Most significantly, we can take note of how these voices, in their disruptive insistence, mark the limits of the symbolic and ideological function of pastoral novels.

Chapter 3

THE "OTHER" PASTORAL: ALTERNATIVE VERSIONS OF FEMALE SUBJECTIVITY IN *LA DIANA* AND *LA GALATEA*

THE central role women play in the constitution and maintenance of pastoral ideality and male specular subjectivity has been well established. At the same time, their stories command considerable textual attention and offer a variety of characterizations and positions vis-à-vis their status as objects of desire. Some characters, such as Selvagia in *La Diana* and Teolinda in *La Galatea*, enter the boundary of the bower seeking solace from their own frustrated relationships. Others, such as Diana and Galatea, put forward eloquent defenses of their rebuke of love. The question then remains of how to interpret the narrative and symbolic significance of these women's tales in relation to homogeneous and idealized male world-view that dominates these texts. Whether as objects of desire or lovers we must consider how women's words and actions function alongside and against the values and ideologies propounded by the pastoral.

The main idea here is to perform a gendered reading of pastoral novels in which the expectations, desires, and aims of the female characters are not automatically considered identical to or perfectly harmonious with those of the shepherds. The practice of love is certainly the predominant theme of Spanish pastoral novels, but this amatory ideality is differently experienced by the women who inhabit the bower. As Steven Hutchinson has stated regarding the Cervantine corpus in general, although "there may be little difference [...] between the ways in which male and female characters express their desires, [...] their experience of desire diverges considerably" (159). We must also consider to what extent this female desire destabilizes, or alternatively, is assumed by the operating amatory fantasy. It is at this interpretative juncture that we now find ourselves in our reading of the pastoral novel.

Female characters in sixteenth-century Spanish pastoral novels traditionally have not been read as especially threatening or subversive to the pastoral social order. Even my own analysis up to this point has defined pastoral women solely as objects of desire. But this interpretation is, as such, fundamentally incomplete. All symbolic structures are bound on occasion to falter and display their limitations. In what follows, I will examine several such instances in *La Diana* and *La Galatea* where female characters' experiences exceed the texts' abstracting specularity and threaten to unsettle the pastoral metaphor. The unanticipated surfacing of female subjectivity complicates my own reading of an aristocratic and patriarchal pastoral ideology. At the same time, I do not agree with the view that the *libros de pastores* can be read as sixteenth-century protofeminist manifestos. As with all successful social systems, the pastoral community effectively contains contrary elements, either by suppressing them or by simply discounting their effects. In her study of American literature, Dale M. Bauer has argued that in texts that reflect a male dominated point of view "there are no interpretative communities willing to listen to women's alien and threatening discourse" within or outside the boundaries of the text (3).[1] Despite the resonance of this statement when examining the form, content, and socio-historical context of sixteenth-century pastoral novels, my aim is to establish just such an interpretative community for female subjectivity in our present critical discourse.

I. In the Beginning there was Garcilaso: The Second Eclogue and the Pastoral Novel

Before moving on to the main part of my argument, I would like to suggest in a brief and preliminary manner that much of the instability reflected in Cervantes's baroque pastoral literature–and to a certain extent even in *La Diana* and *La Galatea*–is already present in one of the first formal pastoral texts in Spanish letters, Garcila-

---

[1] I would like to thank Joyce Tolliver for pointing out Bauer's study. Although the texts and contexts we study are different, Bauer's analysis has been both inspirational to and confirmatory of my own reading of the pastoral.

so's Second Eclogue. There are multiple reasons for including in a study of pastoral novels a discussion of the Second Eclogue. First, the eclogue's length and its inclusion of varied storylines and settings within and outside of the bower is an autochthonous precursor for Montemayor's *La Diana*. Second, its failure to produce a pristine bucolic topography already exposes the difficulty that the pastoral text has in symbolizing the contradictory and conflict-ridden historical context from which it emerges. Finally, by reading the Second Eclogue in this manner, I am rejecting in my own analysis an evolutionary reading of the Spanish pastoral as a progression from ideal to parody. The instability that Cervantes exploited in his later pastoral texts–*La casa de los celos* and *Don Quixote*, for example–were already perceived and made manifest by Garcilaso at the beginnings of the classical pastoral in Spanish Renaissance letters. In fact, as I will show, this same formal and symbolic hesitation in the Second Eclogue's bucolic topography opens the door for a destabilizing female presence in novels such as *La Diana* and *La Galatea*. To be more precise, the supposed failures of the Second Eclogue set a relevant precedent for precisely those moments in the pastoral novel where the idyll cannot keep outside of its borders the "otherness" embodied by the female subject.

The Second Eclogue is the most problematic and the least studied of Garcilaso de la Vega's works. Even though it was composed in the same three-year span as the First and Third Eclogues (1533-36),[2] the Second Eclogue is often considered an immature work, strained by an unsuccessful mixture of the pastoral and the epic.[3] Despite Bernard Gicovate's and Inés Azar's excellent attempts to rescue this poem from critical neglect, current studies of Garcilaso still noticeably privilege the First and Third Eclogues. Editors, critics, and readers alike almost unequivocally settle on the perfected bucolic aesthetic of these allegedly later efforts. My aim is not to re-

---

[2] Rafael Lapesa offers the following dates: the "Second Eclogue", 1533 and early 1534; the First Eclogue, 1534; the Third Eclogue, 1536. Bernard Gicovate questions this dating scheme by pointing out that given the length of the poems and the multiple segments that each contains, in all probability they were written more or less in a simultaneous fashion. For this reason he counters the notion of an evolution between the Second Eclogue and the First and the Third.

[3] For example, Elias Rivers states that, "Garcilaso's first experiment with the pastoral [...] was extremely ambitious, though not wholly successful. In this work [...] he tried to write a pastoral work which would be simultaneously epic, tragic and comic. [...] As such it has been extremely difficult for critics to interpret" (51).

peat Gicovate's and Azar's position and champion the Second Eclogue as equal or superior to the other two.[4] Instead, I would argue that the eclogue's apparent failure tells us much about Garcilaso's complex understanding of the symbolic promise offered by the pastoral fantasy. As I have already suggested, I believe we can read the Second Eclogue as a work whose engagement with the pastoral ideal exposes the falsity of this literary escape. Through a jarring counterpoint of the bucolic and the epic, Garcilaso vividly renders those aspects of social existence that the idyll formally excludes and represses: violence, unbridled sexual desire, and the unresolvable contradictions and conflicts of history. Azar's comparison of Albanio's desperate plight to the Duke of Alba's heroic life makes a case for a moralizing reading of the text. As I advance my own analysis, I want to make clear that I also understand the Second Eclogue to have a moral subtext. The issue is not whether Garcilaso is here preoccupied with the repercussions of unchecked human desire. He undoubtedly is. Yet, in my opinion, the poet does not make available a way out of the predicament of conflict, whether at a personal or broader historical level. The Second Eclogue represents a world where spiritual and physical struggle pervades all human activity, outside as well as inside the bower. The apparent promise of a future restitution of order does little to erase the stain of violence that marks both Albanio's and Alba's histories.

From its very beginning, Albanio's "horrible historia" 'sad tale' (Ln. 154.140; 202) is marked by a violent undertone not conducive to bucolic fantasy.[5] The shepherd's recollection is a detailed account of his and Camila's happier days as hunters. Azar has amply demonstrated the way in which Garcilaso's transformative imitation of

---

[4] Azar makes this point especially forcibly in the closing paragraph of her study: "Sólo en el contexto de una especie literaria flexible y multiforme–la pastoral–y de una forma de expresión proteica–el discurso–esa vasta tarea de conciliación era posible. Discurso y pastoral constituyen el ámbito dialéctico de esa *armonía discorde* que la *Égloga II* consigue por medio de un enciclopédico esfuerzo humanístico, el más complejo–si no el más logrado estéticamente–de toda la obra de Garcilaso" 'Only in the context of a flexible and multiform genre–the pastoral–and of a proteic form of expression–the speech–was that vast task of conciliation possible. Speech and pastoral constitute the dialectic atmosphere for this discordant harmony that the "Second Eclogue" achieves through an encyclopedic humanist effort, the most complex–if not the most aesthetically pleasing–of Garcilaso's entire corpus' (137; my translation).

[5] All translations of the Second Eclogue are largely based on J.H. Wiffen's 19th century translation. Upon occasion, I slightly altered or modernized the text in order to facilitate comprehension.

Sannazaro's *Arcadia*'s focuses upon the cruel enjoyment of the hunt within the peaceful boundaries of the bower:

> Ubicado en su nuevo contexto, el gozo del cazador se convierte en paradójico comentario humano a la desdicha de las aves prisioneras [...]. Es este contraste paradójico de desdicha y gozo lo que el texto de la égloga subraya, apartándose por completo de su modelo. La desviación no es casual, porque gozo y desdicha son los términos del cambio de fortuna de Albanio, y el violento contraste entre ambos es quizás el más ajustado resumen de toda su historia. (107)

> In this new context, the pleasure of the hunter becomes a paradoxical commentary on the misfortune of the captive birds [...]. It is this paradoxical contrast of calamity and pleasure what the eclogue underlines, separating itself completely from its model. The deviation is not casual, because happiness and sadness are the terms which mark Albanio's change of fortune, and the violent contrast between these two is possibly the most accurate summary of the whole story. (my translation)

The shepherd's golden past is ironically characterized by the sadistic pleasure that the couple attained in wreaking havoc upon the pristine *locus amoenus*. Instead of being one with their surroundings, Camila and Albanio avidly pursue a seemingly helpless nature: "¿Qué bosque o selva umbrosa no fue de nuestra caza fatigada?" 'What heath or leafy waste / Of forests, has not heard our hunting cry?' (Ln. 186-7. 141; 203). The viciousness of Albanio and Camila's pastime is palpable in several ways. Albanio admits that their predilection for preying on birds stemmed from the comparable ease of the exercise: "Cualquier caza a entrambos agradaba, / pero la de las simples avecillas / menos trabajo y más placer nos daba" 'Hunting of all kinds charmed, but that the most / Of simple birds, snared ever with least cost / Or toil' (Lns. 200-3. 141; 203). Far from meeting any material need or moral imperative, Albanio and Camila's outings simply fulfilled their wish for a cheap thrill: "de vida ociosa y blanda, / pasábamos el tiempo alegremente" 'When August heats were past, a different sport, / But no less idle, we were wont to court, / To pass the day with joy' (Lns. 237-8. 142; 204). This idea is reiterated in statements such as "sin fatiga era cumplido nuestro intento" 'Alive we captured, which was done with ease' (Ln. 246. 142; 205) and "a su pesar [los pájaros] y a mucho placer nuestro, / que así d'un mal ajeno bien s'empieza (se deriva)" 'Much to their [the birds] mischief, and to our delight' (Lns. 258-9. 143; 205). Untouched by the suffering of their prey, Albanio and Camila's relationship is patently founded upon selfish and inconsequential gratification.

The tension between idyllic harmony and the brutality of the shepherds is a symptom of the violence latent in the amatory ideals of the genre. Gicovate has correctly identified the conflict that lies at the heart of the eclogue: Garcilaso's belief in "the perfection of nature and contrasting this macrocosm of unity with the blemishes human beings can bring to its order" (85). Gicovate also refers to Albanio's responsibility for allowing what had been an innocent friendship to become an unsettling carnal desire that has no place within the bucolic amatory fantasy (83). Not without irony, Albanio finds his fate to be equal to that of the birds of prey.[6] Hunted and haunted by his desire for Camila, he ends up trapped, desperate, and fighting for his sanity and his life. But unlike the birds, Albanio's predicament is of his own making. It is as if the perverse enjoyment evoked by the hunt is transposed to his relationship with Camila. As he confesses to Salicio: "[B]asta saber que aquesta tan sencilla / y tan pura amistad quiso mi hado / en diferente especie convertilla, / en un amor tan fuerte y tan sobrado / y en un desasosiego no credible / tal que no me conosco de trocado. / El placer de miralla con terrible / y fiero desear sentí mesclarse [...]" '[E]nough to know / that this fond friendship, this divine-faced foe, / So pure from passion, undisturbed by fears, / To different color changed my rising years. / My ill star shone; the spirit of unrest, / And love, excessive love, my soul possessed; / So deep, so absolute, I no more knew / Myself, but doubted if the change were true. / Then first I felt to mingle with the stir / of sweet sensations in beholding her, / Fearful desires that on their ardent wings [...]' (Lns. 314-21. 145; 207). A noteworthy component of the shepherd's indecorous desire is that he shares with Camila the same bloodline: she is from Albanio's "sangre y agüelos decendida" 'From my [his] own ancestors remotely sprung' (Ln. 171. 140; 202).[7] Just as he had wantonly abused the purity of his relationship with the bucolic

---

[6] This is the central theme of Roger Boase's article "The meaning of the Crow-Hunting Episode in Garcilaso's *Égloga Segunda* (II. 260-95)."

[7] The original is composed in the third person "his."

landscape, Albanio has corrupted a love that was founded upon both sentimental and familial ties.

Violence pervades what is left of Albanio's contact with nature and with Camila. After Camila's stern rejection the shepherd abandons his herd punishing nature once more. The most pointed in a series of images is that of the hungry calves who wail upon finding "las tetas secas ya de las hambrientas / madres" 'Finding their udders no refreshment yield' (Lns. 510-1. 150; 213). Not surprisingly, nature itself turns aggressive towards the desperate lover. As is often pointed out in comparing the Second Eclogue to Sannazaro's *Arcadia*, Albanio's suicide attempt is not attenuated by the hopeful sign of two loving doves. Instead, as the shepherd readies himself for a fatal fall, the wind pushes him back and denies him any relief. Admittedly, this intervention of nature saves Albanio from eternal damnation. But unlike the source text, the shepherd receives no comfort and instead is doomed to live out the rest of his life with his "grave cargo" 'grave pangs' (Ln. 670. 155; 218).

Violence also extends to the remaining contacts that Albanio has with Camila, as well as with Salicio and Nemoroso, who try to rescue him from his desperate state. Undeterred by the reprehensibility of his desire, Albanio tries to subdue Camila when he finds her asleep by the fountain where they last met. Albanio looms over the shepherdess envisaging her as if she were dead, "ella está agora como muerta" 'And hers is slumber deep as death' (Ln. 795. 159; 224), and in so doing reveals the aggressive attitude in his approach. He holds her forcefully even as she awakens and demands to be set free: "Suéltame ya la mano, que el aliento / me falta de congoja" 'Let go my wrist! / Scarce can I breathe; let go, I do insist!' (Lns. 832-3. 160; 226). Characterized by reproaches and lies, the strained encounter ends when Camila tricks Albanio into letting her go. Any remnant of the innocence of their past friendship is eradicated and Albanio is consumed by an even deeper madness. Forsaken by his own mind, the shepherd imagines himself violently separated from his own body, dead to himself and to the world around him. In a twist that underscores the shepherd's underlying narcissism, Albanio turns his obsession to his own image in the fountain where earlier Camila's semblance had been identified as the source of the shepherd's desire. When the shepherds try to force him away, Albanio physically attacks Salicio, effectively ending any illusion of a functioning community among the shepherds.

Salicio screams and Nemoroso miserably blunders in his new role as intermediary, trivializing the severity of Albanio's hostility. It is in the midst of this confusion and conflict that we last hear of Albanio as he falls asleep for a second time.

As if Albanio's turbulent story were not sufficient, Garcilaso's examination of the underbelly of the pastoral dream intensifies in the later part of the eclogue when Nemoroso tells of the military and political prowess of the Alba family. Reminiscent of Albanio's torrid story of misplaced desire, this segment brings to the fore elements that undermine the bucolic fantasy: the violence of war and the trappings of court life. According to Azar's moral reading of the Second Eclogue, Fernando de Alba's exemplary active and intellectual life is a defining counterpoint to Albanio.[8] If Fernando embodies qualities such as nobility, honor, and self-control, Albanio alternatively is cast as a morally degraded being that has confused carnal appetite for true love (135). In sum, Azar's interpretation of the Second Eclogue argues that Nemoroso's eulogy of Alba sets the example that Albanio needs to and will follow. Aided by Severo, Alba's teacher and a well-known magician, Albanio will undoubtedly be cured from his madness. Consequently, the future promises a renewed bucolic harmony: "la cesación de la desdicha y del conflicto, el desenlace de la historia, la certeza del orden y, también, el final del poema" 'the cessation of desolation and conflict, the denouement of the story, the certitude of order and, also, the end of the poem" (137; my translation).

Yet there remain some problems with Azar's claim of a restitution of harmony in this bucolic scene. To start with, Albanio's cure is never realized. When the Second Eclogue ends, Albanio remains asleep in the confused slumber of his own madness. The value of Severo's therapy is also at issue. Although not much critical atten-

---

[8] Azar argues that, "Vida activa y gozo sensible, sabiamente alternados por obra de la reflexión, constituyen la clave de la vida de Fernando. Esa equilibrada coincidencia de vida intelectual, activa y voluptuosa es precisamente el modelo humano postulado por la concepción humanística [...]" 'Active life and sensible pleasure, wisely alternated with reflection, constitute the key to Fernando's life. The equilibrium between the intellectual, the active, and the voluptuous aspects of life is precisely the human model offered by humanist understanding [...]' (30; my translation). She also describes the magician Severo as the "creador y conservador del orden" 'creator and preserver of order' and Nemoroso as "devuelto al orden moral por las artes de Severo" 'returned to the moral order through Severo's magical arts' (119; my translation).

tion has been paid to this detail, the magician's treatment for a broken heart is to transform love or desire to hate: "en un punto remueve la tristura, / convierte'n odio aquel amor insano, y restituye'l alma su natura" 'He in an instant cures, removes the pain, / Converts impassioned frenzy to disdain, / Sadness to smiles, and on the soul's tuned keys / Rewakes its old familiar melodies' (Lns. 1092-4. 168; 240). Nemoroso, who has already undergone Severo's therapy, now only sees "la vileza / de lo que antes ardiendo deseaba" 'what I before with such a gust / had grasped for gold, to be but worthless dust' (Lns. 1123-4. 169; 241). All that the reader is left with, therefore, is a *locus amoenus* where lust is replaced by disgust.

I would suggest that Alba's exemplariness is not the magic bullet that Azar understands it to be. The eclogue is nowhere directly critical of Fernando de Alba, Garcilaso's military commander and court benefactor. Nevertheless, whether we categorize this segment as eulogy or as epic, we must admit that an account of a life framed by the trials of war and the politics of the court milieu is hardly appropriate material for a pastoral scene. In fact, as it is typical of many pastoral texts, early in the eclogue Garcilaso employs the convention of the *desprecio de corte*. When Salico first enters the scene he declares,

>¡Cuán bienaventurado
>aquél puede llamarse
>que con la dulce soledad s'abraza,
>y vive lejos d'empacharse
>en lo que al alma impide y embaraza!
>No ve la llena plaza
>ni la soberbia puerta
>de los grandes señores,
>ni los aduladores
>a quien la hambre del favor despierta;
>no le será forzoso
>rogar, fingir, temer y estar quejoso.
>   (Lns. 38-50. 136-7)

>How highly he may rate
>His fortunate estate,
>Who, to the sweets of solitude resigned,
>Lives lightly loose from care,
>At distance from the snare

>Of what encumbers and disturbs the mind!
>He sees no thronged parade,
>No pompous colonnade
>Of proud grandees, nor greedy flatterers vile,
>Ambitious each to sport
>In sunshine of a court;
>He is not forced to fawn, to sue, to smile,
>To feign, to watch of power each veering sign,
>Noticed to dread neglect, neglected to repine. (197-8)

Though Salicio's pronouncement may seem disconnected from the much later introduction into the eclogue of Alba's life, it seems clear that Garcilaso is here setting the stage for the failure of both the pastoral and the epic as escape. In the first part of the eclogue, Salicio's *alabanza de aldea* is quickly deflated by Albanio's lunacy, which turns the *locus amoenus* into a space of violent and chaotic desperation. In the second part, the venerable noble cannot free himself from the pride, pretense, and corruption that characterize the court milieu. Nor can we overlook the brutality and constant threat of untimely death that characterizes a military man's life. By putting side by side Albanio's lustful madness and Alba's heroic yet besieged life, Garcilaso denies the reader or *oyente* the full payoff of either the pastoral escape or the spiritual uplift of the epic.

Garcilaso's version of the Alba family is organized as a praiseful account of military valor and impeccable nobility; they are all "Marte en guerra, en corte Febo" 'At court a Phoebus, and a Mars in fight' (Ln. 1190. 171; 244). Still, just as earlier in the eclogue Garcilaso draws attention to the cruel enjoyment of the hunt within the pastoral topography, here he underscores the viciousness and bloodshed that the hero's life demands. The amount of suffering and death that the Alba family witnesses, causes, and suffers exacts a very high human price. For example, Fernando's father brave death is framed by the bloody spectacle formed by his enemies' rolling heads and exposed entrails:

>Unos en un bruto lago de su sangre,
>cortando ya el estambre de la vida,
>la cabeza partida revolcaban;
>otros claro mostraban, espirando,
>de fuera palpitando las entrañas,

> por las fieras y estrañas cuchilladas
> d'aquella mano dadas. (Lns. 1241-8. 173)

> The price of their temerity; these lay
> In deep disorder, some whose vital threads
> He had already slit, with cloven heads,
> Wallowing in blood; some silent dying; some
> Yet breathing free, not wholly overcome,
> Showed palpitating bowels, strangely gored
> By the deep gashes given by his sharp sword. (246)

The elder Alba's valor and eternal fame is framed in the eclogue by a graphic image of the carnage and mayhem of war.

Like his grandfather and father, Fernando is an exceptional warrior. Yet his career is fraught by illness, resentment, and disappointment. Whether describing his sickly "débil presencia" 'gaunt form of Sickness stands to sight' (Ln. 1457. 180; 252) as he enters Paris, the "envidia carcomida" 'sickening Envy' (Ln. 1559. 183; 255) of those who covet his skill and valor, or the frustration he experiences when his thirst for Turkish blood is left unquenched (Ln. 1662-3. 186), Fernando's experiences are defined as much by disillusionment as by victory. Even the account of Fernando falling in love with his future wife, doña María Enríquez, includes the unfortunate memory of a duel defined as a "batalla fiera" '[furious] fight' (Ln. 1389. 178; 250) that the young Alba had to accept in Burgos in 1524. True, Alba's marriage is recalled as a source of good fortune. María Enríquez is an "esposa / dulce, pura, hermosa, sabia, honesta" 'Virtuous, pure, and beautiful young bride' (Ln. 1418. 178; 251), and Fernando's desire for his wife is not in question: "Apenas tienen fuera a don Fernando, / ardiendo y deseando estar ya echado;" 'Anxious to be admitted, scarce the choir / Of nymphs could check Fernando's forward fire' (Lns. 1415-6. 178; 251). Nonetheless, marital bliss is quickly interrupted by the duties of the warrior, as the loving husband departs with Charles's army to Vienna. Certainly, Fernando's triumph over the many obstacles he faces while away contributes to his status as a virtuous hero. At the same time, it seems evident that Garcilaso's account of Alba's deeds is tainted by the poet's own negative experiences as a soldier and a courtier. As I mentioned in an earlier chapter, Cruz has analyzed the way in which Garcilaso's poetry reflects an increasing "demoralization" with his participation in imperial warfare and his role as intercessor in the court ("Arms versus Letters," 195).[9] In a reading of the Latin ode to Sepúlveda, Cruz notes the animalistic and predatory quality that distinguishes Charles V and which reveals the poet's identification with the "vanquished" ("Arms versus Letters" 198). I would argue that Garcilaso's representation of the Alba family's predilection for the "cruda guerra" 'war's fires abroad' (Ln. 1223. 172; 245) can be read in a similar fashion. In a powerful simile, Fernando's pursuit of the Turks is compared to a ferocious hunting dog who has found his prey:

> Con animosa hambre y con denuedo
> forceja con quien quedo estar le manda,
> como lebrel de Irlanda generoso
> qu'el jabalí cerdoso y fiero mira;
> rebátase, suspira, fuerza y riñe,
> y apenas le costriñe la atadura
> qu'el dueño con cordura más aprieta:
> Así estaba perfecta y bien labrada
> la imagen figurada de Fernando
> que quien allí mirando lo estuviera,
> que era desta manera lo juzgara.
>   (Lns. 1664-74. 186)

> His sword in unbelieving blood; with bold
> And eager action, not to be controlled,
> He struggles with the king; as the fierce hound
> Of generous Erin, on the spring to bound
> After the bristly boar, restricted, whines,
> And quarrels with the leash that scarce confines
> His passionate desire and fleet-foot flight,
> Which makes his master draw the string more tight
> So, imaged to the life, contending stand
> The fix to fly, he settled to withstand; (258-9)

Upon his return to his homeland and his beloved wife, the duke has to repress or "enajenar" the "muerte, daños, enojos, sangre y guerra" 'Death, dangers, doubts, vexations, wounds, and war' (Ln. 1710. 187; 260) that he has both suffered and promulgated. It is this clash between valor and violence, between love and death, that

---

[9] See also, "Self-Fashioning in Spain."

Alba's story reveals, and which in this text neither the pastoral fantasy nor the epic can resolve. To the contrary, as I have here argued, it is as if Garcilaso is stressing the inability of either genre to repress the conflict that underlies human experience. There is no escape, bucolic or heroic, from the trauma of history.

The Second Eclogue ends with Nemoroso and Salicio debating whether they should awaken Albanio from his sleep. The next day they will take their "enfermo compañero" 'distracted friend' (Ln. 1856. 192; 264) to Severo where he will be cured. Yet this promise of future order is at once undercut by the threat of Albanio's demented state. With night falling and the shepherds heading home, Albanio remains a figure associated with violence and death. Accordingly, Salicio's final farewell to Nemoroso is qualified by the fear that Albanio may well throw him off a cliff to his death: "Yo lo haré, que al hato iré derecho, / si no me lleva a despeñar consigo / d'algún barranco Albanio, a mi despecho" 'I will; I will; unless in my despite / Albanio hurl me down some breakneck dell' (Lns. 1882-3. 192; 265). Whether we read this final passage as a comedic turn or as a dire warning of things to come, the Second Eclogue cannot be said to end on an uplifting note. Albanio, like Alba, is a man bound by human desire and frailty and he imperils the worlds in which he exists.

Garcilaso's Second Eclogue should not be read as his beginning and unsuccessful attempt at the pastoral mode. In other words, it should not be deemed simply as a blunder or negligible practice run. Rather, it is my opinion that in the Second Eclogue the poet acknowledges the repressed underside of the bucolic dream, the contradictions and conflicts that pervade the historical subtext. As a result, even before the birth of the pastoral novel in Spain, Garcilaso's eclogue subtly contests the validity of the idyll, whether as a literary escape or as a living practice. As such, it presents itself as a problematic yet inescapable precedent for all Spanish pastoral texts that follow from Jorge de Montemayor's *La Diana* onwards and long before Cervantes's deconstructive parody in *Don Quixote*.

II. Montemayor's *La Diana* and the Female Subject: Transgression and Reinscription

La Diana is not only the first and most imitated narrative in Spanish pastoral literature, it contains arguably the most varied representation of women among all texts produced up to that point in Spanish literature. Critics have differed in their investigation of this aspect of the text. As I have previously quoted, Wardropper asserts that in *La Diana* the feminine point of view receives "its fullest expression in the Spanish Renaissance" (142). Wardropper bases this statement mainly on the large number of women that appear in the text and their numerous interventions in the action. However, his analysis assumes that feminine participation in the text automatically signifies the dominant function of a feminine point of view. Hence, he does not distinguish between the idealization of women as objects and when that idealization is disrupted by subversive elements in the female characters' behavior. Johnson reaches a separate conclusion by proposing that, although initially *La Diana* seems to be a text where women freely enact their own desire and subvert social expectations, the potential for subversion is eradicated by incorporating (and annulling) women's desire into "el orden patriarquista" 'the patriarchal order' ("Amor-Aliqua Vincit" 180; my translation). I will work within and between these two opposing views and examine episodes in *La Diana* and *La Galatea* where the feminine point of view erupts, at times contributing to and at times momentarily challenging the preponderance of this "orden."

From the largely absent Diana to the ever present and controversial Selvagia, women in Montemayor's text act out highly disparate modes of behavior. On occasion, female characters openly express their passion for other women, cross-dress, and actively pursue reluctant male counterparts. Together these elements create a gap between what the male narcissistic fantasy requires and what many of these female characters actually do. Recalling Bauer's assertion regarding interpretative communities, one of the more telling characteristics of *La Diana* is that while most instances of apparent feminine defiance to pastoral ideality are narrated in great detail, neither the narrative voice nor fellow male characters acknowledge them as unsettling. It is as if Sireno and Sylvano were unable or unwilling to admit the implications of these disruptions for the lover's identity, communal unity, and aesthetic harmony. Instead, the persistence of female agency is conveniently ignored by the dominant male perspective.

How then can we interpret the presence of female subjectivity in *La Diana*? How does it fit within a male narcissistic structure that requires its erasure? The need to repress that which threatens the subject's and society's coherence is at the center of all human endeavors. By the same token, these elements often manage to resurface or return, at times emerging in the form of bothersome events or conditions. Mostly they appear indirectly in forms that, even if unsettling, can be appropriated or manipulated by the operating socio-symbolic system. As will become clear, I view the surfacing of female subjectivity in the bower as a return of the repressed. At times this return seems to imperil the pastoral fantasy. At other times, it is effectively absorbed. To think of female subjectivity in this manner allows for a more nuanced reading of *La Diana* as symbolic act. The female voice and the disruption that it signifies can be associated with the nagging referent of history, summoning that which the idyll aims to leave behind: the traumas, conflicts, and contradictions that lie unresolved at the core of social existence. To be more specific, when these women characters speak or act in a way that does not reproduce their ideality, they expose the underside of the pastoral fantasy. They make apparent the constructed and false nature both of their perfection and that of the idyll. From another, more positive, perspective, their appearance also may offer a way forward to the possibility of alternative fantasies that call for the inclusion of difference—whether gender, racial, religious, or class—within the bower, and by extension in society at large. As we shall see, this "other" pastoral makes its mark only to be finally proscribed in Montemayor's text. Its presence provides, however, a profitable analytical route for reading the underside of the pastoral. Let us examine some examples in *La Diana*.

Belisa's story well illustrates the way in which feminine desire can complicate the amatory structure. At a first glance, Belisa seems to embrace her position as object of desire. Loved by both Arsileo and his father Arsenio, she is defined by her function as mirror for their respective identities as perfect lovers: "Y era la más extraña cosa que se vio jamás, pues así como se iba más acrecentando el amor con el hijo, así con el padre se iba más extendido el afición, aunque no era todo de un metal. Y esto no me daba lugar a desfavorecelle, ni a dejar de recibir sus recaudos" 'It was the strangest thing to see how, as love increased for the son, so it extended to the father, though they were of different natures. But this did not cause to disfavor Arsenio, or to keep me from accepting his gifts' (250; 142).[10] We first meet her alone and grieving the death of her lovers. Corrupted by jealousy and frustration, Arsenio has killed his son and himself. Belisa has been left behind with no one for whom to be beautiful, young, and virginal. Consequently, she finds herself without proper function in the pastoral amatory fantasy. She is a willing object bereft of a place within the male structure of desire that has defined her up to this point.[11]

Then again, Belisa's conformity is not as straightforward as it may first appear. One troubling aspect of Belisa's behavior is the way in which she consciously imperiled her position as a virtuous object. Even though Belisa could have chastely met with Arsileo in public view of other *aldeanos*, she makes available the intimacy of her garden window, aggressively pursues her lover's company, and asserts her desire to possess him. In her confession to the shepherds, Belisa acknowledges her miscalculation, aware that her eagerness to illicitly meet with Arsileo gave cause to the tragedy:

---

[10] Belisa ends her story with an almost identical statement of her pain for the loss of both Arsileo and Arsenio, confirming the value that both men's idealization held for her: "¡Ay Arsileo, cuántas veces temí sin pensar lo que temía! [...]. ¡Ay Arsenio, que no me estorba la muerte de tu hijo dolerme la tuya, que el amor que contino me mostraste, la bondad y limpieza con que me quesiste, las malas noches que a causa mía pasaste, no sufre menos sino dolerme de tu desastrado fin; que ésta es la hora que yo fuera casada contigo, si tu hijo a esta tierra no viniera!" 'Alas, Arsileo, how often I feared not knowing what I feared, [...]. Alas, Arsenio, may your son's death not keep me from grieving yours, for the constant love you showed me, for the goodness and purity you loved me with, the sleepless nights you spent for my sake, I can do no less than to grieve your untimely end; for by now I would have been married to you, if your son had not come along!' (252-3; 144).

[11] Grosz argues that from a psychoanalytic point of view what women find almost inevitably in romantic love is a complete objectification characterized by their homogenization and erasure as specific subjects: "She strives to be affirmed as a unique, desirable, special subject, an individual distinct from all other women; yet romantic love relations involve, instead, 'putting her on a pedestal' (the projection of man's narcissistic self-conception) and/or a reduction to the position of sexual object (receptacle of active masculine desire). What is more clearly affirmed is not her subjectivity but her ability to be reduced to desired object, which she shares in common with all women in patriarchy [...]. In this sense she is interchangeable with any other woman" (134).

> ¡Ay desdichada de mí!, que no acabo de entender a qué propósito lo puse en este peligro [a Arsileo], pues todos los días, ahora en el río, en el soto, llevando a él mis vacas, ahora al tiempo que las traía a la majada, me pudiera él muy bien hablar, y me hablaba los más de los días. *Mi desventura fue causa que la fortuna se pagase del contento que hasta entonces me había dado, con hacerme que toda la vida viviera sin él.* (251, my emphasis)

> Alas! wretched me, for I cannot begin to imagine to what purpose I put him in jeopardy, because every day, be it in the field, or by the river, or in the copse where I brought my cows, or returning them to the fold, he could have talked to me, as he did most days. *My misfortune was the reason for Fortune to repay me for the happiness it had given me so far, by making me live the rest of my life without him.* (143, my emphasis)

Unable to contain her passion, Belisa exceeds Arsileo's objectifying gaze and endangers her function as a perfect object. Before her relationship with Arsileo, Belisa had proudly protected her image as a chaste woman. By inviting Arsileo to her window and making her own desire manifest, she imperils both her own ideality and his ability to reflect upon her his own identity as a chaste and sacrificial lover. Her perfect specularity muddled, Belisa pays the high price of loneliness and unhappiness. Tarnished and desolate, she flees to the pastoral landscape:

> Pues como yo mezquina vi el desventurado caso, sin más pensar, como mujer sin sentido, me salí de casa de mis padres y me vine importunando con quejas el alto cielo, y inflamando el aire con sospiros, a este triste lugar, quejándome de mi fortuna, maldiciendo la muerte que tan en breve me había enseñado a sufrir sus tiros, adonde ha seis meses que estoy sin haber visto ni hablado con persona alguna, ni procurado verla. (252)

> When I, wretched one, saw this luckless mishap, without thinking, like a woman bereft of my senses, I fled from my father's house and came to this sad place, wearying the heavens with my complaints and filling the air with sighs, lamenting my fortune, cursing death, who had so quickly shown me how to suffer from his stings; so I have been here six months not seeing nor speaking to anyone nor trying to. (143)

Belisa joins the shepherds in their journey persuaded by the promise of Felicia's magic. Initially, Sireno, Sylvano, and the narrator's vocal admiration of her beauty offers a faint hope for love within the boundaries of the bower. Her second chance at being a proper object of desire is only fully realized in Book V; there it is revealed that neither Arsileo nor his father is dead, and that the entire incident has been an illusion magically concocted by an evil sorcerer, Alfeo. He too once had been in love with Belisa, and now jealous of her love for Arsileo and her appreciation of Arsenio punishes her by calling on demons that take their form and act out the gruesome murder and suicide scene.

> Alfeo, con sus hechizerías ha dado causa al engaño en que hasta agora has vivido y a las infinitas lágrimas que por esta causa has llorado, porque, sabiendo él que Arsileo te había de hablar aquella noche, que entre vosotros estaba concertado, hizo que dos espíritus tomasen las figuras de Arsileo y de su padre, y queriéndote Arsileo hablar, pasase delante de ti lo que viste, porque pareciéndote que eran muertos, desesperases o a lo menos hicieses lo que heciste. (333)

> [T]hat this same Alfeo and his spells caused the deceit you have lived with until now, and the endless tears you have shed for it, because knowing that Arsileo had arranged to speak to you that night, he had two spirits take the form of Arsileo and his father and when Arsileo spoke to you, you thought you saw what happened. So that thinking them dead, you would despair, or at least do what you did. (186)

With the sorcerer's deception discovered Belisa regains her place happy to perform her function as Arsileo's beloved. During her stay in the bower she reflects upon her mistakes, does penance for her sins, and regains a suitable place in the amatory fantasy. But there is a price to be paid in exchange of Belisa's reformation. In her reunion with Arsileo, Belisa regains her lover but loses her voice. Barely able to speak, her final words illustrate the cost of returning to a specular relationship with Arsileo: "Conténtate con saber el extremo en que tu fingida muerte me puso, y por él verás la gran alegría en que tu vida me pone" 'Be content to know what sorrow your feigned death caused me and know of the joy I receive seeing you alive' (336; 188). Johnson reads this repression of feminine desire as a general trend in *La Diana*: "El movimiento, tanto lírico/psíquico como narrativo/físico, del libro de Montemayor, tal como lo leo yo, tendrá como fin el intentar encauzar el deseo (léase la mujer deseante) por los canales 'normales,' reducir a estas ovejas errantes al rebaño, imponer la autoridad del pastor" 'The movement, both lyrical/psychic and narrative/physical, of Montemayor's book, as I see it, has as its aim to direct desire (read desirous woman) into the 'normal' channels, bring back these lost sheep to the flock, impose the authority of the shepherd' ("Amor-Aliqua Vincit" 169; my translation). In Belisa's case this channeling takes the form of the sorcerer's punishing spell and the stripping away of her manifest desire for Arsileo. Only after being properly penalized for actively manifesting her own desire, is she allowed to regain her position as ideal–and silent–object of Arsileo's desire.[12]

A number of female characters in *La Diana* follow patterns that parallel Belisa's transgressive impulses as well as her ultimate acquiescence. In the Book I Selvagia is first introduced as a shepherdess who has been "muy quejosa de amor" '[she] complains of love' (134; 66). She has lost her lover and tries to join Sireno and Sylvano in their laments. Yet, in contrast to the shepherds' characterization as loyal and virtuous, the narrator wonders whether Selvagia is truly suffering from love or whether "se burla con el desengaño" 'she feigns her disappointment' (134; 66). With Selvagia's sincerity made suspect, the tone is set for the rest of the scene where the three characters debate the capacity of women to love. Sylvano argues that the beloved, even when perfect, cannot be expected to fully match the male lover's devotion. Even with their ideal beauty and chastity, women easily forget, are inconstant, and do not possess the same capacity for suffering.[13] In her response, Selvagia cogently questions

---

[12] Arsenio, when faced with Belisa's flight and his son's love for her, decides to retreat to one of his properties and casts "todas las cosas del mundo en olvido" 'all worldly cares into oblivion' (336; 188).

[13] With this indictment Sireno and Sylvano deny any possibility of women fully joining their community of pastoral lovers; Selvagia is permitted to tag along with the shepherds but is not considered by Sireno and Sylvano as a worthy and equal practitioner of love. The two shepherds mock her when she first approaches them, ironically laughing at the song of love she had just recited: "Después que la pastora acabó de cantar se vino derecha a la fuente a donde los pastores estaban, y entre tanto que venía, dijo Sylvano, medio riendo [...]" 'After the shepherdess stopped singing she approached the spring where the shepherds stood, and as she came, Sylvano said, jokingly [...]' (135; 67). Furthermore, the particularities of the female characters' stories separate them from the group dynamic found between Sireno and Sylvano, who have strictly defined themselves as chaste and loyal lovers of the now married Diana.

this assumption. She reminds the shepherds that both women and men fall out of love for the same reasons: "Son cosas que el amor hace y deshace; cosas que los tiempos, y los lugares las mueven, o les ponen silencio" 'These are things that love does and undoes, things that time and place set to motion or doom to silence' (137; 68). Women, like men, are vulnerable to the ravages of time and space. Selvagia also asserts that women not only can be the most sincere of lovers, but that their "entendimiento" is so keen that they could "enseñar a vivir a los hombres, y aun los enseñaran a amar, si fuera el amor cosa que pudiera enseñarse" 'teach men how to live and even teach them to love, if love were something that could be taught' (138; 69). Following this logic, Selvagia proceeds to accuse men of intentionally misconstruing women's actions. They expect women to exist in the "más bajo estado en la vida" 'lower state in life' and force upon them prescriptions that only serve their interests, or "lo que pide vuestra inclinación" 'what your inclination desires' (138; 69):

> Mas con todo esto creo que no hay más bajo estado en la vida que el de las mujeres, porque si os hablan bien pensáis que están muertas de amores, si no os hablan, creéis que de alteradas y fantásticas lo hacen, si el recogimiento que tienen no hace a *vuestro propósito* tenéislo por hipocresía. No tienen desenvoltura que no os parezca demasiada, si callan decís que son necias, si hablan que son pesadas, y que no hay quien las sufra; si os quieren todo lo del mundo creéis que de malas lo hacen, si os olvidan y se apartan de las ocasiones de ser infamadas decís que de inconstantes y poco firmes en un propósito. Así que no está en más pareceros la mujer buena, o mala, *que en acertar ella a no salir jamás de lo que pide vuestra inclinación.* (138, my emphasis)

> But even so, I believe there is no lower state in life than woman's, because if they speak well of you, you think them dead with love; if they do not speak to you at all, you think them proud and flighty; if their shyness *does not suit you*, you call it hypocrisy; they have no candor but you think it excessive; if they are quiet, you say they are stupid, if they talk, you think them tedious, that no one can stand them; if they love you more than anything in the world, you believe they do it out of malice; if they forget you and withdraw from situations which may cost them their reputations, you say they are inconstant and disloyal. So that there is no such thing as a good or bad woman *except for one who does not flee from what your inclination desires.* (69, my emphasis)

This is a pronouncement within my analysis of pastoral love that could be interpreted as drawing a distinction between the narcissistic fantasy of the shepherd and other nonspecular types of connection. Contrary to the prevailing amatory fantasy, Selvagia's apology calls for a complex feminine position distinct from that which is usually clouded by the narcissistic necessities of the shepherd-lover. Within the male pastoral fantasy, women make possible an imaginary fullness for the male lover. They are vilified as inconstant and cruel in order to further extol the shepherd's capacity to love faithfully. Of course, the figure of woman characterized both as a perfect object and as an embodiment of vice thoroughly displaces the experiences and desires of real women. As Selvagia points out, women can hardly counteract the conditions that subordinate their agency to men's need for specular wholeness. This speech is for this very reason a significant moment in *La Diana* and points towards an alternative configuration of gender ideology and its injunctions. Regrettably, although praised for her "entendimiento y viveza de ingenio" 'understanding and liveliness of wit' (138; 69), Selvagia's reasoning is completely discounted by Sylvano and Sireno. Instead the shepherds insist upon calling her "hermosa" 'fair' (138; 69), conscripting her to the abstract ideality assigned to all other women in the text.[14]

Ironically but not unexpectedly, Selvagia eventually gets caught up in Sylvano's abstracting idealization and, as her earlier speech predicts, is unable to counteract her new lover's narcissistic gaze. Selvagia's inescapable destiny as an interchangeable object of desire is flagrantly exposed when Diana returns and Sylvano sings in her honor even though he now claims to love Selvagia. By this point Selvagia seems to have little choice but to remain an object for Sylvano, trapped by the limited roles that pastoral ideology provides for female characters: "A todos pareció bien lo que Sylvano decía, aunque Selvagia no estaba muy bien en ello, mas por no dar a entender celos donde tan gran amor conocía, *calló por entonces* [...]" 'What Sylvano said seemed like a good idea, though Selvagia did not think so, but so as not to display her jealously amid such great love, *she kept quiet* [...]' (353; 197, my emphasis).

Diana is the most obvious example of the erasure imposed on

---

[14] "Hermosa" in *La Diana* is an empty description, employed indiscriminately for all the women in the text.

women in this text. An object *par excellence*, Diana is often named, described, talked about, and made into an image that displaces her physical presence. Her entrance is postponed until Book V, after Sireno and Sylvano have been cleansed by Felicia's magic water. Even as they continue to sing laments in her honor, the shepherds explicitly admit the lack of connection they feel for the real person that now stands before them. As a *desamorado*, Sireno focuses on extending his membership in the pastoral community through his poetic practice. Sylvano, in turn, literally exchanges one object for another–Diana for Selvagia. Diana here comes to embody Selvagia's protest in Book I: She is a woman both idealized and vilified for the benefit of her lovers. Upon her return, she is harshly judged by Sireno and Sylvano and is barred from reclaiming her place within the pastoral community. In her marriage she has not fared much better, hounded by the unrelenting jealousy of her husband:

> Con celos voy al ganado,
> con celos a la majada,
> y con celos me levanto
> contino a la madrugada.
> Con celos voy al ganado,
> y en su cama acostada,
> si le pido de qué ha celos
> no sabe responder nada.
> (Lns. 29-36. 324)

> With Jealousy I go to my flocks
> With jealousy to the pen,
> And with continual Jealousy
> I arise at dawn.
> I dine at Jealousy's table
> I sleep in his bed.
> I ask of whom he is jealous
> He does not know how to answer. (180)

To her credit Diana does protest her former lovers' condemnation. When Sireno solicits Diana's admission of guilt, the shepherdess reacts with indignation, certain of her innocence in the matter of her marriage. First, Sireno's yearlong absence gave her license to forget him as she thought herself forgotten: "olvidé y fui olvidada" 'I forgot and was forgotten' (Ln. 14. 324; 179). Second, she had a duty to obey her father: "¡Desculparme yo, Sireno, si la primera culpa contra ti no tengo por cometer, jamás me vea con más contento que el que agora tengo! ¡Bueno es que me pongas tu culpa por haberme casado, teniendo padres! [...] ¿Y qué parte era el amor, adonde estaba la obediencia que a los padres se debía?" "'If I offended you first and pardoned myself," said Diana, "may I never know more happiness than I do know. It is a good thing to blame me for having married, since my parents forced me!" [...] "And what role could love play," said Diana, "if I had to obey my parents?"' (352; 197). Regardless of her good intentions, Diana finds herself in a double-bind: her actions are determined by a conflicting patriarchal structure that demands obedience to her father yet loyalty to her lover. Diana's remark, "¡Desculparme yo!," expresses frustration with her position as an object trapped and used by lover, father, and husband alike.

Unfortunately, as in Selvagia's case, her complaint proves ineffectual. Sireno masterfully transforms Diana's powerlessness against her father into proof of his own superiority:

> ¿Mas qué parte eran los padres, la obediencia, los tiempos, ni los malos o favorables sucesos de la fortuna para sobrepujar un amor tan verdadero como antes de mi partida me mostraste? ¡Ah Diana, Diana, que nunca yo pensé que hubiera cosa en la vida que una fe tan grande pudiera quebrar! ¡Cuanto más, Diana, que bien te pudieras casar y no olvidar a quien tanto te quería! (352)

> But how can parents, obedience, time, and good or bad twists of Fortune overcome a love as true as the one you showed me before I left? Ah, Diana, Diana, I never thought anything in the world could shake so firm a faith! So much so, Diana, that you could have married and still not forgotten the one who loved you. (197)

Despite Diana's quandary, Sireno exploits her alleged betrayal. Moreover, Diana's upset response to her present state–at times proud, at times jealous, and at times sad and confused–is described by the narrative voice as erratic and unworthy. In her last appearance (Book VI), all that Diana can do is weep, overpowered by the impossible nature of her position and further objectified by the narrative voice:

> En cuanto los pastores esto cantaban, estaba la pastora Diana con el hermoso rostro sobre la mano, cuya manga, cayéndole un poco, descubría la blancura de un brazo que a la de la nieve escurecía, tenía los ojos inclinados al suelo, derramando por ellos unas espaciosas lágrimas, las cuales daban a entender de su pena más de lo que ella quisiera decir: y en acabando los pastores de cantar, con un sospiro, en compañía del cual parecía habérsele salido el alma, se levantó, y sin despedirse de ellos, se fue por el valle abajo [...]. (357-8)

> While the shepherds were singing this, the shepherdess Diana stood with her fair face cupped in her hand, whose sleeve, having fallen a bit, revealed the whiteness of an arm that would darken snow; her eyes were cast upon the ground, upon which spilled many tears, and she knew that her grief was greater than she wished to admit; and when the shepherds stopped singing, with a sigh that seemed to take her soul with it, she arose, and without taking leave of them, went towards the lower valley braiding her golden hair, and her hat clung to a branch as she arose. (201-2)

This last description is especially revealing of the ideological prescriptions of the pastoral. Diana's case thus epitomizes the suffocating condition of women within the pastoral space and within patriarchy in general. Her worth is measured solely by her capacity to be a specular surface upon which the shepherds can construct their own narcissistic fantasies. Yet, her situation is presented to the reader as a desirable ideal, cunningly manipulating the text's reception. As promoted through the character of Diana, women are the fortunate recipients of their lovers' constant devotion, even if they can never equal their virtuous nobility. Consequently, they should consider their status as idealized objects of desire as auspicious.[15] It

---

[15] There have been many interpretations of Diana's role in the context of pastoral love and harmony, some more positive than others. For Anthony Perry Diana represents, "a fallen ideal; ...The name 'Diana' thus represents the two poles of virtue, the idealized and the unrealized particular. If it is difficult to deny that the title refers to the earthly Diana, each mention of the name is a disturbing reminder of the gap between mythical perfection and reality" (228). José C. Pérez views her even more severely by proposing that she embodies "los poderes nefastos [del amor]" 'the malevolent power [of love]' (62; my translation). According to the critic, Diana's actions show, "[que] el deseo de dominar es más fuerte que el amor, que su satisfacción consiste en rendir a los hombres por medio de su belleza, y nada más. Una vez que los tiene bajo su dominio su placer concluye" 'the hardest desire to

is here that *La Diana*'s symbolic representation of gender hierarchies finds, from my point of view, its finest expression.

Duarda, the Portuguese shepherdess who appears in Book VII, offers a final and fascinating case of female agency and its containment within the pastoral topography of *La Diana*. When Duarda first appears she has already declared herself free of all her emotional and imaginary attachments to her lover, Danteo. Duarda had hoped to be considered an equal in their affairs, a request which seems to distance him. As Duarda explains to her friend Armia, just days before Danteo's wedding they had promised each other eternal love. Her only request was to wait until a more propitious time to ask her father for her hand in marriage: "Conténtate, Danteo, con que yo soy tuya y jamás podré ser de otro, por cosa que me suceda. Y pues yo me contento con la palabra que de ser mi esposo me has dado, no quieras que a trueque de esperar un poco de tiempo más, haga una cosa que tan mal nos está" 'Be content, Danteo, to know that I am yours and can never be another's, no matter what happens. And I am happy you have given your word to be my husband; do not wish that instead of waiting a little longer we do something unseemly!' (363; 205). He nonetheless proceeded to marry Andresa, alluding to his father's authority as grounds for his betrayal. Although Danteo's actions could be compared to Diana's (they both marry influenced by the wishes of their fathers), I would say

---

control is love, since its satisfaction consists of submitting men through beauty, and nothing else. Once under its spell pleasure subsides' (63; my translation). To the contrary, David H. Darst offers an extremely positive interpretation of the character by asserting that Diana, "alone appears to be motivated by a will of her own in the narrative, a creature who assumes responsibility for her actions and who, at the end of Book VI, through the author's very human and sympathetic description of her disappearance from the narrative, comes alive as an individual conscious of her own existence" (187). Johnson offers a much more subtle interpretation, viewing Diana as a transgressor to pastoral love due to what he interprets to be her indifference to her lover's pleas: "La transgresión o erotismo practicada por Diana consiste en la ausencia de amor: en su indiferencia, en su libertad, en su estar exenta. La soledad/saudade que expresa hacia el final, al ver que Sireno y Sylvano ya pueden vivir indiferentes a ella, marca el comienzo de su entrada a la órbita fálica, su puesto bajo control" 'The transgression or eroticism practiced by Diana consists of the absence of her love: in her indifference, in her liberty, in her being exempted. The solitude that she expresses towards the end, when Sireno and Sylvano can be indifferent to her, marks the beginning of her entrance into the phallic order, her being put under control' ("Amor-Aliqua Vincit" 181; my translation). As I have tried to make evident, my interpretation of Diana's situation departs from all the above. She in fact cannot be judged as saint or as vixen, but just as a woman whose continued objectification obstructs of her right to be a complex, unique, and desiring subject.

that their cases differ substantially. Diana found herself without a marriage promise, Sireno had been gone for months, and her father preferred Daranio's wealth to Sireno's devotion. In this case, Duarda had willingly and happily accepted Danteo's proposal. Three short days later, Danteo married Andresa, rebuffing Duarda's confessed love for him and his marriage promise to her.

Recognizing her fungible status in Danteo's eyes, Duarda decides to regain her liberty and to be no longer defined by Danteo's objectifying desire: "Pues si eso es así que quien es de una persona no puede ser de otra, *yo la hora de ahora me hallo mía y no puedo ser de Danteo*" "'If it is so,' replied Duarda, 'that a person cannot belong to another, *I now belong to myself and cannot belong to Danteo*'" (363-4; 205, my emphasis). Her friends Armia and Felismena initially interpreted this discursive position as extreme and dangerous. They are seduced by Danteo's proclaimed pain and solitude as a widower. Still, both women eventually come to admire Duarda's lucidity in her evaluation of Danteo's actions. For example, when Duarda demonstrates the disparity between Danteo's words and his actions, Felismena wishes she could have seen the falsity of her own lover's words: "No trates, Armia, de sus palabras, trata de sus obras, que por ellas se ha de juzgar el pensamiento del que las hace. Si tú te enamoras de canciones, y te parecen bien sonetos hechos con cuidado de decir buenas razones, desengáñate, que son la cosa de que yo menos gusto recibo y por la que menos me certifico del amor que se me hace" "'Do not discuss his words, Armia,' said Duarda, 'discuss his deeds, because his thoughts must be judged according to them. If you become enamored with words and think that carefully written sonnets are good arguments, you deceive yourself, for they are what please me least and least assure me of his love'" (368; 208). Duarda exposes the lover's duplicitous nature, leading Felismena to conclude, "Desdichada de mí que no supe yo aprovecharme deste consejo" 'And I am wretched for not taking this advice' (369; 208). Even Armia, who continues to defend Danteo's renewed pursuit of Duarda, cannot help but admire her *discreción*, to the point where she frankly desires to be a man so she could honor Duarda and love her "más que a mí" 'more than myself' (362; 204).

At the end of the episode, Duarda rejects Danteo's plea outright, asserting her will and denying him, with her frank analysis of the situation, any hope of possessing her: "Deixame gozar de miña libertade e nao esperes que comigo poderas gañar o que por culpa tua perdeste" 'Let me enjoy my freedom and do not hope to regain what you lost through your own fault' (370; 209). Unlike any other female character in the text, she demands an autonomous and unencumbered agency. Duarda's hard-won freedom from love, to her own surprise, transforms her into a self-assured subject. This accounts for her staunch refusal to conform to the usual etiquette between pastoral lovers, or what the narrator perceives as her "terrible respuesta" 'sharp reply' (370; 209). Interestingly enough, Duarda's affirmation of her independence is diminished in two very important ways in a later and revised edition of *La Diana*. First, the 1574 Venice edition incorporates a response from Danteo, granting him the last word and reasserting his position as the more virtuous of the two, thereby dissipating the subversive effect of Duarda's position. In this version, Danteo claims to have remained faithful and unflinching in his love for her (regardless of his marriage to Andresa) and by inference accuses Duarda of inconstancy. Danteo's revisionist response ends with a declaration of the permanence of his love, making use of a well-known pastoral convention of eternalizing the lover's words on the bark of an oak tree:

> En un roble escriví un día
> crezca la firmeza y fe,
> y agora quando passé,
> vi lo que crecido avía,
> causóme gran confusión,
> y dixe por qué razón
> en la rústica corteza
> crece la fe y la firmeza
> que hallo en mi corazón?
> (ftn. 31. 371)[16]

> I wrote on an oak tree one day
> may faith and constancy grow,
> and now as I passed by,
> I saw how much it had grown,
> causing me great confusion,
> and I questioned the reason why
> on the rustic bark of a tree

---

[16] For the full text added in the 1574 edition, see Asunción Rallo's edition of *La Diana* (ftn. 31. 370-1).

the faith and constancy grow
that also grow in my heart? (my translation)[17]

Second, and also an addition to the original episode, the narrative voice confirms Danteo's characterization of Duarda as flawed, introducing the next episode in the plot with the assertion: "Estando pues el pastor portugués muy metido en acusarle de su inconstancia, oyeron a una parte del prado muy gran ruido" 'When the Portuguese shepherd was busy accusing her inconstancy, they heard in another part of the meadow a very loud noise' (ftn. 31. 371, my translation). The subject is again broached literally in the last scene of *La Diana* where the narrative voice declares that there is still hope for Duarda's repentance, implicitly positing the need that she accepts her role as Danteo's beloved. Defusing any lingering anxiety that Duarda's refusal may cause, the couple's story is linked to the marriage ceremonies in Felicia's castle, foreshadowing a reconciliation between the Portuguese lovers in the promised but never produced "segunda parte": "Allí fueron todos desposados con las que bien querían, con gran regocijo y fiesta de todas las ninfas y de la sabia Felicia, a la cual no ayudó poco Sireno con su venida, aunque della se le siguió lo que en la segunda parte deste libro se contará, juntamente con el suceso del pastor y pastora portuguesa, Danteo y Duarda" 'There they were married to their beloveds, with great rejoicing and festivity by all the nymphs and the sage Felicia who had helped the shepherd Sireno more than a little since his arrival, though what came of it will be told in the second part of this book, as well as what happened to the Portuguese shepherd and shepherdess, Danteo and Duarda' (377; 212). Marriage in *La Diana*, like pastoral love in general, is defined not as a mutual endeavor but as the possession of a female object of desire: "fueron *todos desposados con las que bien querían.*" The text's overriding and final masculine perspective offers a comforting dénouement for Duarda's story, reassuring the reader by tendering the gift of future marital "bliss." The prospect for Duarda is the loss of an independence she so forcefully had tried to safeguard; the disruptive effects of her position are truncated. With the abstracting objectification of all female characters successfully perpetuated, the symbolic containment of conflict and contradiction is secured.

---

[17] The added text found in the footnote of Rallo's edition is not available in the Mueller translation.

One more aspect of feminine behavior in *La Diana* that begs to be examined is the homoerotic desire that becomes apparent between female characters. Frequent and in some instances described in detail, these encounters are entirely passed over by the male pastoral community and the narrator. Likewise, homoerotic desire among women characters in *La Diana* has been completely ignored, derided, or made unthreatening by most critics. Some of the most notable examples are Menéndez Pelayo who uses adjectives such as "extravagante," "monstruosa," and "desagradable" 'extravagant, monstruous, and unpleasant' to describe Selvagia's story (273; my translation); López-Estrada who views Felismena and Celia's attraction as "un cierto confusionismo" 'a sort of confusion' ("Introducción"; my translation); and Avalle-Arce who asserts that "el homosexualismo latente en algunos episodios sí debe provenir del platonismo" 'the latent homosexuality in some of the episodes must come from Platonic ideas' (ftn. 35. 83; my translation). Wardropper's assessment falls within the same categorization: "this undercurrent of homosexuality is a result of the Platonic belief that love is caused by the sight of beauty" (139). This Platonic view taken by Wardropper and Avalle-Arce has guided many critics who assess the subversive value of these episodes as minimal. A recent example is Adrienne Martin who argues that,

> Lo que importa, según mi relectura, es la filosofía del amor que admite el amor homosexual basado en la persecución de la belleza. [...] [D]ebido a la base filosófica de la narración, el homoerotismo femenino y la heterosexualidad son contiguos, complicando así la mitología del deseo. Por esta situación [...] el episodio que acabo de discutir no es, en última instancia, transgresivo. [...] El fragmento no produce significados, y consecuentemente ha sido insignificante para el autor, lector y crítico. [...] [S]e convierte en amenaza llena de significado sólo cuando la homosexualidad es una posibilidad sentimental y social [...].
> (104-5)
>
> What matters, according to my own rereading, is the philosophy of love that admits homosexuality based on the pursuit of beauty [...]. Given the philosophical basis of the narration, feminine homoeroticism and heterosexuality are contiguous, complicating the mythology of desire. For this reason [...] the episode I have just discussed is not in the final analysis transgressive. [...] The fragment does not produce meanings, and consequently it has

been insignificant for the author, reader, and critic. [...] It can become a threat full of meanings only when homosexuality is a sentimental and social possibility. (my translation)

Nevertheless, although in the period homosexuality was accepted as a natural practice among the ancients, it is not altogether condoned as part of a Neoplatonic amatory practice. In Ficino's *Commentary*, for example, homosexuality falls under one of the vulgar types (Speech VI, Chapter 6). This is a complicated subject, given that Neoplatonic philosophy stresses the spiritual enlightenment reaped from the contemplation of beauty, regardless of its source. But, as we well know, Neoplatonism is a Christian reevaluation of a mixture of classical and early Church writings on the topic of love. If it did not exclude the physical union of its lovers whose physical enjoyment of each other's beauty led them to reflect upon God's perfection, it did label homosexuality as a sexual practice exclusively defined by the satisfaction of bodily urges.

As my own analysis shows, I agree that the episode does not ultimately shake the narrative's dominant heterosexual paradigm. However I believe it is important we recognize the mechanism of repression that determines our reception. Homoerotic desire is treated, in my opinion, as that which is opposite and which has to be radically erased, or at least wholly ignored, not as a Neoplatonic manifestation of contiguous male-female and socially sanctioned desire. The return of homoerotic desire, nonetheless, further reveals this text's symbolic aims. The enunciation of this type of female desire enacts a difference that pastoral ideality cannot comprehend, accept, and that it struggles to repress thoroughly.

The most prominent homoerotic exchange in *La Diana* is the encounter between Selvagia and Ysmenia at the feast of the temple of Minerva.[18] There is very little that can be debated about Selva-

---

[18] The significance of Minerva for the encounter is not explicit. The *aldeanos* of Selvagia's region have a feast and worship the goddess once a year, and customarily women are left in the temple to revel alone. Minerva is the Roman goddess of wisdom, defensive war, spinning, weaving, and the arts of peace. One possible connection between Selvagia and Minerva is that the goddess is not attracted to men and only comes into contact with one when tricked by Neptune (or Poseidon) to go to Hephaestus's home. Hephaestus had been told that Minerva wanted to have violent love made to her, which he tried unsuccessfully to do. The general significance of Minerva to the pastoral genre is much easier to establish given the goddess's pacifist character, her reluctance to use arms, and partiality to solving conflict through dia-

gia's desire for Ysmenia. From the moment she sees this woman enter the temple, Selvagia openly acknowledges her passion and relishes immediate physical contact. When the reader first hears of these lovers their encounter is told as a transitory and now past event, diffusing the threat this type of libidinal configuration may pose. Selvagia is in Sireno and Sylvano's village, where her father has sent her, suddenly and without explanation. Her amatory situation has also changed: she now claims to love Ysmenia's cousin, Alanio. Despite the apparent heterosexual channeling of Selvagia's desire, the story she recounts pushes the prescriptions on gender and sexuality traditionally found in the early modern pastoral convention.

Selvagia begins her tale with a description of her province, an impeccable bucolic setting: "La vida de esta provincia es tan remota y apartada de cosas que puedan inquietar al pensamiento que si no es cuando Venus, por manos del ciego hijo, se quiere mostrar poderosa, no hay quien entienda en más que en sustentar una vida quieta, con suficiente medianía, en las cosas que para pasalla son menester" 'Life in this province is so remote and secluded from things that disturb thoughts, that unless Venus wants to manifest her power through the actions of her blind son, no one undertakes more than to live a quiet and measured life in the manner necessary to sustain it' (139; 69). With this account of her origins, Selvagia clearly establishes both the innocence of her upbringing and the exhilaration of love. The night before the official celebrations are to begin, the women enter the temple and are left to revel on their own until the next morning. When a group of women from a nearby village arrives, Selvagia admires their beauty and looks forward to spending the night with her new friends:

> Estando, pues, como digo, en compañía destas amigas mías, vimos entrar por la puerta una compañía de hermosas pastoras a quien algunos pastores acompañaban; los cuales dejándolas dentro, y habiendo hecho su debida oración, se salieron al hermoso valle, porque la orden de aquella provincia era que ningún pastor pudiese entrar en el templo, a más que dar la obediencia, y se volviesen luego a salir [...] Y la causa desto era porque las pastoras

---

logue. For a detailed account of Minerva/Athena's story see Robert Graves's *The Greek Myths: 1*, pages 96-100.

y ninfas quedasen solas, y sin ocasión de entender otra cosa, sino celebrar la fiesta regocijándose unas con otras, cosa que otros muchos años solían hacer, y los pastores fuera del templo en un verde prado que allí estaba, al resplandor de la nocturna Diana. (140, my emphasis)

Being then, as I said, in the company of my friends, we entered through the door and saw a bevy of fair shepherdesses accompanied by shepherds, who, leaving them inside, and having said their prayers, left for the pleasant valley, since the law of the land decreed that no shepherd could enter the temple, but had to perform his duty and leave [...] *And the reason for this was so that the shepherdess and nymphs could be left alone without distraction to celebrate and rejoice with each other*, with the shepherds outside the temple in a green valley nearby, under the splendor of nocturnal Diana, *a custom others had observed for many years.* (70, my emphasis)

In the temple, Selvagia has the good fortune of having Ysmenia sit beside her, "para que yo [Selvagia] fuese desventurada *todos los días que su memoria me durase*" 'for whose sake I [Selvagia] would suffer for *as long as her memory lasts*' (140; 70, my emphasis). Ysmenia's face is partially covered with a veil and Selvagia is immediately enraptured by her eyes. A flirtatious game of coy looks begins when, finally, Ysmenia's "hermosa y delicada mano" 'the prettiest and most delicate hand' (141; 70) reaches out and touches Selvagia. Their first words are heartfelt and playful, especially Selvagia's who offers Ysmenia her hand, her heart, and her soul, and teasingly wonders, "¿Cómo puede ser pastora que siendo vos tan hermosa os enamoréis de otra que tanto le falta para serlo, *y más siendo mujer como vos?*" "How can it be, shepherdess, that being so lovely you fall in love with one who is not, *and what is more, a woman like yourself?*" (141; 71, my emphasis). This admission of the risqué nature of their desire corroborates the difference between their lives outside of the temple and the erotic freedom they find within. Ysmenia's response, although somewhat conventional, confirms the reciprocity of their emotional and libidinal longing: "¡Ay pastora, que el amor que menos veces se acaba es éste, y el que más consienten pasar los hados, sin que las vueltas de fortuna, ni las mudanzas del tiempo les vayan de la mano!"' "'Alas, shepherdess," she replied, "this is the kind of love than never ends and goes beyond fate and is not subject to changes in Time or Fortune"' (141; 71). Having admitted their sexual attraction, Selvagia and Ysmenia fall into each other's arms, consumed by their passion and unaware of any of the celebrations happening around them: "Y después de esto los abrazos fueron tantos, los amores que la una a la otra nos decíamos, y de mi parte tan verdaderos, que ni teníamos cuenta con los cantares de las pastoras, ni mirábamos las danzas de las ninfas, ni otros regocijos que en el templo se decían" 'And after this the embraces and our loving speeches were many, and for my part, so in earnest, that we paid no heed to the songs of the shepherdesses, nor to the dances of the nymphs, nor to the other ceremonies that were taking place in the temple' (141-2; 71). It is important to note that in the rest of Montemayor's text there is no other scene that comes close to the emotional and physical intensity these two women share.

The conditions under which Selvagia and Ysmenia's relationship evolves dictate that it be contained. Soon after their romp, Ysmenia falsely claims that she is a man, "Alanio," dressed as a woman, therefore reinscribing her previous actions. Yet Selvagia who can barely speak ("tan fuera de mí que no supe respondelle" 'I [Selvagia] remained so beside myself that I did not know what to say' [143; 72]) remains enthralled by her desire for this hybrid feminine being and responds to "Alanio" as a woman:

> Hermosa pastora, que para hacerme quedar sin libertad, o para lo que la fortuna se sabe, tomaste el hábito de aquella quel de amor a causa tuya ha profesado, bastara el tuyo mismo para vencerme, sin que con mis armas propias me hubieras rendido. Mas ¿quién podrá huir de lo que su fortuna le tiene solicitado? [...] Plegue a Dios que uses tan bien del poder que sobre mí has tomado, que pueda yo sustentar el tenerme por dichosa hasta el fin de nuestros amores, los cuales de mi parte no le ternán en cuanto la vida me durare. (143-4)

> Fair shepherdess, in order that I may not live in liberty, or for whatever reason Fortune knows, you donned the dress of one to whom I have declared my love, your own weapons would have conquered me without your having to defeat me with mine. But, who can escape from what Fortune has in store for them? [...] I pray to God you use the power you have gained over me, that I may call myself happy until the end of our love, which, for my part, I would not end as long as I lived. (72)

Selvagia, to a certain degree, consents to Ysmenia's 'maleness,' yet insists on calling "him" "hermosa pastora." As the tale progresses the amatory plot convention is dizzyingly stretched, reflecting the text's necessity to bring these female characters back into the fold. Selvagia finds out Ysmenia's deceit, but only after falling in love with the true Alanio, Ysmenia's cousin and veritable double. Selvagia's love is in this manner conveniently displaced to an adequate recipient. Both her textual audience and the reader meet her cleansed of her passion for another woman, lamenting a now unrequited and chaste love for Alanio. Selvagia's first-person narration may initially suggest that, by canceling out the narrator's point of view, her story comes to us uncensored. However, the text's narrative and psychological progression does what the narrator's absent voice cannot: it diffuses and eventually removes Selvagia's agency. Sireno and Sylvano's response to Selvagia's story is equally dismissive of her alternative desire. Aware of her experiences at Minerva's temple, they only recognize Selvagia's suffering for Alanio and invite her to model her chaste laments after their own: "Hermosa Selvagia, grandísimo es tu mal, pero por mayor tengo tu discreción. Toma ejemplo en males ajenos si quieres sobrellevar los tuyos; y porque ya se hace tarde, nos vamos al aldea y mañana se pase la siesta junto a esta clara fuente donde todos nos juntaremos" '"Fair Selvagia, your sorrow is great, but I judge discretion to be greater. Take other men's sorrow as example, if you want to overcome yours, and since it grows late, let us go back to the village, and tomorrow we will spend the noon hour near this clear spring where we all gather"' (156-7; 81). Ironically, Sireno and Sylvano's gracious acceptance of the shepherdess may also implicitly refer to and intend to restrain her deviancy. Is Selvagia's "grandísimo mal" her desire for Ysmenia? Is the suggestion that she imitate "males ajenos" an injunction that she reproduce acceptable heterosexual desire?

As Johnson reminds us, Selvagia's transformation can only be partially trusted:

> La tensión establecida en el texto entre el deseo transgresor de dos mujeres y las exigencias de la sociedad disminuye y casi casi desaparece. La desviación se rectifica. El tuerto se endereza. Casi casi, porque no hace falta ser Freud para observar que enamorarse de alguien muy parecido al primer objeto erótico significa no la superación, sino la supervivencia de aquel deseo primitivo. ("Amor-Aliqua Vincit" 171)
>
> The tension established in the text between the transgressive desire of two women and the expectations of society is lessened

and almost disappears. The deviation is rectified. The error is straightened out. But only almost, because we do not have to be Freud to observe that to fall in love with someone very similar to the first object of love signifies not the elimination but rather the survival of that first desire. (my translation)

Selvagia's desire is only cosmetically rectified because it is transferred to an identical copy of Ysmenia. Of no less importance is the way in which Selvagia's recounting of her past noticeably focuses not the present state of affairs–her love for Alanio–but on the night of passion that she shared with Ysmenia. Despite the text's best efforts, Selvagia does not rid herself of or reject her homoerotic longing. For this reason, the only way in which her transgression can be thoroughly expurgated from the pastoral scene is through Felicia's magic. Interestingly, Felicia does not resurrect Selvagia's relationship with Alanio. That would imply an endorsement of her lesbian attraction for Ysmenia. Instead, the shepherdess's past is thoroughly erased. She is given and accepts the role of Sylvano's properly abstracted object of desire.

A second instance of lesbian desire is equally revealing. Felismena's story initially seems to perfectly fit the pattern of pastoral love: she is a lover suffering a beloved's rejection. A city dweller, she enters the bower desperately looking for her beloved Felis, whom she has not seen in two years. Still, when the details of Felismena's journey are revealed we soon find out that her libidinal desire for Felis temporarily takes an unexpected turn when she enters into a relationship with Celia, Felis's new love interest. Felismena's most significant attribute is that she is a strange hybrid of feminine and masculine qualities. Her beauty recalls that of Venus but her corporal strength and facility with arms pertain to the realm of Mars.[19] The events of her story play upon this indeterminacy in her character. Abandoned by her lover, Felismena dresses as a man, secretly follows Felis to the court, and becomes his page, Valerio. Initially, Felismena views Celia as the enemy. Yet, in an unexpected twist, these women's relationship is soon entangled by Celia's attraction to Valerio. Felismena takes advantage of this turn of events and subtly seduces the lady. But she gets caught up in the game. As she plays

---

[19] As mentioned in Chapter One, Felismena's birth is directly linked with a curse and a blessing from Venus and Pallas respectively.

out the part of Valerio, Felismena develops feelings of admiration and love for Celia:

> La señora Celia la tomó [una carta de don Felis] y puso los ojos en mí, de manera que yo le sentí la alteración que mi vista le había causado, porque ella estuvo tan fuera de sí, que palabra no me dijo por entonces. [...] Señora–le respondí yo–la ventura que a esta corte me ha traído no puede dejar de ser muy mejor de lo que nunca pensé, pues ha sido causa que yo viese tan gran perfición y hermosura como la que delante mis ojos tengo; y si antes me dolían las ansias, los sospiros y los continuos desasosiegos de don Felis, mi señor, *agora que he visto la causa de su mal, se me ha convertido en envidia la mancilla que dél tenía.* (214, my emphasis)
>
> Lady Celia took it [Don Felis's letter] and looked at me, and I saw my presence caused a change in her, for she was so beside herself she could not speak a word. [...] "Lady," I replied, "the fate that brought me to this court has been better than I had ever imagined, for it has given me the opportunity to see much perfection and beauty as I see before me, and if my Lord Don Felis's longings, sighs, and continual unease pain me, *now that I see the cause of his unease, the pity I felt for him now turns to envy.*" (118, my emphasis)

As Valerio, Felismena finds in Celia a woman worthy to be her rival and her lover making for an inescapable erotic charge. We cannot dismiss the fact that Celia believes that she is in love with a man, that Felismena is "man-like" in her martial abilities, or that she seems to be perfectly interchangeable with Felis, even in her name. Still, Felismena never occupies the position of a man nor does she speak as if she were a man. She enters the bower as a woman whose masculine qualities are most saliently demonstrated in her ability to shoot well an arrow, but who is constantly praised for her delicate and exquisite feminine beauty and demeanor. And it is this duality that is paralleled in her love for Felis and Celia.

Much like Selvagia and Ysmenia's encounter, Felismena and Celia's meetings lack the usual restraint maintained between lovers. Admittedly flirtatious, Celia confesses her attraction for Valerio while Felismena playfully encourages her advances. The following exchange, in which Celia finds out that Valerio had known Felismena, is revealing:

> ¡Y cómo!–dijo Celia–¿conociste tú a Felismena, la dama a quien tu señor en su tierra servía?
> Sí conocí–dije yo–[...]. Verdad es que era vecina de la casa de mi padre, pero visto tu gran hermosura, acompañada de tanta gracia y discreción, no hay por qué culpar a don Felis de haber olvidado los primeros amores.
> A esto me respondió Celia ledamente y riyendo: Presto has aprendido de tu amo a saber lisonjear.
> A saberte bien servir–le respondí–querría yo poder aprender, que adonde tanta causa hay para lo que se dice, no cabe lisonjear. (214-5)

> "And how," said Celia, "did you come to know Felismena, the lady your master served in your land?"
> "I knew her," I said, [...] "It is true she was my father's neighbor, but seeing your great beauty, accompanied by so much grace and wisdom, there is no reason to blame Don Felis for having forgotten his first love."
> Celia replied merrily to this and said, laughing, "Your love has quickly taught you to flatter."
> "I would like to learn to serve you well," I replied, "for when there is so much truth behind what is said, there is no room for flattery." (119)

Although Celia is not aware of Valerio's true identity, the homoerotic tension between the two becomes an integral part of Felismena's story and its reception. Felismena fully understands the effect her words have on Celia, enjoys the lady's attention, and encourages Celia's transgressive desire.[20] Felismena's contradictory actions are equally provocative, juggling between her love for Felis, the letters she delivers for him, the pleasure she gets from Celia's attention, and the deep pull she feels for the lady. Ultimately, she finds herself

---

[20] The possibility of Felismena's sexual conquests as "Valerio" is initially establecida in the tale when Fabio, another servant of Felis, invites him out to town: "que comer, y beber, y vestir y cuatro reales para jugar, no os faltarán, pues mozas como unas reinas haylas en nuestra calle, y vos, que sois gentil hombre, no habría ninguna que no se pierda por vos" 'As to food, drink, and clothing, and four *reales* in pocket money, they will not lack us, as well as wenches like queens who live in our street, for you are an attractive young man and not one of them would not fall for you' (209; 115). Felismena's response to Fabio's proposal is playfully ambiguous, and is accompanied by a laughter that celebrates Fabio's libertine attitude, "cuán naturales palabras de paje eran las que me decía" 'how natural were the words the page spoke' (210; 115).

in a wonderfully transgressive double-bind: the better she performs her role as Valerio, the more she seduces and is seduced by Celia. Unable to choose between the two prospects, Felismena lives "en la mayor confusión del mundo" 'in a state of great confusion' (217; 120). In the end the decision is made for her when Celia reaches the (logical but incorrect) conclusion that Valerio's only interest is that of a go-between: "Desdichada de mí, oh Valerio, que en fin acabo de entender cómo engañada vivo contigo. No creía yo hasta agora que me pedías favores para tu señor, sino por gozar de mi vista el tiempo que gastabas en pedírmelos. Mas ya conozco que los pides de veras, y que pues gustas de que yo agora le trate bien, sin duda no debes quererme" 'Wretched me, oh Valerio, for you now come to know how I live deceived by you. I did not believe until now that you were asking me favors for your lord, but rather to enjoy my sight while you asked them. But now I realize that since you are asking for them in earnest, and that you would appreciate it if I treated him well, you do not, without a doubt, love me' (218; 121). Distraught by her perception of Valerio's indifference, Celia dies soon after.[21]

Celia's death ultimately offers the pastoral community and the reader a way of avoiding Felismena's indeterminacy. But the problem is not easily solved. Felismena loves both Felis and Celia and cannot (or does not want to) decide between the two. Her reaction to Celia's accusation is evidence of the fluidity of Felismena's desire: "Y con esto se me quitó delante [...] y cerrando tras sí la puerta, *ni bastó llamar suplicándole con mis amorosas palabras que me abriese y tomase de mí la satisfacción que fuese servida, ni decille otras muchas cosas en que le mostraba la poca razón que había tenido en enojarse para que quisiese abrirme*" 'And with this she departed [...] locking the door behind her. *Nor did it do me any good to call her, begging her with loving words to open the door and be satisfied in knowing that I would serve her, and other things I said to her to show her how little reason she had to be angry and to open the door*' (218-9; 121, my emphasis). Felismena's tears and "amorosas palabras" confirm her passion for Celia, who had "poca razón [...] en enojarse." Celia's death is as traumatic to her as Felis's disappearance had been. Felismena openly laments the loss, painfully aware of the

---

[21] Concerning the controversy over whether Celia commits suicide, dies of sadness, or even dies at all see Juan Montero.

now lost potential of their relationship: "Pues de mí no digo nada porque de una parte, la desastrada muerte de Celia me llegaba al ánima" 'As for me, I said nothing, for while on the one hand, Celia's wretched death touched my soul' (219; 121). Rhodes has categorized Felismena's behavior as masculine, and therefore not part of the possible "feminist" content of the text: "Felismena [...] is not as much a credit to womanhood as she is to manhood: her power at arms and even her speech habits are decidedly masculine and aggressive, to say nothing of the fact that a woman falls in love with her and dies of that love" ("Skirting the Men" 148). I would propose that Felismena's story once again marks the text's resistance to alternative manifestations of female agency; or perhaps, even more pointedly, its resistance to a desire that floats the line between male and female, contesting the essential nature of gender categories. From this angle, her story can be seen as a return, even if temporary, of that other side of the pastoral metaphor.

In Book VII of *La Diana* we encounter a final case of homoerotic attraction in the friendship of Duarda and Armia. As already described above, Duarda rejects Danteo's pleas, while Armia insistently argues in his favor. Paradoxically, there is an erotic undercurrent in their friendship that filters through Armia's pleas for Danteo's case. More to the point, there are moments when Armia's words reveal themselves as a personal plea for Duarda's love, and not as an advocacy of the disloyal shepherd. Still, as in all other cases of female homoerotic desire, the text is able to diffuse and/or repress this exchange's destabilizing effects by focusing Duarda's past relationship with Danteo and his renewed interest in her. As a result, Armia's longing for Duarda is confused, even in her own consciousness, with Danteo's efforts to recapture his beloved.

Regarding these episodes, Johnson has concluded that *La Diana* offers its contemporary audience an opportunity to explore the contentious feelings aroused by lesbian desire and its presence in a rigid patriarchal culture: "la tensión entre fascinación y repugnancia provocada por la posibilidad de un encuentro homosexual, entre el deseo que no reconoce límites y el terror a este mismo" 'the tension between the fascination and the disgust provoked by the possibility of a homosexual encounter, between a desire that knows no limits and the terror of the same' ("Amor-Aliqua Vincit" 174; my translation). Perhaps for a segment of the contemporary and modern reading audience this may hold true. Still, the net result is that repugnance and purgation win out over voyeuristic fascination. The "terror" that homoerotic desire among women represents is effectively disarmed under the cover of legitimate (male and narcissistic) love. As in Selvagia's case, the text refuses to directly recognize Felismena's complex desire. The shepherds and the narrator acknowledge only her love for Felis, purging once more the particular elements that do not fit within the logic of feminine ideality and pastoral love. Like her fellow female characters, her ultimate role is to be an object of desire for Felis, with whom she is chastely reunited at the end of *La Diana*. What we find is a deliberate tactic of glossing over, deauthorizing, and negating any form of alternative agency that does not conform to the symbolic and ideological prescriptions of these narratives. We could argue that these narratives show their audience how to productively repress, or at least ignore, those "other" desires and wipe out any unsettling effects to a conventional and binary gendering of subjects.

A way of reading through or beyond these strategies of containment in *La Diana* is to stress the striking difference between these women's manifest desire and the shepherds' amatory fantasy. If the pastoral lover, as a narcissistic lover, depends on the specular abstraction of the beloved, these female characters seem to indulge in the confusing and overwhelming experience of immediacy. None of them mediate their desire through conventional idealization and sublimation in poetic practice. Instead, in their limited encounters they seem to revel in the presence of the other as something to be reckoned with and recognized. The pattern established in these women's stories depends upon their touch and on their one-on-one exchanges and confessions. To this effect, Tamsin Lorraine has spoken of the possibility of "fusion" between equal subjects, which she defines as an alternative feminist position to the objectification and specularity of narcissistic love:

> [F]usion could happen any time the subject relinquishes the position of imposing objectivity on the other and allows the object the status of subject–that is, allows the "object" to set the boundaries on meaning. The subject allows herself to be shaped by the object: Repetition of self-representations is suspended in order to merge with the object-as-subject. [...] [T]he feminine position allows for a suspension of disbelief, for the nonjudgmental merging of two into one that requires a reciprocal shaping on the part of both in order to fit each other and make contact. This requires a

suspension of the Symbolic order–not a "you are like (or unlike) me" but an "I am you and you are me" that takes place simultaneously; an oscillation of perspectives that finally ends in merging both without losing either. (96-7)[22]

If we follow the logic of Lorraine's proposition, we can see in *La Diana* the emergence of a substitute form of love. Closer to the "merging with the object-as-subject," these women's stories may be interpreted as Jamesonian "utopian" moments through which alternative subject positions emerge, even if quickly to be contained by the idealizing and objectifying forces of male narcissism and specularity.[23] In *La Diana*, pastoral harmony is thus ultimately (even if precariously) retained, but not without having its limits strained by the insistence of feminine desire, difference, and agency. As I argued in the previous chapter, pastoral novels' symbolic function, to resolve any underlying conflicts or contradictions, ultimately succeeds and accordingly instructs. But not before its assumptions and prescriptions are tested by the otherness represented by an alternative female subjectivity.

III. *La Galatea*: The Pastoral Community Revisited

In *La Galatea* female agency and desire is made manifest through a series of episodes where women, separate and alone, put into action their own version of the pastoral social order. One remarkable aspect of *La Galatea* is the variety of positions that female characters are allowed to occupy vis-à-vis the pastoral amatory fanta-

---

[22] It is important to note that Lorraine's account of "fusion" is not exclusive to men or women, but to what she calls the "feminine position" (97). She separates herself from critics such as Luce Irigaray by proposing that symbolic positions taken by men and women are not or need not be exclusionary: "Just as there are times when men relate to women as more than their mirror reflection of men, there are times when women represent themselves according to the logic of the same" (77). Both men and women can, in her opinion, partake of this alternative form of identity and subjectivity. I have, in my own analysis talked about the masculine narcissistic position and the feminine position as represented respectively by men and women. I have done so given the traditional patriarchal ideology present in *La Diana* and *La Galatea*, as in pastoral texts in general.

[23] Thinking of both men and philosophers as narcissistic subjects, Grosz proposes that, "To acknowledge the *independent* otherness of feminine pleasure beyond the service of orgasm and production involves giving up the coercive control and self-definition the masculine and the meta-theoretical provide for themselves" (179).

sy. While some reject outright their lovers' pleas others aggressively go after them, clearly transgressing the rules of demure and chaste behavior prescribed by conventional amatory codes. Notwithstanding these differences, female characters often come together and share their experiences within the otherwise homogeneous idyll. In repeated instances women meet, talk about their lives, and support each other without ever expecting to mirror each other's points of view or feelings. Fernández-Cañadas de Greenwood has demonstrated how women's speech in *La Galatea* breaks with the idealizing mechanisms that characterize male discourse: "Mientras que los hombres parecen estar preocupados con el tema de la perfección [...], las pastoras [...] se expresan por medio de estrategias retóricas y personales que están lejos de coincidir con el paradigma de perfección" 'While the men seem preoccupied with the topic of perfection [...], the shepherdesses [...] express themselves by way of rhetorical and personal strategies that are far from coinciding with the paradigm of perfection' ("Las mujeres en la semántica de *La Galatea*" 55; my translation). Where male characters adopt common rhetorical strategies, female characters engage in a much more immediate and individualized expression of their emotions:

> La conclusión parece ser la siguiente: la variedad e intensidad de los sentimientos afectivos expresados ordenadamente por los poetas pastores, tiene un correspondiente en los modelos sicológicos femeninos. [...] La complejidad de personalidades femeninas a su vez se refleja en la ingeniosidad de sus discursos. Mientras que los personajes masculinos son casi uniformemente receptivos, preocupados por el efecto de su expresión en perfecto y justo equilibrio, las figuras femeninas son más multifacéticas, y aplican el "discreteo" para expresar, a su manera diferente, la variedad y genuina comprensión de los sentimientos. (Fernández-Cañadas de Greenwood, "Las mujeres en la semántica de *La Galatea*" 58)[24]

> The conclusion seems to be the following: the variety and intensity of sentiment expressed in an orderly manner by the shepherd poets, has a corresponding pattern in the female psycholog-

---

[24] Marcela Trambaioli has also emphasized how Cervantes's pastoral novel is notably engaged in the creation of a "juego de perspectivas y contrapuntos que determina la originalidad cervantina dentro del género pastoril" 'game of perspectives and counterpoints that determines the Cervantine originality within the pastoral genre' (53; my translation).

ical models. [...] The complexity of the female personalities is reflected in the wit of their discourses. While the male characters are almost uniformly receptive, preoccupied by the perfect and balanced effect of their poetic expression, the feminine figures are multifaceted, and use the rhetoric of discretion to express, in a different manner, the variety and genuine comprehension of their emotions. (my translation)

At a more fundamental level, I would argue that this disparity reflects the appearance of two distinct social formations within the Cervantine bower. Whereas the pastoral male community reproduces a single identity under the rubric of "enamorados" for all its members, female characters resist such discursive or psychological homogeneity. They instead consistently offer each other companionship and recognition, regardless of their status as willing objects, *mujeres esquivas*, or pursuant lovers. When we take a broad view of *La Galatea*, the male lovers' amatory project is privileged by the narrative voice as well as in the overall focus of the stories told. Even so, this marginal configuration of the female community is a fascinating feature of this text and one well worth examining. In *La Diana* I cannot find the same type of diverse yet united feminine community. Although for much of the text Selvagia, Felismena and Belisa share the space with Felicia's nymphs, the two groups never are conceived as one unit. It is clear that Felicia's world is separate and that the nymphs will never fully understand or share the other female characters' experiences. Selvagia, Felismena, and Belisa, for their part, never associate separately and never are required to negotiate any difference. On the other hand, *La Galatea*'s feminine community can be read as this text's most original and significant utopian impulse, an alternative group formation that embraces the multiple boundaries of meaning repressed by male pastoral society.

Galatea, described as a *mujer discreta* and *esquiva* by the narrator, rejects Elicio's advances, which she interprets as diminishing of her value as an individual: "En menos me tendría yo si en más le tuviese" 'I would hold myself in less account, if I held it in more' (206; 32). Alban Forcione has pointed out how this statement "muestra la firmeza de una mujer que percibe claramente que hay posibilidades de degradación en toda obediencia a las reglas y la retórica del cortejo que adoptan sus interlocutores masculinos" 'demonstrates the strength of a woman who clearly perceives the possibility for degradation in the obedience to the rules and rhetoric of courtship adopted by the male interlocutors' ("Cervantes en busca de una pastoral auténtica" 1016, my translation). More to the point, Galatea's words reflect an acute awareness of the objectification that she suffers in the shepherd's pleas: the more Elicio loves and idealizes her, the less she exists as a desiring individual. She is, therefore, caught in a trap. Galatea's *discreción* and *esquivez* offer her suitors a way of structuring their self-worth as faithful and sacrificial: "la afirmación de independencia de Galatea es interpretada forzadamente por sus admiradores dentro de una mitología de amatoria tradicional y su retórica correspondiente" 'Galatea's declaration of independence is interpreted by her admirers within the mythology of traditional love and its corresponding rhetoric' (Forcione, "Cervantes en busca de una pastoral auténtica" 1017; my translation). Her attempts to have her will recognized utterly fail, as she inadvertently plays the part of perfecting mirror for Elicio and Erastro. By Book VI, Galatea has relinquished her initial–even if ineffectual–defiance when forced to seek Elicio's help in the face of an arranged marriage. This final episode in *La Galatea* dismantles her agency and provides all the male characters in the text with an occasion to prove and improve their individual and collective narcissistic selves as heroic and loyal lovers.

As an antidote to the objectification she endures from her male counterparts, Galatea resorts to building a community with other women by seeking out and preferring the company of other shepherdesses. In her first encounter with Elicio and Erastro it is clear that she would rather spend her time elsewhere: "Yo te prometo, Elicio, que no por huir de tu compañía ni de la de Erastro he vuelto del camino que tú imaginas que llevaba, porque mi intención es pasar hoy la siesta en el arroyo de las Palmas, en compañía de mi amiga Florisa, que allá me aguarda, porque desde ayer concertamos las dos de apacentar hoy allí nuestros ganados" 'I assure you, Elicio,' replied Galatea, 'that it was not to shun your company or that of Erastro that I have changed the way you think I was taking, for my intention is to spend the noontide of today by the stream of palms, in the company of my friend Florisa, who is awaiting me there, for as early as yesterday we two agreed to graze our flocks there today' (205-6; 32). Even though they berate her, Galatea leaves her suitors behind and seeks Florisa, "de la cual fue con alegre rostro recebida como aquella que era su amiga verdadera y con quien Galatea sus pensamientos comunicaba" 'by whom she was received with joyous mien, as being her true friend, and she to whom Galatea was willing to tell her thoughts' (208; 33). From then on, the two shepherdesses frequently meet up with other female characters, distancing themselves physically and psychologically from their male suitors. In the process, they expand their own horizons by unconditionally accepting a diversity of women members into their inner circle.

The tolerant nature of the female community in *La Galatea* is reflected in Galatea's and Florisa's acceptance and support of Teolinda's desperate search for her absent lover. Although also initially a *mujer esquiva*, Teolinda's story positions her as a direct opposite to Galatea. She eagerly accepted Artidoro's attentions and repeatedly met with him. Faced with his impending departure to another village, Teolinda refused to simply fall into the usual pattern of chaste loyalty. Discounting any expectations of silence or discretion, she solicits a pledge from her lover:

> Y así, después que mis ojos dieron licencia que los suyos amorosamente me mirasen, no estuvieron quedas las lenguas ni dejaron de mostrar con palabras lo que hasta entonces por señas los ojos habían bien claramente manifestado. En fin, sabréis, amigas mías, que un día, hallándome acaso sola con Artidoro, con señales de un encendido amor y comedimiento, me descubrió el verdadero y honesto amor que me tenía; y, aunque yo quisiera entonces hacer de la retirada y melindrosa, porque temía, como ya os he dicho, que él se partiese, no quise desdeñarle ni despedirle; y también por parecerme que los sinsabores que se dan y sienten en el principio de los amores son causa de que abandonen y dejen la comenzada empresa los que en sus sucesos no son muy experimentados. *Y por esto le di respuesta tal cual yo deseaba dársela*, quedando en resolución, concertados en que él se fuese a su aldea, y que, de allí a pocos días, con alguna honrosa medianía me enviase a pedir por esposa a mis padres. (240-1, my emphasis)

> And so, after my eyes gave leave for his most beauteous eyes to gaze on me lovingly, our tongues were not still, nor failed to show with words what up till then the eyes had so clearly declared by sign. Finally, you must know, friends, that one day when I found myself by chance alone with Artidoro, he disclosed to me, with tokens of an ardent love and courtesy, the true and honourable love he felt for me; and though I would have wished

to play the reluctant prude, yet, because I was afraid, as I have already told you, that he would go, I did not wish to disdain him nor to dismiss him, and also because it seemed to me that the lack of sympathy, inspired or felt at the beginning of a love-affair, is the reason why those who are not very experienced in their passion, abandon and leave the enterprise they have begun. *Wherefore I gave him answer such as I desired to give him.* We agreed in the resolve that he should repair to his village, and a few days after should by some honourable mediation send to ask me in marriage from my parents; (52-3, my emphasis)

Resisting the role of "melindrosa" and considering Artidoro a less experienced lover than she, Teolinda takes charge of the situation and asks him to marry her. Above all, Teolinda seems to want to avoid the usual amatory prescription of forlorn or absent love and its sublimation through poetic expression. She wants a fulfilled marriage, meaning full recognition from and contact with a husband and not an abstracting relationship with a distant poet lover. Although wedding celebrations are common in pastoral texts, marriage as a fully realized social institution is not a part of the bower as developed in these narratives. As I discussed in the previous chapter, matrimony is a proposition that seems possible only as a future and as yet unrealized state for the lovers. Marriage unions do not easily fit into an ideology of love that is structured around the specular absence of the beloved. Thus, Teolinda, with her impetuous arrangement of her own engagement to Artidoro, seeks an alternative to the standard distanced amatory relations between the shepherds, as well as, I would propose, a channel through which to affirm herself as an equal partner and subject to her husband.

In Cervantes's pastoral society the matter of public honor cannot be elided. Concerned with how "los ociosos ojos y lenguas parleras" 'idle eyes and chattering tongues' (240; 52) might damage her reputation, Teolinda's many conversations with Artidoro are maintained with "recato, secreto y honestidad" 'reserve, secrecy, and modesty' (240; 52). Nevertheless, her request of Artidoro's hand, even if secret, puts her on dangerous ground and tests the limits of acceptable feminine modesty. Cervantes draws attention to her lack of caution when Leonarda, Teolinda's twin, first meets Artidoro. In a case of mistaken identity, Leonarda chastises the couple for what she perceives as a breach in decorum: "apenas podía formar palabra para responderle, pero al fin respondí de la suerte que su atrevimiento merecía, y cual a mí me pareció que estábades vos, hermana, obligada a responder a quien con tanta libertad os hablara" 'I could scarcely form words to answer him, but at last I replied to him in the way his boldness deserved, and as it seemed to me you, sister, would have had to answer anyone speaking to you so freely' (243; 54). Teolinda's active desire defies the ideals of female chastity and discretion of traditional pastoral ideology, and of society at large. Yet, as should be expected, Teolinda's indiscretion is soon contained by the text. Similar to Belisa in *La Diana*, Teolinda oversteps her boundaries and pays for it with the disappearance of Artidoro from her life. In spite of her desperate search, Teolinda will never marry or even again see her lover.

Notwithstanding Galatea's and Florisa's rejection of their suitors' advances, never once do they dismiss or reject Teolinda. Moreover, even though Galatea and Florisa have never experienced love, they fully identify with their new friend's disappointment and desperation:

> Con tantas lágrimas acompañaba la enamorada pastora las palabras que decía, que bien tuviera corazón de acero quien de ellas no se doliera. Galatea y Florisa, que naturalmente eran de condición piadosa, no pudieron detener las suyas, ni menos dejaron, con las más blandas y eficaces razones que pudieron de consolarla, dándole por consejo que se estuviese algunos días en su compañía [...]. (249)

> With such tears did the loving shepherdess accompany the words she uttered, that he would have had a heart of steel who had not grieved at them. Galatea and Florisa, who were naturally of a pitying disposition, could not hold theirs back, nor yet did they fail to comfort her with the most soothing and helpful words in their power, counseling her to remain some days in their company [...]. (58)

Faced with Teolinda's sad state of affairs ("la cual iba tan triste y pensativa que era maravilla" 'who went her way so sad and thoughtful that it was a marvel' [250; 58]), Galatea and Florisa try to console and entertain her. They even contribute in her search for Artidoro by hiding her from her family (379-80). Throughout Teolinda's evolving tale, Galatea and Florisa remain her loyal friends, not only supporting her but also urging her to come back and let them know how her search for Artidoro is resolved. Unlike the male community that expects all its members to be of one mind, Galatea and Florisa never once ask Teolinda to relinquish her desire. To the contrary, they become her staunchest advocates. Eventually, she does return but only to inform them how, in yet another case of mistaken identity and deceit, Leonarda (Teolinda's sister) fooled Artidoro into marrying her.[25] Even when cognizant of this appalling outcome, Galatea and Florisa do not scorn or mock her: "y aunque [las lenguas de] Galatea y Florisa quisieron mostrarse expertas y elocuentes en consolarla, fue de poco efecto su trabajo" 'and though the tongues of Galatea and Florisa wished to show themselves skilful and eloquent in consoling her, their toil was of little avail' (619; 310). In a marked difference from the pastoral male community, these three female characters accept each other's position vis-à-vis male desire, sharing their experiences without the requirements of homogeneity or self-same identification.

Another example of Galatea's and Florisa's acceptance of heterogeneity and difference is the case of Rosaura. Like many other characters in these pastoral novels, Rosaura and her lover, Grisaldo, come into the idyll seeking to resolve the love problems they have created for themselves outside of its boundaries at the court. As the story goes, Rosaura loves Grisaldo but refuses to confess it. When she finds out that Grisaldo's father would rather he marry another woman, she decides to provoke Grisaldo's jealousy by pretending to be in love with Artandro. Confused by Rosaura's behavior, Grisaldo acquiesces to his father's wishes. To make matters more difficult, Rosaura's own father decides to give her hand to Artandro. Rosaura flees her father's house, finds Grisaldo in the countryside, and pleads for his loyalty: "Considera, Grisaldo, que en nobleza no te debo nada, y que en riqueza no te soy desigual, y que te aventajo en la bondad del ánimo y en la firmeza de la fe. Cúmpleme, señor, la que me diste, si te precias de caballero y no te desprecias de cristiano" 'Consider, Grisaldo, that in birth I am your equal, that in wealth I am not your inferior, and that I excel you in goodness of heart and in firmness of faith. Fulfill to me, sir, the faith you gave me, if you are proud to be a gentleman, and are not

---

[25] As it turns out, it is Leonarda who ultimately breaks completely with any sense of propriety or loyalty. She had fallen in love with Galercio, Artidoro's identical brother, but since Galercio rejects her she decides to substitute one brother with the other and dupe Artidoro into marrying her, pretending to be Teolinda.

ashamed to be a Christian' (386; 145). When confronted with Grisaldo's recriminations (she had many times refused his hand, had tried to make him jealous by flirting with Artandro, and had disdained him when he informed her of his father's plans), Rosaura persists and relinquishes any semblance of propriety. In a simultaneously sincere and manipulative act of desperation, she attempts suicide. Grisaldo, moved by Rosaura's grief, accepts her proposal and promises her marriage. As witnesses to this encounter, Galatea, Florisa, and Teolinda come out of their hiding place and aid the reconciled lovers. Grisaldo goes off to arrange the marriage with their respective fathers, and Rosaura is left to wait with her female companions.

Although Rosaura's story of love, deceit, and manipulation puts her in a completely different category from her newfound friends, Galatea's understanding and approval of Rosaura is remarkable. A lady of the court, Rosaura brings a radically different perspective to the bower. She has dealt with love as a sport to be played through trickery and false indifference, skills that Galatea does not possess. When abandoned, she chases her lover and conspicuously contrives their encounter in order to regain Grisaldo's favor. If Galatea intends to maintain independence and singularity by staying away from her suitors, Rosaura willingly participates in a game of deception and jealousy with two lovers, Grisaldo and Artrando. When this strategy backfires, Rosaura throws herself into a masterfully theatrical performance to seduce her estranged lover. Regardless of these differences between them, Galatea enthusiastically takes in this lady of the court. She offers Rosaura companionship until Grisaldo's return and excuses their indiscreet behavior:

> No más, no más, señores, que, adonde andan las obras tan verdaderas, no han de tener lugar los demasiados comedimientos. Lo que resta es rogar al Cielo que traiga a dichoso fin estos principios, y que en larga y saludable paz gocéis vuestros amores. Y en lo que dices, Grisaldo, que Rosaura venga a nuestra aldea, es tanta la merced que en ello nos haces, que nosotras mismas te lo suplicamos. (392)

> 'No more, no more, my friends, for where deeds are so true, excessive compliments must find no place. What remains is to pray Heaven to lead to a happy end to these beginnings, and that you may enjoy your love in a long and beneficent peace. And as for

what you say, Grisaldo, that Rosaura should come to our village, the favor you do us therein is so great, that we ourselves beg it of you.' (149-50)

If Rosaura finds in Grisaldo's marriage proposal the satisfaction of her desire, she finds in Galatea an unconditional friend: "no sentiré mucho la ausencia de Grisaldo estando en vuestra compañía" 'I will not much regret Grisaldo's absence, when I am in your company' (392; 150). Galatea's female community accepts even this most extreme of cases.[26]

Going back to Lorraine's proposition, the feminine community in *La Galatea* could be interpreted as another example of subject-to-subject relationships or fusion. Never expecting to be identical with and always accepting of each other's particular subject position or boundaries of meaning, *La Galatea*'s female community emerges as an important contrast to the prevailing expectations of sameness in pastoral social formations. Although on multiple occasions male characters invade this feminine space, Galatea and her female companions always manage to regroup, share their unique stories, and support each other regardless of the trajectory their stories have taken. While individual manifestations of feminine desire are routinely repressed, the female community thrives as an independent and dissimilar entity. Galatea and her group offer a conflicting understanding of community within the bower. Through this community's persistence, the symbolic representation of pastoral homogeneity is, if not radically destabilized, at least shown not to be exclusive. To be more exact, this female community allows for a measure of difference that, through contrast, illustrates the repressive mechanisms that make the shepherds' community possible. Its insistent alterity points to the other side of the pastoral fantasy.

---

[26] There are many other women's stories that develop throughout *La Galatea*. Gelasia's extreme *esquivez*, Nísida's rational approach to love, Blanca's humble acceptance of her fate in love, and Leonarda's cruelty and deceit are the most notable examples. These characters are all welcome and active members of Gelatea and Florisa's community.

IV. CERVANTES PERFORMS THE FEMALE POETIC VOICE: *ENFADOSAS SUEGRAS* AND OTHER FEMININE COMPLAINTS IN *LA GALATEA*

Of the ninety-two poems in *La Galatea*, Cervantes includes fifteen sung by women characters that manifest, even if in a restricted fashion, an autonomous female voice. Reflective of the heterogeneity found within the female community, these poems make patent the multiple and dissimilar positions occupied by the shepherdesses. In these passages Cervantes, as a poet, inhabits the female psyche and gives voice to what is otherwise silenced.[27] In making this claim, my idea is not to read *La Galatea* as going against the symbolic aims of the pastoral that I have described so far. Rather, what these women's poems do is introduce, much like the female community itself, a series of alternative subject positions that are marginalized by the male pastoral society.

In their introduction to *Tras el espejo la musa escribe: Lírica femenina de los Siglos de Oro*, Julián Olivares and Elizabeth S. Boyce present three essential ways in which women poets of the Golden Age appropriate the male poetic tradition that precedes and surrounds them: they either faithfully imitate, carefully manipulate, or overtly subvert the model (16-95). They see women poets as reworking traditional classical, medieval, and Petrarchan amatory conventions and giving a clear voice to a heretofore mostly absent female subjectivity. Following this logic, a fascinating issue in the study of women's poetry that remains concerns how one is to read the adoption of a female voice by a male poet. A phenomenon read-

---

[27] I will refrain from engaging in the ongoing debate concerning Cervantes's place within the poetic canon of Golden Age literature. Critics such as José Manuel Blecua, Francisco Ynduráin, and, most recently, Mercedes Alcalá Galán and Adrienne Martin have argued for a reevaluation of Cervantes's talent as a poet and his contributions to late sixteenth and early seventeenth-century poetic theory. What is of interest to this analysis is the way in which these critics feature as some of Cervantes's best poetry that of *La Galatea*, specifically the poetry sung by women characters. Blecua considers Gelasia's sonnet not only the finest poem in *La Galatea* but also Cervantes's most eloquent effort in this form. Moreover, in the first volume of his anthology *Poesía de la Edad de Oro*, the only poem he includes from Cervantes's pastoral text is Teolinda's *villancico*, "En los estados de amor / nadie llega a ser perfecto, / sino el honesto y secreto" 'Whosoever by much striving / would the perfect lover be / *honour needs and secrecy*' (380; 50). Likewise, Alberto Sánchez favors Galatea's first poetic intervention and Gelasia's final rejection of love as the two best poems found in the text.

ily found in classical and medieval literary traditions, early modern poetry of this sort most often perpetuated male fantasies and feminine stereotypes. Yet, in specific instances we can acknowledge the unanticipated effects that the 'female' voice–as filtered through the discursive lens of a male poet–may bring about. Thaïs E. Morgan suggests the possibility that a male-authored text that speaks the feminine can in fact textually produce a space for feminine agency. The assertion that male authors appropriate "the category of femininity in order to strengthen their own authority" must be tempered by a consideration of how some may instead, perhaps unconsciously, "critique masculinity through adopting a feminine (and in some cases, potentially feminist) position in the system of sexual difference" (Morgan 3). Jonathan Goldberg builds on this analytical position by reminding us that the phrase "writing as a woman" (used so frequently in feminist criticism), "does not guarantee the gender of the author"; for "to write as a woman must involve the revelation that woman is not a self-evident or tautological category, indeed, that it may have no ontological ground" (136-7). To "write as a woman" is, from this perspective, a practice that assumes multiple and variable significations that can be equally adopted by both male and female writers. If so, the regulatory effects of the author's gender are largely irrelevant (Goldberg 138).

This assumption of an "other's" voice by a male author leads to the view that gender categories are discursively produced, maintained, and performed: "When the constructed status of gender is theorized as radically independent of sex, gender itself becomes a free-floating artifice, with the consequence that *man* and *masculine* might just as easily signify a female body as a male one, and *woman* and *feminine* a male body as easily as a female one" (Butler, *Gender Trouble* 10). Seemingly fixed and immutable, binary gender divisions are understood by feminist theorists as the effect of a patriarchal discourse (the Foucauldian law or Lacanian symbolic) that not only produces these categories but also depends on their continued reiteration in order to sustain itself as law.[28] Yet, it is in the nature of discourse that the repetition or citation of gender categories is al-

---

[28] Butler's criticism of essentialist feminism, the desire of many feminist thinkers (Wittig, Kristeva, etc...) to "return" to an existence untouched by patriarchal ideology or to understand and defend the category of "woman" as one that is whole (Showalter, Irigaray) resides in her belief that both sex and gender are produced by discourse and maintained in their reiteration by "sex/gendered" subjects.

ways threatened by the possibility of conscious and unconscious error or misappropriation. The discursive performativity of the law is thus never as predictable as one might assume. In other words, heteronormative gender identifications can rarely be perfectly "performed" or lived out by any given subject. It is in this gap between prescribed and lived experience where Judith Butler posits a possibility for fluidity, transformation, and agency for the subject. In much the same manner, the effects of gendered representations in literary and cultural texts, even if ideologically driven, can hardly be controlled or predicted. In an analysis of a feminine poetic voice, this point can be of great importance. A male author can well adopt or perform a female voice in order to restate a limited and marginalized position for women in society, but the final effects of that mimicry are unpredictable and may end up being read instead as an affirmation of female agency. Performativity is not necessarily a willed transgression of a determined gender category. To the contrary, to perform the female voice is both a working within and through the prescriptions that determine this category. The emphasis is not in identifying moments where a radical transcendence of the law or ideology occurs, but where a "problematic" citation of the law's parameters and demands seems to emerge: "This critical task presumes, of course, that to operate within the matrix of power is not the same as to replicate uncritically relations of domination. It offers the possibility of a repetition of the law which is not its consolidation, but its displacement" (*Gender Trouble* 40). The fifteen poems sung by women in *La Galatea* could be understood to represent and perform the feminine in ways that both confirm and destabilize the expected parameters of feminine behavior. Butler's concept of performativity offers a way to understand the identificatory mechanisms displayed in pastoral poetic discourse, its operating gender ideology, and the rifts that are repressed and that emerge in its articulation of the female voice.[29]

From a literary and historical perspective, Margit Frenk has written about a type of poetic transvestism through which a variety

---

[29] Fernández-Cañadas de Greenwood includes in her analysis of *La Galatea* a similar interpretative position by asserting that "De manera intencional o no, Cervantes ha dado a sus pastoras una 'diferente voz,' un significado que les corresponde y que las diferencia" 'whether intentionally or not, Cervantes has given his shepherdesses a different voice, a meaning that belongs to them and that differentiates them' ("Las mujeres en la semántica de *La Galatea*" 58; my translation).

of female identities were developed in male-produced popular Spanish poetry. In her view these female voices "suelen diferir de las proyectadas por la voz lírica masculina y de las expresadas en fuentes no poéticas" 'often differ from those projected by the masculine lyrical voice and from those expressed in none poetic text' (94; my translation). The resulting register includes women who are in love, staunchly reject love, or lament their deception in love. Rooted in medieval folklore, these images are reproduced in an early modern "literatura urbana" ("urban literature") or "folklore urbano" ("urban folklore") allowing for "una voz femenina fuerte, avasalladora, que impone una imagen de mujer consciente de sí misma y capaz de hacer valer su voluntad" 'a strong female voice, overwhelming, which imposes an image of woman conscious of herself and able to make her will known' (100; my translation). Frenk's conclusions confirm the theoretical proposition of critics such as Morgan and Goldberg. In other words, the discursive construction of female agency marks its presence in a poetic tradition that largely excludes women authors. Cervantes's own pastoral poetic practice, I would argue, follows this pattern. Although classical, courtly, and Renaissance amatory traditions are fundamental to the Spanish pastoral novel, the use of these popular sources in *La Galatea* makes available an alternative space for female agency. Their inclusion in the Cervantine poetic inventory generates a surprising effect: the ability to stave off the abstracting mechanisms on which pastoral amatory convention and the lover's identity depends.

The poems sung by female characters can be divided into two broad categories: Galatea, Florisa, Belisa, and Gelasia reject love, while Teolinda, Nísida, and Blanca indulge in its effects, both positive and negative.[30] This even distribution of feminine positions towards love contrasts with the attitudes of their male counterparts. As I argue in the previous section, a key difference between male and female communities in *La Galatea* is the homogeneity of the

---

[30] I will not discuss Galatea and Nísida's last poems. The poems appear towards the end of Book VI, when the shepherds gather to play a game of guessing or "enigmas" where they have to figure out what the speaker is describing. Because of their content, these two poems do not lend themselves to the present analysis. Also, I have left out of my analysis Calíope's praise of the poets for similar reasons. Her celebration of famous men, although beautifully constructed, does not add to my present argument, given its formulaic structure and Calíope's lack of development as a character in the text.

first compared to the variety of nuanced and even contradictory perspectives we find in the second. While the male community constructs a sole identity, the female community forfeits psychological, emotional, or ideological coherence in favor of a diverse and inclusive group. This allowance of difference extends to the text's poetic structure, so that one poem sung by an *enamorada* always follows a poem sung by an *esquiva*.[31]

Galatea, and Florisa's poems in Book I forcefully represent the position of the woman who rejects love. But whereas in the courtly tradition feminine chastity is typically characterized by an extreme sense of virtue accompanied by a cold heart, in the voices of Galatea and Florisa chastity is defined anew: they do not cast off love simply because they are cruel or proud, but because love, from their viewpoint, inevitably is conditioned by the childish and selfish nature of the male lover. Florisa declares how many men call themselves lovers but only very few–none that she knows–understand the true meaning of love:

> Éste mil bienes del amor pregona;
> aquél publica de él vanos cuidados;
> yo no sé si los dos andan perdidos,
> ni sabré al vencedor dar la corona:
> sé bien que son de amor los escogidos
> tan pocos, cuanto muchos los llamados.
> (Lns. 9-14. 236)[32]

> Here on Love's countless blessings does proclaim,
> Love's fruitless cares another makes known.
> I cannot say if both be brought to shame,
> Nor yet to whom to give the victor's crown.
> This much I know: that many Love by name
> May call, yet few are chosen for his own. (49)

For Florisa, to reject love is not a question of virtue or spite, but an act of self-defense consciously adopted in order to preserve her sense of worth and the tranquility of the bower. We should pre-

---

[31] The only way in which this pattern may be disrupted is in the sequence where the two sisters, Nísida and Blanca, sing immediately subsequent sonnets. Nísida and Blanca are described as almost identical in appearance and character and their sonnets share the topic of faith in love–allowing us to consider these two poems as one extended elaboration of the same thought. As a result, for all practical purposes, the pattern above described remains undisturbed.

[32] The source of Florisa's verses is Matthew 20:16.

sume, according to the logic she follows in her song, that if she were to find true love she would acquiesce. Given her lack of satisfaction, Florisa's questioning of the honesty or genuineness of the shepherds' feelings makes her particularly troublesome to the male pastoral community. Except when referring to the unbridled lust felt by savages, love is never cast as insincere in the pastoral fantasy. Faithfulness, constancy, and nobility are the mainstays that anchor the genre's idealizing foundation. Florisa's complaint challenges this supposition. If we recall Butler's description of the unstable and duplicitous nature of "performance," we could argue that Florisa problematically "cites" the position of the unwilling and unavailable object of desire. Her rejection of love can and does allow her admirers to assume their own positions as chaste and virtuous subjects. At the same time, her declaration momentarily displaces the privileged status of male love and its implied supremacy over female cold-heartedness and fickleness. Her performance reproduces the position of an *esquiva*, but with a difference that negates the integrity of pastoral love and posits a "truth" beyond the lover's narcissistic laments.[33]

Galatea, the central female character in the text, echoes and confirms Florisa's grievance, rejecting love outright in her first poetic intervention:

> Su *fuego* enfriará mi casto intento,
> el *ñudo* romperé por fuerza o arte,
> la *nieve* deshará mi ardiente celo,
> la *flecha* embotará mi pensamiento,
> y así, no temeré en segura parte
> de Amor el *fuego*, el *lazo*, el *dardo*, el *hielo*.
> (Lns. 9-14. 207)

> My chaste intent will chill the burning flame,
> The knot I shall break through by force or art,
> My glowing zeal will melt away the snows,
> The arrow shall fall blunted by my shame,
> And thus nor noose nor fire, nor frost nor dart,
> Shall make me fear, safe in secure repose. (33)

---

[33] Begoña Souviron López goes so far as to conclude that, "Cervantes ensaya con el prototipo de pastora que se resiste a aceptar el amor, convirtiéndose la defensa del 'libre albedrío' de la mujer en el núcleo filosófico de esta obra" 'Cervantes develops the prototype of the shepherdess that resists love, transforming her into the defender of feminine free will within the philosophical nucleus of the text' (132; my translation).

Undeniably, this poem refers to a Petrarchan Italianate amatory tradition, casting Galatea as cruel and conveniently chaste. At the same time, this complaint is uttered by a feminine voice that is radically absent from that tradition. Galatea's declaration, I would argue, can therefore be understood as a challenge to the disingenuous artificiality she perceives in the male lovers. The images developed in these last verses move from the conventional to the less predictable. Her intellect acts as a shield against Cupid's arrow: "la flecha embotará mi pensamiento." Much like Florisa, Galatea's problematic reiteration of the amatory convention produces a gap in pastoral convention through which her intelligence and will, disregarded by her lovers Elicio and Erastro, begins to emerge.[34]

This unique position is carried through to Book V, where Galatea bitterly denounces her father's decision to marry her to a man she has never met and certainly does not love:

> ¡Oh justa, amarga obediencia,
> que, por cumplirte, he de dar
> el sí que ha de confirmar
> de mi muerte la sentencia!
> [...]
> Ved si es el combate fiero
> que dan a mi fantasía,
> si al cabo de su porfía
> he de querer, y no quiero.
> ¡Oh, fastidioso gobierno,
> que a los respetos humanos
> tengo de cruzar las manos
> y abajar el cuello tierno!
> (Lns.10-16 / 25-32. 509)

> Just obedience, hard to bear!
> For I have the 'yes' to say
> In obedience, which some day
> My death-sentence shall declare;
> [...]

---

[34] Although the role of *mujer esquiva* dictates that she, eventually, will fall in love, Galatea is only forced to acquiesce to Elicio's advances when she faces an undesirable marriage. Given *La Galatea*'s unfinished ending, it is hard to tell whether she would in fact eventually truly fall in love with the shepherd.

> Lo! The battle cruel doth prove,
> Which they wage against my thought,
> If, when they have fiercely fought,
> I love not, yet needs must love;
> Oh displeasing power of place!
> For, in reverence of the old
> I my hands must meekly fold
> And my tender neck abase. (218-9)

Despite her function as an ideal and abstracted object of desire for the pastoral community, Galatea forcefully condemns her father's unfair decision in front of the gathered pastoral community. He is a "[s]evero padre" 'cruel sire' (Ln. 41. 510; 219), concerned only with satisfying his own interests: "Gocé mi libertad / en mi temprana sazón; / pero ya la sujeción / anda tras mi voluntad" 'In my happy girlhood's hour / I enjoyed my liberty, / But, alas! Now slavery / O'er my will asserts its power' (Lns. 21-24. 509; 219) and, "Mira que es cosa sabida / que a mí me quitas la vida / con lo que a ti satisfaces" 'Lo! The truth is known full well, / That thou from me life dost steal / In fulfilling thy desire' (Lns. 42-44. 510; 219).[35] Unlike the eloquent, idealized suffering of the shepherds, Galatea here gives voice to the real pain and consequences she will have to endure as unwilling wife:

> Ya triste se me figura
> el punto de mi partida,
> la dulce gloria perdida
> y la amarga sepultura.
> El rostro que no se alegra
> del no conocido esposo,
> el camino trabajoso,
> la antigua, enfadosa suegra.
> Y otros mil inconvenientes,
> todos para mí contrarios,
> los gustos extraordinarios
> del esposo y sus parientes.
> (Lns. 49-60. 510)

---

[35] Perhaps not surprisingly, this lament is typically categorized as a sad example of Cervantes's bad poetic form. This opinion, at least in part, stems from the resistance of the reader and the critic to accept any type of poetic register that violates the ideality of the high pastoral convention. This is a position that, in turn, limits the critics' ability to examine Cervantes's complex and provocative use of the popular sources at hand. See Maxime Chevalier.

> Now I picture in its gloom
> The sad hour when we must sever,
> The sweet glory, lost for ever,
> And the mournful, bitter, tomb;
> Unknown husband's joyless face,
> Troubles of the toilsome road,
> And his aged mother's mood,
> Peevish, for I take her place.
> Other troubles will begin,
> Countless heartaches will annoy,
> When I see what gives joy
> To my husband and his kin; (219)

Breaking away from idealized representations of love and sacrifice, Galatea expresses her frustration at the actual conditions that frame women's existence. Calling to mind Frenk's analysis of female agency in popular poetry, Aurora Egido has here identified a reiteration of folkloric themes usually seen as antithetical to the refined pastoral practice: "Galatea es [...] la voz que clama contra las tiranías impuestas por el matrimonio forzado. Sus versos aluden al tema folclórico de la enfadosa suegra y a los inconvenientes de entrar por casamiento a formar parte de una familia de desconocidos" 'Galatea is [...] the voice that speaks against the tyranny imposed by arranged marriages. Her verses allude to the folkloric theme of the bothersome mother-in-law and the inconveniences of entering, by way of marriage, a family full of strangers' (42; my translation). Forcing its way into the discursive inventory of this text, Galatea's lament exposes the undeniable reality of marriage: she will lose her "dulce gloria," gain her "amarga sepultura" (echoes of Garcilaso's "dulce primavera" and "tiempo airado" in Sonnet XXIII) and in the meantime be "rewarded" with a mother-in-law and a husband's whims. Galatea's song at once acknowledges her traditional duty towards her father *and* undercuts or displaces patriarchal authority by denouncing the unfair nature of this arranged marriage. She will perform the role of the obedient daughter, but not before denouncing the injury that she will suffer as a consequence and lamenting the agency from which she is being deprived.

Galatea and Florisa open a space for alterity in the bower by voicing their doubts about love and lamenting its damaging effects. As I described earlier, Teolinda joins Galatea and Florisa's community but as a woman who pines for marriage with her estranged lover: "Entonces acabé yo de entregarme de todo en todo a todo lo que el Amor quiso, sin quedar en mí más voluntad que si no la hubiera tenido para cosa alguna en mi vida" 'Then at last I yielded myself all in all to all that love demanded, without there being left in me more desire than if I had never had any for anything in my life' (220; 40). Her lyric interludes, accordingly, unveil her agency as desiring female:

>Si el deseo desfallece
>cuando la esperanza mengua,
>al contrario en mí parece,
>pues cuando ella más desmengua
>tanto más él se engrandece.
>Y no hay usar de cautela
>con las llagas que me atizan:
>que, en esta amorosa escuela,
>mil males me martirizan
>*y un solo bien me consuela.*
>   (Lns. 15-24. 211-12)

>Though desire should cease to be,
>What time hope is on the wane,
>Yet'tis not the same in me.
>My desire does remain,
>Though my hope away does flee.
>'Gainst the wounds my soul that blight
>I can take nor care nor thought,
>Martyr to my hapless plight,
>In the school where Love hath taught,
>*One thought only brings delight.* (35)

This lament expresses a typical lover's plight: Desire has only increased as her hope dwindles. Yet in Teolinda's case the disconnect between passion and its realization propels her to stubbornly pursue her lover. Now abandoned, she clings to her obsession, disregarding all familial and societal considerations:

>Mi alma de las carnes se despega,
>siguiendo aquella que, por hado extraño,
>la tiene puesta en pena, en mal tamaño,
>que el bien la turba y el dolor sosiega.

> Si vivo, vivo en fe de la esperanza,
> que, aunque es pequeña y débil, se sustenta
> siendo a la fuerza de mi amor asida.
> (Lns. 5-11. 250)

> To dwell within my flesh my soul does cease,
> Following his soul that by some mystic fate
> In plain has placed it, and in woe so great
> That happiness brings strife, and sorrow peace.
> If I do live, 'tis hope that makes me live,
> Hope, that, though slight and weak, does upward mount,
> Clinging unto the strength my love doth give. (59)

Far from being a silent and absent other to the departed Artidoro, Teolinda's poetic voice announces her desire and despair. Although this position may not seem subversive to our modern eye, her willingness to risk her reputation because of her frankness strains the limits of chaste idealization. These verses' destabilizing force resides precisely in the repetition of conventional amatory rhetoric from the mouth of a female character who manifests her *own* particular desire. In performative terms, we could say that Teolinda's citation of this language manipulates and challenges the gender codes and values that it is meant to reproduce.

In *La Galatea* Nísida's and Blanca's story also stands out in a similar fashion. Disguised as religious pilgrims, Nísida and Blanca are sisters searching respectively for their beloveds, Timbrio and Silerio. The only problem is that both men love Nísida, making Blanca's journey an especially risky endeavor. Even if they find Silerio, he may continue to reject Blanca in favor of Nísida. Luckily for Blanca, Silerio acquiesces and their reunion proves to be a happy one. Still, it is important to note that only because of Nísida's and Blanca's determination is this ending possible. They refuse to stay at home and long for their absent lovers. Again, I am not arguing that Nísida and Blanca radically challenge the amatory conventions that underlie the thematic and ideological structure of this text. Rather, that within and through their problematic citation of gender roles and poetic convention, they surprisingly manage not only to make their own desire known but in doing so unsettle the injunctions that require women's chaste passivity. This is especially made evident in their poetic interventions.

In her first song Nísida uses her voice to seduce Silerio (478-9). In the sonnets that follow, Nísida and Blanca relate their experiences and declare their joy and relief at love's newfound realization:

> Yo sé qué es bien, yo sé qué es desventura,
> y sé de sus efectos claro, y siento
> que cuanto más destruye el pensamiento
> el mal de amor, el bien más lo asegura.
> [...]
> [F]ue dura pena, fue dolor tan fuerte,
> que agora no conozca y haga prueba
> que más es el gusto de mi alegre vida.
> (Lns. 5-8 / 12-14. 522)
> Pasó la furia del invierno helado,
> y, aunque el fuego de amor quedó en su punto,
> llegó la deseada primavera,
> donde, en un solo venturoso punto,
> gozo del dulce fruto deseado,
> con largas pruebas de una fe sincera.
> (Lns. 9-14. 522)

> I know what bliss is, what misfortune drear,
> And what they do I know full well; 'tis plain
> That bliss the more builds up the thought again,
> The more Love's sorrow does its strength impair.
> [...]
> Cruel was the anguish, bitter was the taste
> Of sorrow, yet I know and prove that still
> Greater the joy is of this glad today. (227)
> Spent was the fury of the winter's chill,
> And, though the fire of Love its power retained,
> Yet the spring came which I had longed to see.
> Now in one happy moment I have gained
> The sweet fruit long desired by my will
> With bounteous tokens of sincerity. (228)

Their search finally over, Nísida and Blanca indulge in and celebrate the "gozo del fruto deseado." Even though they play a limited role in Silerio and Timbrio's story of friendship and resigned suffering, the sisters' declared enjoyment of love as a reality to take pleasure in–rather than as a lack to be lamented or a threat to be avoided–should be recognized for its subversive import. Nísida's and Blanca's physical and discursive journey represents a female perspective that differs substantially from that of their lovers.

Book VI reclaims the diverse spirit of the female community in a series of poems sung by Galatea, Nísida, and Belisa. Through their verses, these women manifest a variety of opinions that cannot be easily reconciled. Together they account for the multiple ways in which the practice of love determines their conditions as other to their male lovers. Galatea denounces love's fickle nature as a "mortal dolencia" 'deadly pangs' (Ln. 3. 602; 297) that should be avoided. She bolsters her position by pointing out the dishonor that lovers cause when spreading damaging rumors.

> Segura está quien nunca fue querida,
> ni supo querer bien, *de aquella lengua*
> *que en su deshonra se adelgaza y lima*;
>   mas si el querer y el no querer da mengua,
> ¿en qué ejercicios pasará la vida
> la que más que al vivir la honra estima?
>   (Lns. 9-14. 602, my emphasis)

> Secure is she who never was beloved,
> Nor could love, *from that tongue which in dispraise*
> *Of her honor, with subtle glow does gleam.*
>   But if to love and not to love have proved
> Fruitful in harm, how shall she spend her days
> Who honor dearer e'en than life does deem?
>   (297-8, my emphasis)

Nísida follows with a description of love's ability to defeat the will and seduce the emotions. In an autobiographical poem, Nísida relates the force with which love overtook her:

> Valor, honestidad, recogimiento,
> recato, ocupación, esquivo pecho,
> Amor con poco premio lo conquista.
>   Así que, para huir el vencimiento,
> consejos jamás fueron de provecho:
> de esta verdad testigo soy de vista.
>   (Lns. 9-14. 603)

> O'er worth, o'er honour, o'er a mind discreet,
> Shy modesty, a bosom of disdain,
> Love doth with ease achieve the victory;
>   Wherefore, in order to escape defeat,
> Strength from no words of wisdom can we gain,
> Unto this truth an eye-witness am I. (298)

In spite of all the warnings or "consejos" she may have heard, in her experience love was an invincible force. This is an idea often expressed in the Petrarchan and amatory register. But when it comes to the prescriptions that determine a woman's fields of action, the inevitability of love can be particularly damaging to her "valor, recogimiento, recato, ocupación." This is a consequence that Nísida fears she may face; even though she truly loves Timbrio, she still runs the risk of being labeled as unchaste. As a result, Nísida's ode to love quickly takes on multiple meanings, producing a sense of ambiguity and unease in the poem. Where the typical male lover–especially in the pastoral–is seen to gain in virtue by falling (and suffering) in love, women lovers are at risk, unveiling the double standard dictated by gender categories and patriarchal ideology within amatory rhetoric.

Finally, Belisa, a shepherdess who has rejected the shepherd Marsilio's amorous efforts, sings a long poem in which love is radically condemned, among other things, as a "desvarío" and a "falso contento" 'madness' and 'false a good' (Lns. 32-33. 604; 299). Women endowed with free will should hold on to reason and reject love as if it were a "compusición venenosa / con jugo de adelfa amarga" 'Mixed with juice of bitter bay, / Is to it but pleasing food' (Lns. 9-10. 603; 298). This venom will poison her young, innocent psyche and destroy any future claims to agency or independence:

> Mi tierna cervix exenta
> no permita ni consienta
> sobre sí el yugo amoroso,
> por quien se turba el reposo
> y la libertad se ausenta.
> (Lns. 36-40. 604)

> Let my tender neck and free
> Never yield itself to be
> Placed beneath the loving yoke,
> Whereby peace is, at a stroke,
> Slain, and banished liberty. (299)

When considered as a unit, the series illustrates the way in which an emotion that in pastoral literature is understood as pure and ennobling for the shepherd threatens to debase women and rob them of their dignity. Even if these poems are working through the traditional models of the *esquiva* and the *enamorada*, the performative function of the female voice challenges the bind that dictates that women lose whether they reject or embrace their suitors.

The last poem sung by a woman in *La Galatea* is Gelasia's sonnet, a poem that is usually read as one of Cervantes's most inspired. From my point of view the poem's success stems from how it offsets the stereotype of the *esquiva* as a recklessly proud, ill-natured woman who willfully goes against the laws of nature. Gelasia (like Marcela later in *Don Quixote*) is portrayed as rightfully exercising her free will. She pursues her desire to live a serene life, to own her destiny, and not be frustrated by the damaging aftermath of false love. Only by living an unhindered life in nature can she be at peace. A Diana figure, Gelasia completely, almost exuberantly, rejects her lovers' requests: "antes les rogó que no la tuviesen por descomedida en no hacer lo que le mandaban [corresponderle a sus amantes], porque su intención era de ser *enemiga mortal del amor y de todos los enamorados*" 'rather she asked them not to count her discourteous in not doing what they asked her; for her intention was to be *mortal enemy of love and of all lovers*' (459; 185, my emphasis). Much like the mythological figure, Gelasia demands to have her choices respected and asserts her right to live out her own alternative pastoral fantasy:

> ¿Quién dejará, del verde prado umbroso
> las frescas hierbas y las frescas fuentes?
> ¿Quién de seguir con pasos diligentes
> la suelta liebre o jabalí cerdoso?
> ¿Quién, con el son amigo y sonoroso,
> no detendrá las aves inocentes?
> ¿Quién, en las horas de la siesta ardientes,
> no buscará en las selvas el reposo,
> por seguir los incendios, los temores,
> los celos, iras, rabias, muertes, penas
> del falso amor, que tanto aflige al mundo?
> Del campo son y han sido mis amores:
> rosas son y jazmines mis cadenas;
> libre nací, y en libertad me fundo.
> (Lns. 1-14. 615)

> The pleasing herbs of the green shady mead,
> The cooling fountains, who will e'er forsake,
> And strive no more the fleet hare to o'ertake
> Or bristling wild-boar, following on with speed?

> Who will no more the friendly warblings heed
> Of the dear, simple birds within the brake?
> Who in the glowing noontide hour will make
> No more his couch within the woods at need,
> > That he the fires may follow, and the fears,
> > Jealousies, angers, rages, deaths, and pains,
> > Of traitorous Love, that does the world torment?
> > Upon the fields are set my loving cares
> And have been, rose and jasmine my chains,
> Free was I born, on freedom am I bent. (306-7)

Of particular interest is the image of the rose and the jasmine as chains. In a twist of the typical metaphor, she is bound not by an idealized beloved but rather by natural splendor that protects and comforts her.

Ending the cycle of women's poems, Gelasia's declaration of independence is in perfect correspondence with and elaborates Galatea's initial declaration against the effects of love. Gelasia, like Galatea and Florisa, will not succumb to a "falso amor" that she fears will only deprive her of the peace she has found in nature. Her refusal lingers as an example of feminine self-fashioning and independence.[36] As we have seen before, Gelasia's position inevitably feeds into the lover's construction of the self as constant and virtuous despite (and because of) the beloved's cruel rejection. It also questions love's sincerity and establishes the parameters for female agency and freedom within the pastoral geography. Her poetic voice demands a pastoral space where the feminine self can exist free of masculine influence: "libre nací, y en libertad me fundo." And as far as we can tell, her demand is met. Gelasia remains a free agent within the Cervantine *locus amoenus*.

As these examples make evident, *La Galatea*'s women characters often engage in a problematic performance of amatory rhetoric that momentarily knocks off balance their role as abstract objects of desire. In the concluding chapter of *Bodies that Matter*, Butler offers an articulate description of performativity and its potential for displacement of gender categories: "Performativity describes this rela-

---

[36] Although I do not agree with Juan Diego Vila's interpretation of Gelasia–and the other shepherdesses of *La Galatea*–as narcissistic, I do agree with his conclusion that, "tal como Cervantes parece afirmar en muchas de sus obras, a la par del reconocimiento interno de la voluntad femenina siempre se produce, en consecuencia, el acceso a la libertad" 'just like Cervantes seems to affirm in many of his works, the internal recognition of female will brings about, as a consequence, access to liberty' (258; my translation).

tion of being implicated in that which one opposes, this turning of power against itself to produce alternative modalities of power, to establish a kind of political contestation that is not a "pure" opposition, a "transcendence" of contemporary relations of power, but a difficult labor of forging a future from resources inevitably impure" (241). The performance of gender is thus not to be thought of as a radical dissolution of power structures, patriarchal ideology, or symbolic law. Instead, it is a tinkering with, a subversive manipulation and misappropriation of the law as it is produced and reproduced by and through its subjects. This is exactly what I believe happens with female characters, especially in their poetic interventions. The pastoral amatory fantasy and socio-symbolic system it supports is not dissolved or transcended. What we do find is a feminine voice that inhabits the prescribed roles for women within the pastoral and yet produces from "resources inevitably impure" an alternative position. These women characters should not simply be dismissed as a patriarchal colonization of the feminine perspective on Cervantes's part. Instead they function problematically within the overall repression of difference that guides the pastoral's ideological and didactic project. While not moving away from my argument that the Spanish pastoral novel functions as a symbolic act, I believe that there are nonetheless specific instances where pastoral ideology seems to work against itself; where the conventions that define female behavior appear to point, in their reiteration, towards other alternatives, contesting the repressive homogeneity of the bower.

La Diana and *La Galatea* operate on two contesting planes: one that promotes the idealization and abstraction of women to produce the male lover as a privileged and perfectable subject; another in which the difference embodied by women characters, even if thematically and structurally contained, emerges and momentarily challenges pastoral ideology. The first plane relies on the repression of the second in order to sustain a viable male pastoral subjectivity and its corresponding homogeneous community. In this manner, pastoral literature parallels social existence by playing out gender struggles that are ultimately resolved in favor of a male lover whose "superiority" is dutifully favored. This is a message, I would argue, whose ideological import conditioned much of these texts' contemporary reception, and that serves as a powerful and repressive metaphor. Only we, as modern readers and critics of pastoral novels, can finally give their due to those female voices and acknowledge their existence as particular desiring subjects within the bower.

CHAPTER 4

THE METAPHOR UNDONE: CERVANTES'S UNMASKING
OF THE PASTORAL

IN spite of being the first pastoral novel in Spain, *La Diana* is widely considered to be the highest or most developed expression of the pastoral mode for the early modern period.[1] From its first publication it set a standard for authors and readers regarding acceptable formal and ideological parameters for the genre. All the *libros de pastores*, as well as other literary and popular manifestations of the pastoral that follow are said to directly refer to, strictly copy, or otherwise corrupt this pure and original mature form.[2] Although perhaps too absolute, this assessment of *La Diana*'s influence does hold some truth. The availability of and influence exerted by Garcilaso's eclogues throughout the Renaissance and the Baroque cannot be denied. Nonetheless one can as well easily argue that *La Diana*'s generic influence, popularity among authors, and wide impact on its audience was never equaled in Spain by any other pastoral text. Having said this, I would also point out that by the latter quarter of the sixteenth century and beginning of the seventeenth the strict bucolic model enacted in these earlier high pastoral texts had largely been eroded. The public's taste for the genre never completely disappears, as proven by the popularity that Montema-

---

[1] See Avalle-Arce, especially page 13.
[2] The chapter divisions in Avalle-Arce's seminal study reflect this logic. After a section on *La Diana* and a second on Montemayor's followers, the critic moves on to discuss pastoral novels that read exclusively as autobiographies, adds a section on "los raros" (the strange ones) and another on the "italianizantes" (the Italianate ones). He ends with a chapter exclusively on Cervantes who in his view, simultaneously contains all these characteristics and therefore can be considered a class all on his own. For a complete bibliography of all early modern Spanish novels, see López Estrada's *Bibliografía de los Libros de Pastores en la Literatura Española*.

yor and his immediate imitators enjoyed well into the nineteenth century. Rather, it is with most authors that the world view put forth by *La Diana* seems to lose currency. It is as if the pastoral amatory fantasy and the corresponding bucolic ideality that nourished it could just no longer simply be reproduced by authors of the baroque without the critical distance exerted by irony and parody.

In a direct reference to the relationship between history and literature, Elliott argues for a connection between the rise of "realist" literature and the troubled economic and political history of post-Tridentine Spain:

> [O]ne further element was needed to complete the transition to the harsh realism of the late sixteenth century. This was the ability to set the moral and material problems of the individual against his social background. It was the misfortune that overcame Spain in the last ten or fifteen years of the century which somehow suddenly brought the picture into focus, and gave to Spanish authors their acute realization of the unutterable complexity of existence, as they watched with disillusionment and incomprehension the shipwreck of a nation that appeared to have been abandoned by God. (*Imperial Spain* 246)

From his perspective, this "transition to harsh realism" is best exemplified by the waning production of the pastoral novel and the rise of the picaresque. Although Elliott's version of literary history does not fully take into account the long and complex trajectories that both modes occupy in Spanish letters, he is certainly on track in sensing a more direct engagement of the literatures of the late Renaissance and the Baroque with the conditions lived during this period.[3] Regardless of the way in which we account for the decline

---

[3] Avalle-Arce, for example, accounts for this phenomenon by pointing at the inability of pastoral to support the weight of "verismo" (realism), leading authors to disapprove of a genre that "de intención se desase de toda traba actualizadora" 'intentionally disassociates itself from any actualizing impulses' (266; my translation). In an excellent study of the trajectory of Spanish amatory poetry from the Medieval to the Baroque, Edward Dudley attributes the increasing inability of lyrical discourse to sustain its ideality on the changes brought about by the realization that there was little difference, in man and in nature, between truth and artifice: "In effect the Copernican revolution had displaced the reassuring Neoplatonic/Ptolemaic man-centered cosmos that had inspired Garcilaso and Fray Luis. Now, not only was man not the center of the universe, but his human senses no longer revealed to him the truth of nature. [...] It is this hermeneutic break that subverted not only man's

of the pastoral, a number of issues relevant to our present analysis emerge. If, as I have argued, the pastoral novel can be interpreted as an idealizing metaphor for social conflict and gender contradictions in sixteenth-century Spanish society, then we must inquire what happens when the formal and thematic conventions of the genre no longer effectively enact this symbolic function. And we must examine carefully the extent to which these later pastoral texts reproduce, manipulate, or sabotage outright their source's narrativization of the historical referent. It is therefore not unreasonable to understand the demise of pastoral ideality as a challenge both to the genre's formal conventions as well as to the values and prescriptions that Renaissance *libros de pastores* symbolically sanctioned and reproduced.

As Spain entered its now much renowned decline, the pastoral mode seems to progressively lose its ability to symbolically reproduce what was becoming an increasingly difficult and tumultuous historical and social subtext. The period of the 1590s was steeped in crisis, ridden by military defeats, bankruptcy, high mortality rates and depopulation, and the indebtedness and dispossession of the peasantry: "The country felt itself betrayed [...]. Desolate and plague-stricken, the Castile of 1600 was a country that had suddenly lost its sense of national purpose" (Elliott, *Imperial Spain* 299). The end of Philip II's reign and the transition to that of Philip III brought little relief. Speaking to this point, Antonio Feros has characterized Philip III's accession as one already defined by widespread discontent:

> [A]ll estates had grievances against him: the people because of high taxes; the church and various religious orders because of attempts to usurp their jurisdiction and meddle in their affairs and finances; the counselors because the king never consulted or listened to them (he stopped attending the Council of State, for example); and the grandees because they no longer played a role in the government of the monarchy. (50)

Despite recent reconsideration of Philip III and Lerma's motives, aims, and methods, it is impossible to ignore the high level of cor-

---

confidence in his own senses but also in language itself" (186). We could argue that this statement also holds true for the pastoral, demonstrated in its inability to sustain (or buy into) the fantasy without bending under the pressure of the contingencies of human nature and history.

ruption and the disappointing results of many of their programs.[4] By Philip III's death, Spain had shown little progress in the way of resolving its social and economic problems and found itself set in an atmosphere of *desengaño* and trapped by its own failures.[5] Despite Olivares's best efforts, not much would be resolved during the years of Philip IV. Any hope of economic and social reform was quickly thwarted by a return to war with the Netherlands and the resistance to a restructuring of the taxation system by the *Cortes*. In the same manner, Olivares's vision of a "unified and integrated Spanish Monarchy" was equally defeated by the regional traditions and interests staunchly defended by the Aragonese, the Valencians, and the Catalonians. As I pointed out in Chapter One, the Spanish national and imperial landscape was beleaguered by social and economic predicaments throughout the sixteenth century. The significant difference in my analysis is that apparently by the end of the century and the beginning of the next the cultural or literary imagination found the rhetoric of a golden age insufficient, as it stumbled upon the realization of its impossibility and falsity. Within this historical context the literary bucolic fantasy could hardly effectively narrativize the conflicts and contradictions of history. It seems that the only alternative for many authors was to refer to the pastoral topography–and its accompanying amatory ideality–as a corrupted and traumatized space.

I will focus my discussion of this pastoral undoing on two Cervantine texts, *La casa de los celos y selvas de Ardenia* and *Don Quixote*, whose engagement with the pastoral falls precisely within this pattern. Given that Cervantes's first incursion into literature

---

[4] Two telling examples are the abandonment of the Tagus navigation scheme (an engineering project which would have made the Tagus navigable from Toledo to Lisbon) and the expulsion of the Moriscos (1608 to 1614), which comprised a large segment of labor force. For a recent study on the Lerma *privanza* see Feros.

[5] Feros describes a report written in 1618 which extensively lists the "ills" of Philip III's reign: "The council reported that the ills of Castile were: the further decline in the population of Castile (attributed to excessive taxation, large numbers of individuals living at court, and the creation of too many religious foundations and communities); the crisis in agriculture (from the depopulation of the countryside); the fiscal crisis (provoked by, among other factors, the excessive number of financial *mercedes* awarded by the king); and the destruction of justice and increasing corruption in the administration of the kingdom (represented by the sale of large numbers of local and territorial offices). Between 1619-1625 many other memoranda, books, and royal decrees appeared, all addressing the monarchy's problems and offering numerous solutions" (251).

was *La Galatea* we could have expected a much more reverent attitude towards the conventional Renaissance form. At the same time, it is not surprising that Cervantes, in his masterful practice of parodying the genres available to him, did not miss the opportunity to test the limits of what had plainly become a strained literary dream. Maravall has well made this point when he asserts that,

> Cervantes, a prudent and reasonable man, a realist in fact, understood that the dream of a chivalric-pastoral society was senseless in the context of the real, historical world, for both positive and negative reasons: negatively, because of the serious defects of that world; positively, because of new technical, economic, military, and political resources. [...] What he did write [in *Don Quixote*] was a brilliant refutation of that ideal. (*Utopia and Counterutopia* 147)[6]

As it will become clear in the discussion that follows, *La casa de los celos y selvas de Ardenia* and *Don Quixote* exploit the bucolic fantasy's demise with biting irony and at times, to great comic effect. More significantly they exemplify a lasting literary and ideological undoing of the pastoral metaphor in favor of the alternative forms of agency customarily marginalized and repressed by the idyll. De Armas Wilson asserts that "the Cervantes of the *Persiles* newly posits gender as a socially constructed though cultural fiats, through laws or maxims [...]. Always an active disrupter of the signifier, Cervantes was a revolutionary in his use of sexual oppositions as a category for a poetics of the Other" (*Allegories of Love* 43). The critic excellently demonstrates this thesis through a meticulous study of the relation between marriage and love in Cervantes's posthumous work. I would add, nonetheless, that the poetics of the Other is already most effectively and radically enacted in Cervantes's subversive parody of the pastoral, with the unexpected result of elevating female subjectivity and desire to their rightful place within a transformed and renewed pastoral world.

---

[6] Regarding the irrevocable demise of the pastoral rural myth in *Don Quixote*, Maravall adds, "But Cervantes abandoned that dream, so that the image of rural society only materializes in a precise manner in the final chapters, when Don Quixote's career comes to a melancholy end with his defeat, and at that point it can only have the appearance of farce" (*Utopia and Counterutopia* 148).

I. *LA CASA DE LOS CELOS Y SELVAS DE ARDENIA*: THE PASTORAL METAPHOR DISRUPTED

The pastoral aspects of *La casa de los celos y selvas de Ardenia*, a drama composed between 1585-1590, are typically seen as an intermediate text between Cervantes's early imitation of *La Diana* and the pastoral interludes of *Don Quixote*.[7] An at times puzzling imitation of Ariosto's *Orlando furioso* and of its predecessor Boiardo's *Orlando innamorato*, *La casa de los celos* chronicles Reinaldos and Roldán's frustrated chivalric romantic quest for the beautiful Angélica.[8] This main plot is complemented by an Ardenian or bucolic subplot, where the theme of forlorn love is further developed. Yet, contrary to the reader's initial expectations, the pastoral scenes are explicitly concerned with matters of wealth, self-interest, and bullish competitiveness; in other words, the bucolic setting is frankly contaminated by the concerns of the Iron Age where the chivalric adventure develops. Whereas in *La Galatea* social contradictions and tensions are controlled or successfully resolved in favor of an idyllic social formation, in this text they persist and dictate the shepherds' amatory and communal interactions. *La casa de los celos* allows the conditions of history–or at least its manifestations through human greed, cruelty, and ignorance–to enter the bower, bringing to the fore the disturbing referent which the pastoral form intends to ideally reinscribe. Earl Thompson has alluded to *La casa de los celos*'s correlation to the historical context, stating that, "the action of this pastoral episode is developed in order to illuminate Cervantes's interpretation of a changing society" (13). He concludes his argument with the following assertion: "A careful reading of the play indicates that Cervantes seems to lament the lack of pastoral idealism in the Spanish society of his times" (15).[9] Taking an alternative analytical position, Edward Friedman has em-

---

[7] For the dating of Cervantes's early plays see Jean Canavaggio.

[8] De Armas discusses the use of these sources in *La casa de los celos* in his chapter on "Cervantes and the Italian Renaissance" in *The Cambridge Companion to Cervantes*.

[9] Although my own reading of the play depends upon this relation between the text and history, I would stress that "pastoral idealism" is always already engaged with the "lamentable" circumstances of the historical subtext; and that the difference in *La casa de los celos* is that its negotiations are unveiled and assaulted.

phasized the play's distance from objective reality and social circumstance: "*La casa de los celos* glorifies fictional reality and the reality of fiction. Its nuances are based on literary multiperspectivism; the levels on which it operates are primarily literary levels" (127). Yet even if seemingly opposite, Friedman's focus on this play's "self-consciousness" sheds light upon Cervantes's fascination with the way in which literary conventions and codes can be made to better reveal the subjective, paradoxical, and ironic nature of reality (132).

In *La casa de los celos* the utopian propositions inherent to the pastoral fantasy are utterly and negatively debunked. On one hand, we can interpret this as a rather troublesome development, given the solace that the literary idyll promises from social strife and human self-centeredness for the reader. On the other, the play's exploration of class difference, human frailty, and female agency can also be alternatively understood as a particularly exciting shift against the genre's repressive ideology. In other words, instead of exclusively reading the Ardenian scenes as a caustic dismantling of the pastoral dream, we can explore how this text openly speaks to and privileges those other interests typically silenced by the bucolic metaphor.

When we first enter the borders of Ardenia we find Lauso and Corinto, the two shepherd-lovers, lamenting Clori's rejection: "que en tanto que la dulce mi enemiga / se esté fortalecida en su dureza / no hay mal que huya ni placer que siga" 'while my sweet enemy / has found strength in her hardness / that there is no unpleasantness that escapes nor any enjoyment that follows' (II 173-4; my translation). These lovers are forced to grieve their beloved's acceptance of the unseemly but certainly rich Rústico. Within this pastoral topography, where wealth does matter, Lauso and Corinto represent two obsolete figures whose idyllic narcissism is inconsistent with the real social conditions in which they exist. Corinto complains, for example:

> Granjería común amor se ha hecho,
> y dél hay feria franca dondequiera,
> do cada cual atiende a su provecho.
> [...]
> Vuélvese el oro más cendrado en cobre,
> y el ingenio más claro en tonta ciencia,
> si le toca o le tiene el hombre pobre,
> y desto es buen testigo la experiencia. (II 174-5)

> Love has been made into a common exchange,
> and of it there is an open market anywhere,
> where one tends to one's own benefit.
> [...]
> Burnished gold is transformed into copper
> and the clearest wit into dumbed-down science,
> if it touches or is had by a pitiable man,
> and of this I have as witness my own experience. (my translation)

Corinto's awareness of his condition ironically prompts him to wallow in a pathetic self-fashioning where the lover's gold and ingenuity is unfairly transformed into copper and foolishness. The poor shepherd still retains his gold, or virtuous nature, as well as his poetic skill; nonetheless, these are goods that no longer hold their idealized value, whether in the larger social context or in the narcissistic economy of the amatory fantasy. Well within an iron age and unable to make their nobility and chastity count, Lauso and Corinto find themselves displaced and humiliated by the luxuries that Rústico's material wealth can provide. Clori's manifest attraction for the rich shepherd turns her into a contemptible mirror upon which to construct these conventional lovers' narcissistic subjectivity.

Notwithstanding their claim as lovers within the bucolic fantasy, Lauso and Corinto are inadequate examples of the conventional qualities of nobility, virtue, and gentility that the pastoral mode requires.[10] Rústico's comic role serves as a negative foil for these shepherds. In his first and longest intervention we see him sure of him-

---

[10] It is important to point out that by Act III Corinto enters the world of commerce, negotiating a deal with Angélica where he would protect her from Reinaldos and Roldán in exchange for money:

> Corinto: Digo que te llevaré,
> si fuese a cabo del mundo.
> Angélica: En tu valor, sin segundo,
> sé bien que bien me fié.
> Corinto: Haya güelte, y tú verás
> si te llevo do quisieres.
> Angélica: Mira tú cuánto pudieres,
> que eso mismo gastarás;
> que tengo joyas que son
> de valor y parecer. (III 230)
>
> Corinto: I say I will take you, even if to the ends of the world.
> Angélica: In your valor, second to none,
> I well know I can trust.

self, in command of his flock and managing and protecting his assets, causing Clori to admire his "ingenio para mandar acomodado y presto" 'ability to command well and quickly' (II 179; my translation). Rejecting any notion of an inclusive pastoral community, Lauso and Corinto instead relish a vocal and demeaning derision of Rústico. Following the cue of the play's main title, Lauso and Corinto are devoured by jealousy and unable to accept Rústico as an equal and fellow competitor for Clori's love.[11] When Clori first approaches them, Corinto verbally assaults her with a grotesque, impertinent and yet funny, description of her lowly lover:

> Por aquel, digo, desarmado y bronco,
> calzado de la frente y pies ancho,
> corto de zancas y de pecho ronco,
> cuyo dios es el estendido pancho,
> y a do tiene la crápula su estancia,
> él tiene siempre su manida y rancho. (II 177)

> About him, I say, without arms and brusque,
> with wide forehead and feet,
> short in the legs and hoarse,
> whose god is his extended belly,
> and where licentiousness makes its home,
> he always has his flock and shack. (my translation)

These verses are especially acerbic, unfairly associating Rústico with Bacchus and a life of wanton decadence. Ridiculed for his physical appearance and accused of being a drunk, all that Rústico has are his riches made patent by his "manida y rancho." Rústico's unflattering depiction as a stupid, boorish, and unsightly man puts on view the envy that the shepherds-lovers feel towards him as an intruder and as a climber. Nevertheless, the indisputable allure of his

---

> Corinto: Offer your money, and you will see
> that I will take you wherever you desire.
> Angélica: See how far you can
> and the same you will receive;
> for I have jewels that are
> of value and good taste. (my translation)

[11] In his discussion of the play, De Armas highlights the connection between Ovid's abode of envy and Cervantes's title for *La casa de los celos* ("Cervantes and the Italian Renaissance" 36).

capital for Clori challenges the system of values the pastoral convention depends on; in the processes, it exposes the economic pressures and class hierarchies that persist in the bucolic fantasy.

Corinto and Lauso's unflattering pandering of their baser instincts is further displayed when they play on Rústico a series of outrageous and humiliating tricks. Disparaging of the way of life that Rústico represents, they proceed to ridicule him with the first "burla" ("trick"), "que queremos probar de nuestro intento, / por ver si es suya o nuestra la locura" 'that we want prove from our test / who is crazy, he or us' (II 180; my translation). They pretend that there is an exotic American parrot trapped in a tree. When Rústico shows interest in seeing the unusual animal, they tie him to the tree, climb and stomp on him and relish their cunning mischievousness leaving him tied up and hurt. The second time around they exploit his wish for a better singing voice by tying a cord around his neck and nearly strangling him. On both occasions these *burlas* are designed to deride his intellect and abuse him physically. In effect, Corinto and Lauso not only achieve their aim but also invite the audience to participate in their malicious revenge by provoking laughter at the mortification of this fellow shepherd. Evidently, Rústico's inability to anticipate their schemes and his enthusiastic participation in his own deceit confirm his enactment of the *pastor bobo* type, thereby conflating in this text the low and the high pastoral modes.[12] All the same, Lauso and Corinto's burlas overtly disclose the mercilessness of the shepherds, and damage their identity as ideal lovers and poets. In the first instance, they take great pleasure in the act of tying him up and calling him an ass. In the second, the physical violence notably increases with Corinto verbalizing his desire not only to torture Rústico, but in fact to kill him:

> Corinto: [A] otro estirón que le dé,
> estará como ha de estar.
> Rústico: Ladrón, ¿quiéresme ahogar?
> Corinto: No lo sé; mas probaré. (III 210)

---

[12] Dominick Finello argues that *La casa de los celos*, "brings Cervantes's familiarity with the rustic world into line with that of the Spanish tradition by mixing art and authenticity, prefiguring the pastoral of the *Quixote*" (203).

Corinto: With another pull,
he shall be as I wish.
Rústico: Thieve, do you want to strangle me?
Corinto: I don't know if I can; but I will try. (my translation)

Lauso, although maintaining some distance, supports and enjoys Corinto's conduct, declaring both to Rústico and to Clori his unequivocal approval: "La burla ha estado, a lo menos / como al sujeto conviene" 'This trick was well-suited / for the subject' (III 211; my translation). Their deed done, neither Rústico's embarrassment when fooled nor his genuine happiness at being able to please Clori hardly restores the dignity that Lauso and Corinto have taken away from him. Given the state of the matter, one is hard pressed to find in Ardenia a functional idyll. We may be entertained by the shepherds' antics, but this is not a place for bucolic escape. As a shepherd and a fellow suitor of Clori, Rústico should be brought into the fold and included as a member of the community.[13] Instead, Lauso and Corinto's contempt feeds off of Rústico's otherness, revealing the exclusionary homogeneity and the repressive mechanisms that function under the guise of pastoral ideality. Rústico's presence calls attention to those who live, love, and work in the countryside but who are nonetheless excluded from the literary pastoral dream.

In a curious scene, Rústico meets "Amor" ("Cupid"), but can only see a monstrous "niñazo" ("deformed child") instead of Cupid's exquisite child-like figure: "Niñazo le llamo yo, / pues ya le apunta el bigote" 'I call him a grotesque child / with even a mustache' (II 196; my translation).[14] He, unlike his fellow shepherds sees an unidealized version of Cupid's countenance, both grotesque and deceptive. When Lauso and Corinto ask him to move away so that they can show reverence to the love god, Rústico replies with irony, "¡Qué inocencia!" 'What innocence!' (II 195; my translation). The encounter is significant because it underscores in yet another way Rústico's alterity as markedly at odds with bucolic ideality. By challenging the ideal figuring of Cupid, Rústico renders a much less

---

[13] One obvious example of a less refined lover who is nonetheless welcomed into the group is, as previously mentioned, Erastro in *La Galatea*. Apparently, by *La casa de los celos* Cervantes shows no intention to construct an idyll where social and economic difference are ignored and repressed.

[14] In an earlier intervention Rústico had called Cupid a "papagayo" ("parrot") and a "pájaro pinto" ("colorful bird"), an obvious and hilarious reference to the child's wings (II 195).

romantic but much more historical understanding of amatory relations, where love is explicitly both in tension with but undeniably tied to self-interest and social advantage.

As it regards a gendered reading of this text, Clori is the most complex character within Ardenia. Unwilling to buy into Lauso and Corinto's empty amatory rhetoric, Clori consciously and willfully chooses the material comfort that Rústico's labor and wealth assure her. Her material self-interest is derided as the end of "love" and is implicitly compared to the corruption that is found at court.[15] On the other hand, the degradation of pastoral ideality conversely launches a space for the shepherdess's subjectivity. As she herself tells Rústico after he endures yet another embarrassing trick, "Calla, que para aquello que me sirves, / más sabes que trescientos Salomones" 'Be silent, since what for you are good for,/ you know more than three hundred Solomons' (II 182; my translation). Rather than conform as an idealized specular object for Lauso and Corinto, Clori opts for a much more practical and rewarding approach to the amatory exchange: she will marry Rústico and personally reap the material rewards that this union will bare. Most interesting, her purportedly shameful preference for wealth over idealizing love is also the source of her agency, and plays a key role in Cervantes's dismantling of a gender ideology in this text. If Clori chooses Rústico because, like a "Júpiter nuevo" ("new Jupiter") from his hands "llueve plata y oro" ("rains silver and gold")[16] she does so as a protest against the falsity and arrogance of the shepherd-lovers' objectifying discourse (II 177). Unlike any of the female characters we have seen so far, Clori rejects love because she can recognize it as empty and valueless rhetoric:

---

[15] Cupid tells his mother:

> Has de saber, madre mía,
> que en la corte donde he estado
> no hay amor sin granjería,
> y el interés se ha usurpado
> mi reino y mi monarquía. (II 194)

> You should know, mother,
> that in the court where I have been
> no love exists without gain,
> and self-interest has usurped
> my kingdom and my monarchy. (my translation)

[16] This is an implicit reference to the myth of Danae, mother of Perseus by Jove, who came to her as a golden shower (Ovid, *Metamorphoses* IV. 837).

> Con él tengo, Corinto, más ganancia
> que contigo, con Lauso y con Riselo,
> que vendéis discreción con arrogancia.
> [...]
> Quédense los pastores cortesanos
> con la melifluidad de sus razones
> y dichos, aunque agudos, siempre vanos.
> No se sustenta el cuerpo de intenciones,
> ni de conceptos trasnochados hace
> sus muchas y forzosas provisiones. (II 177-8)
>
> With him, Corinto, I can make more profit
> than with you, with Lauso or Riselo,
> who sell discretion with arrogance.
> [...]
> Let the court shepherds keep
> the mellifluousness of their reason
> and their sayings, which even if witty, are always vain.
> The body is not sustained by good intentions,
> nor from sleepless thoughts does it make
> its many and necessary provisions. (my translation)

Moreover, her rebuff of Lauso and Corinto is also motivated by her desire to have her agency taken seriously. By rejecting the specular function of the beloved, Clori positions herself as a demanding presence in Rústico's life and expects to have a dominant role in their relationship:

> Tiene por justa ley el gusto mío,
> y el levantado cuello humilde inclina
> al yugo que le pone mi albedrío.
>   No tiene el rico Oriente otra tal mina
> como es la que yo saco de sus manos,
> ora cruel me muestre, ora benigna. (II 178)
>
> My pleasure is his just law,
> and he prostrates his proud neck
> to the yoke that my will imposes.
>   The rich Orient does not have another
> mine like the one I take from his hands,
> this whether I show myself cruel or kind. (my translation)

Clori's behavior is for the most part depicted as unflattering. For example, her voyeuristic pleasure at watching Lauso and Corinto ridicule her lover is only partially offset by her bringing to a halt the shepherds' "burla" before any real harm can be done to Rústico. Clori is not an innocent wallflower or model for demureness. Her negative characteristics, nonetheless, put forward a representation of feminine subjectivity that cannot be easily erased by pastoral amatory convention. Clori effectively arrests the symbolic mechanisms that would rather have her be a silent and emptied vessel for someone else's desire. When considered within a paradigm of male narcissism, Clori is surely an important contrast to her predecessors and a remarkable precedent for pastoral female characters in the Don Quixote.[17] Regardless of the motivating forces that condition her love for Rústico, it is difficult to deny that the pastoral metaphor with its repressive stance towards female agency and desire is radically assaulted. Clori's preference for the "cadenas de amor" (chains of love) that jingle with coins made of gold, even if unsavory, is a testament to her agency as a self-determining female subject (III 208; my translation).

II. *Don Quixote*: Parody, Female Agency, and the Undoing of the Pastoral Metaphor

In its appearance in *Don Quixote* the idyll, both as a literary convention and as a utopian proposition, is plagued throughout by the often hilarious, highly contaminating elements from the 'real' or unidealized countryside. Some clear examples of this type of invasion and destabilization of the bucolic space are the interventions of rustic shepherds overtly excluded in the high pastoral tradition in general and in Montemayor and his followers in particular. The shepherds baffled by the Knight's jargon (I. 11), as well as Eugenio's rather prosaic tirade against his goat Manchada (I. 50), immediately come to mind. Likewise, Sancho's vocal disparagement of his master's expectation of an egalitarian pastoral community rules out a convincing construction of an idealizing topography within the fictional boundaries of La Mancha. To Don Quixote's request that he be "una mesma cosa conmigo" 'that you may be seen as my equal' and that he eat "en mi plato y bebas por donde yo bebiere"

---

[17] For an interpretation of how Clori can be read specifically as an intermediary figure between Gelasia and Marcela, see Morley Hawk Marks, especially page 134.

'eat from my plate and drink from my cup' Sancho responds, "[C]omo yo tuviese que bien de comer, tan bien y mejor me lo comería en pie y a mis solas [...]" '[W]hen I have enough to eat I can eat just as well, and even better, on my feet and by myself [...]' (I. 154; I. 58).[18] In fact, part of the humor of this response depends on Sancho misidentifying his master's tribute to a golden age with what he thinks is a reference to the luxuries and formalities of an emperor's feast: "[M]ucho mejor me sabe lo que como en mi rincón sin melindres ni respetos, [que] donde me sea forzoso mascar despacio, beber poco, limpiarme a menudo, no estornudar ni toser si me viene en gana, ni hacer otras cosas que la soledad y la libertad traen consigo" 'I can eat a lot better in my own corner, without any fussing or show of respect, [than] at some other table where I have to eat slowly, and not drink too much, and keep wiping my fingers, and not sneeze or cough if I want to, and all sorts of other things that go along with privacy and freedom' (I. 154; I. 58). The squire's confusion is instructive in so far as it highlights the affinity of the bucolic vision with the fineries and demeanor proper to the court milieu. Sancho's rustic pleasures together with the deportment and life experience of the goat herders, explicitly competes with Don Quixote's recollection of an idealized bower he had so enjoyed in his reading of *La Diana* and *La Galatea*. Moreover, it is important to recognize that the clash between the goat herders' lives and the Knight's literary dream is not just another turn of the humorous and the parodic. There is also here an implicit reference to the economic and social subtext characterized by great hardship and dire prospects for the rural underclass.[19] Unlike their literary counterparts, all these shepherds have to offer are a couple of pieces of goat, acorns, and hard cheese (I. 153-5). As I discussed in Chapter One, by the late sixteenth century the opposing interests of the ranchers and farmers, the damage done to the environment, and heavy local and national taxation largely determined the constant struggle to which these poor *labradores* were subject. If the pastoral fantasy, as symbolic act, is meant to produce a comforting metaphor for historical conflict, these episodes in *Don Quixote* alternatively

---

[18] All translations of *Don Quixote* have been adapted from Burton Raffel's translation.

[19] Johnson does an excellent analysis of the rural crisis of around 1600 and its relation to *Don Quixote* in his book *Cervantes and the Material World*, especially in the section titled "The Drama of Sancho's Salary."

show signs of strain within the agrarian economy and landscape. Unlike the pastoral novels *Don Quixote* does not repress the idyll's unbecoming social and material referents.

Don Quixote also reinscribes pastoral convention through the Knight errant's Golden Age speech (I. 11). The speech is provoked by Sancho's hesitancy to adopt a pastoral spirit and share with the knight errant a meal, "como una mesma cosa." Despite his resistance, Sancho is forced to partake of the pastoral fantasy with his "amo y natural señor" 'master and natural lord' (I. 154; I. 58). These are conditions which contaminate the episode with an aggressivity and a differential hierarchy that, even if humorous, uncovers the contradictory foundation of Don Quixote's pastoral stance. This is not to say that Don Quixote's idyll recuses itself from its literary past, especially Ovid's description of the Golden Age in Book I of the *Metamorphoses*.[20] Yet, it imagines a bucolic topography that, upon close examination, seems to be askew; it is evocative of but does not completely conform to the particular generic conventions and ideological suppositions cultivated by the *libros de pastores* to which it refers.

The speech appropriately starts with a description of a place and time where Mother Nature, untouched by human greed, provided for every necessity and where the tyranny of work, property, and competition was unknown: "ofrecía, por todas las partes de su fértil y espacioso seno, lo que pudiese hartar, sustentar y deleitar a los hijos que entonces la poseían" 'under no compulsion of any kind, offered the children who then possessed her, and from every part of her fertile, spacious bosom, whatever might feed, sustain, and delight them' (I. 156; I. 59). Don Quixote imagines his "zagalejas" 'country damsels' unsown, innocent and honest, and untouched by the "raras y peregrinas invenciones" 'strange, exotic creations' (I. 156; I. 59) characteristic of their pompous Iron Age sisters. In an interpretation of the feminine in this speech, El Saffar

---

[20] For example, Don Quixote presents the lack of material interest or competition ("los que en ella vivían ignoraban estas dos palabras de *tuyo* y *mío*" 'those who walked the earth in that time knew nothing of those two words, *thine* and *mine*' [I. 11, 155; I. 11, 59, my emphasis]) and the giving spirit of Nature ("a nadie le era necesario para alcanzar su ordinario sustento tomar otro trabajo que alzar la mano y alcanzarle de las robustas encinas" 'to obtain his daily bread, no one had to trouble himself any more than to lift his hand and gather his food from the sturdy oak trees' [I. 11, 155; I. 11, 59]) as markers of his imagined Golden Age, thus maintaining the general parameters of space and economy found in traditional pastoral literature.

keenly comments on the ideological import of Don Quixote's description of Mother Nature, "nuestra primera madre," 'our original mother' (I. 156; I. 59) as a wholly benign being: "There Don Quixote delivers his Golden Age speech, which reveals him as enveloped in a fantasy of the all-good mother. Although he clearly yearns for a time before the era of father dominance, Don Quixote strips the Great Mother whom he evokes of her dark side. She is all giving but not all powerful [...] she retains only those qualities that are described and attractive to men" ("In Marcela's Case" 163).

By neutralizing Mother Nature's "dark side" and reconstructing her as an "all-good mother," Don Quixote's vision repeats a one-sided and abstracted version of femininity. As such, his version of the Golden Age seems to perpetuate a gender ideology that privileges chastity over any other value, independent agency, or particular desire. When interpreted from this perspective, the speech seemingly reasserts the "desirable" idealized objectification of women that I have shown its literary predecessors enacted and promoted.

Maravall has noted the various ways in which Cervantes transforms Ovid's *Metamorphoses* in the Golden Age speech, most saliently the "conversion of the myth into the goal of a reform movement which seeks its restoration, not as an impossible reproduction of a classical model but rather as a new vision of a natural society to be established in the context of present reality" (*Utopia and Counterutopia* 134-5).[21] However, when compared to Ovid (as well as the sixteenth-century *libros de pastores*) one specific difference emerges. Don Quixote's imagined bower is populated exclusively by "simples y hermosas zagalejas" 'simple, beautiful country damsels' (I. 156; I. 59) who are free from "la amorosa pestilencia" 'the amorous plague' (I. 157; I. 60). The shepherd–as lover, as poet, or as member or this first innocent age–is absent from and unnecessary to the Knight's pastoral brew. Ovid, for example, populates his Golden Age with men who "had no fear of any punishment" (V. 129), "kept their own shores" (V. 136), and "gathered fruit from the arbutus tree" (V. 145). In the Don Quixote's recreated *Edad de Oro*, other than a vague allusion to the members of his imagined idyll as

---

[21] Maravall accurately lists other elements of the transformation as follows: "elimination of all mythological references; reduction of Ovid's four ages to two, in order to intensify the contrast between them; explicit identification of the Iron Age with the present; introduction of the chivalric element" (*Utopia and Counterutopia* 134).

"los que en ella vivían" 'those who walked the earth in that time' (I. 155; I. 59) and "los hijos que entonces la poseían" 'the children who then possessed her' (I. 156; I. 59), there is no direct mention of men. All specific naming in the speech concerns only the feminine: Mother Nature, the *zagalejas*, or the female court successors that now take their place. As it is to be expected, the shepherdesses are characterized as simple and honest. Still, their dress is here associated with a simplicity of word and feeling that constitutes a sharp contrast to amatory discourse produced by Sireno and Sylvano or Elicio and Erastro in *La Diana* and *La Galatea* respectively; Don Quixote's shepherdesses loved as they dressed, "sin buscar *artificioso rodeo de palabras* para encarecerlos [los concetos amorosos]" '[T]hey spoke their thoughts of love from the soul, simply and unpretentiously, exactly as they thought them, *not searching for elaborate verbal circumlocutions to beautify them*' (I. 156; I. 59, my emphasis). It is not clear whom the *zagalejas* loved, given the absence of lovers and the condemnation that Don Quixote ascribes to love as an "amorosa pestilencia." Even so, the "artificioso rodeo de palabras" is clearly a direct allusion to the highly cultivated rhetorical practice of the shepherd-poet, which the Knight rejects in favor of the *zagalejas*' "verdad y llaneza" 'truth and simplicity' (I. 156; I. 59). Ironic as Don Quixote's declaration may seem (he, after all relishes every opportunity to indulge in linguistic artifice), this conceptualization of pastoral discourse marks a shift in the coordinates that demarcate the idyll. Unlike that of Montemayor and his imitators, Cervantes's bower favors women and their "simple" words over the refined rhetoric of suffering and nobility of the shepherd. The exclusion of the shepherd from Don Quixote's imagined pastoral topography thus offers an alluring contrast to its precursors where the male lover-poet and his community function as structural and thematic anchors. Instead, the Golden Age speech posits the feminine as constitutive and even absolute.[22]

---

[22] That it is Don Quixote, a male subject, who envisions the Golden Age as a feminine space is potentially paradoxical. It is in moments like this that one could say Don Quixote's feminine side surfaces. This psycho-sexual ambiguity in the character is postulated by Cruz as Don Quixote's vacillations between the Imaginary and the Symbolic orders: "Oscillating by degrees between the Imaginary and the Symbolic in parts I and II, Don Quixote never fully separates from, or integrates with the chivalric narratives" ("Mirroring Others" 96). These chivalric narratives are, as I have proposed for the pastoral, male centered.

The speech ends with Don Quixote's final praise of the shepherdesses: "Las doncellas y la honestidad andaban, como tengo dicho, por dondequiera, sola y señora, sin temor que la ajena desenvoltura y lascivo intento le menoscabasen, y su perdición nacía de su gusto y propia voluntad" 'Damsels and decency both walked everywhere, as I have said, alone and in charge of herself, unafraid that impudence and lust might attempt to menace them; a ruined woman fell of her own will and desire' (I. 157; I. 59).[23] This conclusion, with its emphasis on choice and will describes women as agents of their own spiritual and biological destiny. If, as I discussed in previous chapters, the convention's amatory structure depends on the absence of the beloved, Don Quixote's world of roaming *zagalejas* enables an alternative conception of the pastoral as an exclusively feminine space. Most significantly, it negates the presence and superiority of the shepherd and his community. In *La Galatea* Cervantes does not deconstruct the convention's prescriptions and ultimately allows for the lover-poet's worldview to prevail. In the Golden Age speech the pastoral paradigm is finally negated. The Knight Errant's imagination allows for a world where the shepherdess as subject finds herself unencumbered by the demands of idealization, narcissism, and sublimation. In fact, it is exactly this difference what distinguishes in his vision the "true" golden age from a much less innocent present state of affairs. I would argue, therefore, that despite the idealized virginal innocence ascribed to these damsels, we should not dismiss the potentially subversive import of Don Quixote's imagined idyll as a bastion for the feminine. Although couched within a discourse that lionizes chastity, we can legitimately read this golden age as an affirmation of an alternative

---

[23] That there is any possibility for "perdición" (perdition) within Don Quixote's imagined Golden Age poses yet another paradox within the speech. As Mujica has indicated: "What is evident in *Witness* and in Renaissance pastoral as well, is the inevitable collapse of the utopian vision. Unfailingly, outside forces or internal passions interfere and destroy the image of harmony. In no pastoral romance is the projection of perfection actually achieved and maintained. Arcadia is an illusion" (*Iberian Pastoral Characters* 6).

With this paradox lying at the core of every pastoral (there cannot be Arcadia without its opposite, be it the *polis* or personal desire), I maintain that Don Quixote's speech is still a liberating one for the female subject. Since a kernel of instability or perversion is always at the heart of the *locus amoenus*, the female's capacity to deal with it as a coherent unified subject–rather than an erased and scattered object/mirror–is most significant for a reading of the Golden Age speech as a subversion of the traditional pastoral genre.

feminine other, this time surfacing in the imaginary world created by our Knight.

As we advance to a reading of the Marcela, Leandra, and Sanchica interludes, I must emphasize the importance that the Golden Age speech has in establishing a referent for female pastoral characters in the rest of *Don Quixote*. As I see it, Don Quixote's speech opens a textual space that makes it possible for these female characters to affirm their agency beyond male objectification and idealization, countering the idealized absence that they are conventionally expected to perform. In other words, Don Quixote's imagined golden age establishes a renewed referent, which both foreshadows and legitimizes Marcela's personal and economic independence, as well as Leandra and Sanchica's command of their libidinal desires.

In addition, it is important to point out that unlike the knightly world that Don Quixote's imagination valiantly engenders for himself, the pastoral episodes in *Don Quixote* are hardly able to reproduce their source literary models. None of the shepherd-lovers that appear or the women that they love can be classified as true idealized shepherds. From the outset, the shepherd-lover in *Don Quixote* is cognizant of putting on a disguise that takes its cues directly from literary tradition. Certainly in *La Diana* and its imitators characters are regularly introduced who again take on a pastoral disguise. Nonetheless, these characters come into a world that articulates its idealized state as authentic, and come into contact with shepherd-lovers that are its autochthonous citizens. To the contrary, the pastoral world in *Don Quixote* is already articulated as a deliberate yet fragile fiction contaminated by a highly taxing Iron Age reality.

As often noted, Marcela is one of the most controversial female characters in the Cervantine canon. By all appearances she possesses all the qualities of the perfect pastoral object of desire: she is young, beautiful, has taken on the dress of a shepherdess, and chastely rejects love. From within pastoral convention, her character fits perfectly her suitors' narcissistic imperative. Led by Grisóstomo, the lovers take to the countryside to sing laments in her honor and celebrate their identity as noble lovers. By the same token, the events that surround this interlude are characterized by death, anger, and disharmony. Contrary to what I have described as the profitable fashioning of the shepherds as suffering and constant,

Grisóstomo's desperate plunge into death and his friends' spiteful badgering of Marcela prevent the bucolic fantasy–as articulated in *La Diana* and *La Galatea*–from fully taking hold. Instead, the members of the pastoral community find themselves with a dead lover's body and the problem of how to account for, honor, and bury it. Grisóstomo's suicide does a great disservice to the image of the shepherd as perfect or "whole" pastoral subject and he leaves behind his community in disarray.

The unnamed shepherd who announces Grisóstomo's death also introduces Marcela's story. The very first description of Guillermo "the rich man's" daughter labels her as an "endiablada moza" 'damned Marcela' (I. 161; I. 63), a categorization that seems to be related as much to her staunch rejection of love as to her ability to maintain her personal and financial independence. The orphaned and sole daughter of a rich peasant, Marcela has assets–material and physical–that have been sought from an early age by the men of her village, including her priest uncle who zealously "safeguards" the "ganancia y granjería que le ofrecía el tener la hacienda de la moza dilatando su casamiento" 'the profits he earned from her estate, while they waited for the girl to get married' (I. 165; I. 65). Even so, Marcela's strategies of evasion effectively keep in check these outside interests. Initially she consistently casts off her lovers' requests citing her youth and inexperience. Once she has reached a suitable age for marriage, she abandons her uncle's house, takes on the pastoral dress, and goes to live among shepherdesses. Pedro, one of the shepherd-lovers who follow Grisóstomo, relates the rest of Marcela's story. He tells how she first goes to the countryside against the wishes of those who desired to keep her under their control: "Pero hételo aquí, cuando no me cato, que remanece un día la melindrosa Marcela hecha pastora; y, sin ser parte su tío ni todos los del pueblo, que se lo desaconsejaban, dio en irse al campo con las demás zagalas del lugar y dio en guardar su mesmo ganado" 'And then, when you couldn't have expected it, suddenly there was fickle Marcela, turned into a shepherdess. And no matter what her uncle and everyone else in town did to talk her out of it, she made up her mind to go out in the fields with the other shepherdesses and take care of her own flocks' (I. 165; I. 65). It is significant that Marcela's story is exclusively told by male voices that tell and construct her life as a series of inexplicable acts. This narrative condition is well within pastoral convention. But in Marcela's case the story told by a series of male voices that includes the narrator is one clouded by bewilderment and annoyance at her unexpected and unbecoming behavior. Dismissive of her uncle's "protection," and reluctant to become anyone's wife, Marcela's flight into the countryside is thus interpreted as an affront to all that is expected of such a beautiful, available, and rich maiden. In fact, what Pedro seems to be accusing Marcela of is trickery, as if her youthful beauty and avowed inability to carry "la carga del matrimonio" 'the responsibilities of marriage' (I. 165; I. 65) were disingenuous tools of rhetorical artifice and deception. In more concrete terms, the degree of agency her flight manifests contradicts the supposed sweet innocence and frailty she had personified in the minds of her suitors, earning her the title of "melindrosa."[24]

In a moment of great irony but well within pastoral convention, Marcela's flight unwittingly incites her admirers, "cuántos ricos mancebos, hidalgos y labradores" 'how many rich bachelors, gentlemen and farmers' (I. 165; I. 65), to follow her and establish their own community of literary shepherds. But from its inception, this pastoral fantasy unravels. The task for these lovers is to faithfully reproduce the collective harmony and high lyrical practice modeled in the literary tradition. Instead they are perplexed by Marcela's defiant conduct and find themselves stumped. They resort to an endless repetition of insults: "y así, no saben qué decirle, sino llamarla a voces cruel y desagradecida, con otros títulos a éste semejante, que bien la calidad de su condición manifiestan" 'and they don't know what to say to her, except to call her cruel and ungrateful, and other things like that, which is in truth how she acts' (I. 166; I. 66).[25] Their pastoral sojourn, instead of a showcase for their nobility and poetic talent, is tellingly cast as a "pestilence," corrupted and unbecoming:

---

[24] Covarrubias defines melindre and melindrosa as follows: "Un género de fruitilla de sartén hecha con miel; comida delicada y tenida por golosina. De allí vino a significar este nombre el regalo con que suelen hablar algunas damas, a las quales por esta razón llaman melindrosas" 'A type of fruit sauted and sweetened with honey; a delicate candy. From this we came to define the way in which some women often speak in an affected manner' (798; my translation).

[25] Among the more severe insults we find Marcela called, "enemiga mortal del linaje humano" 'mortal enemy of the human race' (I. 178; I. 72), "fiera" 'wild fiend' (I. 179; I. 72), and "pastora homicida" 'murderous shepherdess' (I. 168; I. 67).

Y con esta manera de condición hace más daño en esta tierra que si por ella entrara *la pestilencia* porque su afabilidad y hermosura atrae los corazones de los que la tratan a servirla y a amarla; pero su desdén y desengaño los conduce a términos de desesperarse, y así, no saben qué decirle, sino llamarla a voces cruel y desagradecida, con otros títulos a éste semejante, que bien la calidad de su condición manifiestan. Y si aquí estuviédeses, señor, algún día, veríades resonar estas sierras y estos valles con los lamentos de los desengañados que la siguen. (I. 166)

And yet, living this way, she does more damage, here on this earth, than if she carried the plague, because her pleasantness and her beauty draw the hearts of those who deal with her, and then they court her, and they love her, but her scorn and honesty drives them to despair, and they don't know what to say to her, except to call her cruel and ungrateful, and other things like that, which is in truth how she acts. And were you to stay around here, señor, some day you'd find these hills and valleys echoing with the moans of disappointed lovers. (I. 66)

Marcela decides to live "libertad y vida tan suelta y de tan poco o de ningún recogimiento" 'such a free life, with so little protection–or none at all' (I. 165; I. 65), even if tempered by her "honestidad y recato" 'virtue and chastity' (I. 166; I. 65). It is evident that Cervantes is here exploiting the "paradox of love" for the benefit of parody. If the beloved's *recato* insures her desirability, her staunch material and psychological will and independence transform this tenuous bower into a place of confusion. Much to these shepherds' dismay, Marcela's attitude and her manipulation of prescribed female roles sabotage the successful reproduction of the narcissistic model of the *libros de pastores* they had so avidly read. In *La Galatea* the pastoral community appropriates and profits from Gelasia's zealous attitude by transforming her refusal into fodder for poetic pleasure. But unlike the fictional worlds of *La Diana* and *La Galatea*, *Don Quixote*'s devolves into a pathetic and destructive disillusionment that is finally materialized in Grisóstomo's *real* death. From a similar perspective, Forcione has framed Marcela and Grisóstomo's episode as a "consummation" of *La Galatea*: "With the death of Grisóstomo and the vanishing of Marcela, Cervantes has quite literally ended his rewritten Galatea and with it any possibility of erotic pastoral, clearly disclosing the fictive nature of the love and the object of love which animate it and the emptiness of the poetic tradition it honors" ("The Consummation of *La Galatea*" 64). In other words, the Marcela and Grisóstomo episode ends *La Galatea* because it ends the illusion of a world where idealized love and poetry could in fact fill the world and produce whole subjects.

This community's failure to operate within the bounds of the literary fantasy is manifested in a variety of ways. Unlike their literary predecessors, these shepherds see each other as rivals in Marcela's conquest: "y todos los que la conocemos estamos esperando en qué ha de parar su altivez y quién ha de ser el dichoso que ha de venir a domeñar condición tan terrible y gozar de hermosura tan estremada" 'But everyone who knows her is just waiting to see where her arrogance ends, and who'll be the lucky man to get the job of trying to tame such a fierce temper, trying to enjoy such fantastic beauty' (I. 167; I. 66). Expressing their love with words such as "domeñar" and "gozar," they structure their desire according to a set of expectations much more in tune with the attitudes attributed to the *corte* than with the literary and bucolic *aldea*. Marcela's stalwart attitude only makes things more difficult for Grisóstomo and his fellow shepherd-lovers. She is a defiant object and therefore, an imperfect mirror upon which to reflect their imagined wholeness. As a result, Grisóstomo's desperate song reads as an unconvincing repetition of pastoral conventions. He rambles on a succession of complaints that in the end do little either to satisfy his desire to possess Marcela or to support pastoral ideality:

> En todo hay cierta, inevitable muerte;
> mas yo, ¡milagro nunca visto!, vivo
> celoso, ausente, desdeñado y cierto
> de las sospechas que me tienen muerto,
> y en el olvido en quien mi fuego avivo,
> y, entre tantos tormentos, nunca alcanza
> mi vista a ver en sombra a la esperanza,
> ni yo, desesperado, la procuro; (I. 182)
>
> And death is certain, inevitable, always waiting.
> But some incredible magic keeps me alive,
> Though jealous, and absent, and fiercely disdained, convinced
> Of suspicions I know will bring me death, so sure
> Of being forgotten that I burn still more desperately.
> And all surrounded with torment, I see not even

> A shadow of a shadow of hope–and worse: my heart's
> So deeply desperate I never even look, (I. 74-5)

Bitter and unable to find solace with his fellow lovers, Grisóstomo is a disappointing shepherd-lover. Contrary to the literary model he is imitating, he contaminates his fantasy with cynicism, egotism, and violence: "Yo muero, en fin; y porque nunca espere / buen suceso en la muerte ni en la vida, / pertinaz estaré en mi fantasía" 'And so I'll die. And knowing that nothing good / Can happen, either in life or death, still / I'll always love you: at least my love will live' (I. 183; I. 75). Grisóstomo's suicide, like Don Quixote's own troubled knight errancy, reveals the impossibility of living out a literary dream. Sieber has well described Grisóstomo's misunderstanding: "Grisóstomo interprets [Marcela's disdainful behavior] as a sign of literary convention, as an exterior crust to be broken through, whereas in reality, it is Marcela's very being. [...] In sum Grisóstomo perceives too late that Marcela's role is Marcela in fact, that her rejection is not part of pastoral convention" (193). Due to the inability of the male pastoral fantasy to realize itself under such conditions, Grisóstomo has no other choice but to compose trite verses and ultimately commit suicide, marking a breach with the genre's symbolic commitments. Although "muerte de amor" is a fundamental discursive convention of the genre, death's actual occurrence destroys any possibility for the perpetuation of the amatory fantasy. It threatens to deplete the male community of forlorn lovers and introduces an element of chaos and violence that fundamentally contradicts the idyll's representational and ideological aims.[26]

Try as it may, this makeshift community cannot reproduce the perfecting nobility, comradeship, or aesthetic harmony so highly

---

[26] In other words, if all the shepherd lovers who contemplated suicide or claimed to be dying of love actually did, the pastoral space would be desolate and unimaginable. Referring to Grisóstomo's suicide, Poggioli thus states: "Yet, besides being a Christian, Grisóstomo was a shepherd too, and any reader well acquainted with the pastoral tradition will immediately realize that his suicide is a literary transgression as well as a mortal sin [...]. In brief, within the economy of the bucolic genre, Grisóstomo's suicide is no less arbitrary and unique than Marcela's decision to become a shepherdess in order to deny even more fully the rule of love" (170).

Sieber takes a somewhat different perspective by privileging the perpetuity offered by the poetic word: "Grisóstomo triumphs over death and history by giving himself over to poetry. [...] The poem survives to draw the verbal world around Grisóstomo, keeping him from the grasp of history and the ravages of time" (190).

valued in pastoral novels. Ambrosio, Grisóstomo's closest pastoral companion, puts his own interests before his friend's and tries to take Grisóstomo's now vacant space by defending Marcela's "buen crédito y buena fama" 'modesty and virtue' (I. 184; I. 76): "Y con esto queda en su punto la verdad que la fama pregona de la bondad de Marcela; la cual fuera de ser cruel, y un poco arrogante, y un mucho desdeñosa, la mesma envidia ni debe ni puede ponerle falta alguna" 'So Marcela's reputation for virtue, so generally acknowledge, must stand unshaken: even envy neither can nor should find fault with her, no matter how cruel she may be, and prouder than necessary, and a great deal too disdainful' (I. 184-5; I. 76). But, like Grisóstomo, he fails to produce a coherent and harmonious amatory discourse. Playing upon the absurd contradictions with which amatory discourse defines women, the ironic humor in this declaration cannot be missed. Despite the community's intent to honor their friend's memory, at the end we have an "every man for himself" scenario, with each and every one of these "shepherds" hoping to do what Grisóstomo could not: possess Marcela. Grisóstomo and his friends aim to live out a literary fantasy. But this symbolic project is sabotaged by their inability to erase their own insufficiencies and egotistical instincts. This is an idyll turned sour through its insertion into history; its collapse underscores–rather than represses–the unresolvable and conflictive desires that haunt relations between men and women, and which the pastoral metaphor had in the past been able to erase under the guise of love.[27]

There is another aspect of Marcela's behavior that is seen as singularly disruptive to the pastoral endeavor. As Poggioli points out, Marcela enters the bucolic space only to display more decisively than before her rejection of the "rule of love" of objectification and idealization (170). Of particular interest is that Marcela's repudiation does not result in her hiding from her suitors or denying them her company. Instead, Marcela willingly offers Grisóstomo, as well as all her other suitors, equitable friendship: "Que, puesto que *no huye ni se esquiva de la compañía y conversación de los pastores, y los trata cortés y amigablemente*, en llegando a descubrirle su intención

---

[27] Avalle-Arce asserts that Grisóstomo does succeed in inserting himself in a literary world, and that he makes that fantasy coincide with his "historical" existence. Nonetheless, he modifies his opinion when he adds that, "su vivir literario está inmerso en una circunstancia histórica, de ahí la presentación pendular y ambivalente" (262).

cualquiera dellos, aunque sea tan justa y santa como la del matrimonio, los arroja de sí como un trabuco" '*She doesn't avoid either the shepherds' company or their conversation, and she treats them courteously and pleasantly,* but if she finds they have any designs on her, even if it's as honest and upright as matrimony, she hurls them away like a cannon' (I. 166; I. 66, my emphasis). Although, again, her rejection of love falls well within the parameters of the convention, her direct and willing interaction with the pastoral community confuses its endeavor. Enjoying male friendship ("*no huye ni se esquiva de la compañía y conversación de los pastores*"), Marcela expects to be treated as a peer or as an equal subject. She forcefully throws the shepherds from her side only when they insist on defining her as an object of their love. Otherwise, she seeks their company and treats them "*cortés y amigablemente,*" undermining a rigid characterization as a cruel harpy. She expects the unexpected: male companionship without objectification.[28] Unfortunately, this is a notion that her suitors cannot accept but that proves to be highly disruptive to their own efforts at male bonding and community building. Instead they depict her as a tease and cannot decide whether to celebrate or condemn her unexpected behavior.

In a pastoral interlude beleaguered by irrationality, discord, and death, the most astonishing moment arrives when Marcela, perched high on a rock, delivers her famous speech. She appears from nowhere as a dissonant voice that stops the pastoral scene in its tracks, denouncing an amatory discourse that is intent on framing and limiting her *own* particular pastoral fantasy. Yvonne Jehenson explains the strategy and impact of the speech:

> What Marcela has done is taken the intellectual tools of patriarchy, used them to her cause, and turned them against their inventors. [...] Marcela is encoded within a system, a genre where the female has been silenced: she has either departed, has never existed, or is centralized as *object* of the males' desire or laments.

---

[28] As argued in the previous chapter, Cervantes's Galatea does share the pastoral topography with the shepherds. Yet, in contrast to Marcela, Galatea does not actively try to establish an unromantic friendship or partnership with her suitors. She does not respond to their demands for love but also never actively expects them to see her as anything other that an object of desire. Moreover, by the end of the text she is forced to grudgingly give into her role as "beloved" when she elicits Elicio's help in rescuing her from an arranged marriage.

> It is this tradition that Cervantes explodes and he does this through Marcela's act of speech. (27)

Notwithstanding its contestatory tone and rhetorical acuity, the effect of Marcela's speech remains the topic of some debate. In spite of its significant manipulation of "the intellectual tools of the patriarchy," for many, including Jehenson, the pastoral fantasy is only partially and momentarily disrupted by Marcela's "act of speech." From this perspective, Marcela is caught up in a strictly male dominated space that up to this moment of rhetorical bravado has offered her no opportunity to affirm her subjectivity and that re-objectifies her as soon as she departs from the funeral. Even after her speech the shepherds continue to pursue her and insult her. If we follow this logic, it could be argued that it is exactly Marcela's apparent failure to thoroughly deconstruct the male amatory fantasy that forces her into textual oblivion, never to be heard of or seen again. This is a reading that would place the interlude much closer to the ideological effect that I described regarding *La Diana* and *La Galatea* than to an undoing or explosion of the pastoral metaphor in *Don Quixote*. In other words, her absence could be interpreted as facilitating her objectification and the corresponding male narcissism. But there is an alternative way to understand Marcela's speech, its context, and its repercussions. There is no question that Marcela disappears and that her denunciation does not force her lovers to disband and altogether discard their pastoral stance. Yet, to otherwise infer that this male pastoral community continues to prosper unchanged despite Marcela's jarring intervention would require us to not differentiate between parody and its fictional referent, between the source texts and their disarticulation in *Don Quixote*. It is not the same to read a pastoral novel than to read the Marcela interlude. The evidently acerbic and pathetic tone employed throughout is an integral part of the operating parody. It reveals the contradictory and conflictive underside of the bucolic dream, thereby exposing its constructedness and frailty. For this reason what is significant about Marcela, her speech, and her disappearing act into the forest is not whether there is evidence of a submission to the pastoral fantasy, which as I have shown, is here already corrupted and veritably inoperable. What is of value in this episode is how this woman's words, acts, and agency fit into Cervantes's dismantling of the mode's formal characteristics and ideological values. In this text the pastoral fails to symbolize the tensions and disillusionment present in seventeenth-century social experience.

Marcela's speech only reiterates what she has already expressed through her acts: a refusal to sacrifice her own pastoral fantasy in order to promote its male counterpart. Her situation is structured by Cervantes as a series of traps. She is expected to choose between her desire to live as an independent subject in the forest and her assigned role as an object of desire for Grisóstomo and his fellow lovers. Or, rather, she must choose between her flight into a pastoral feminine space similar to the one alluded to by the Knight Errant in his *Edad de Oro* speech and the pastoral fantasy produced in sixteenth-century novels. From the shepherds' point of view, Marcela is made to bear the blame for Grisóstomo's death and is simultaneously cast as object of desire and as target for the lovers' hate. When she shows up at Grisóstomo's funeral Ambrosio accuses her of extreme cruelty and callous pride yet paradoxically promises her eternal obedience. From Marcela's perspective, she is simply trying to carve out a space where she can live as she wishes. Her address to this haphazard community is by and large a defense of her rejection of Grisóstomo and of the extended group of lovers. More specifically, Marcela's speech unveils the symbolic mechanisms and patriarchal rationale that uphold the pastoral fantasy at the cost of female subjectivity. She does not come to confirm the lovers' objectification, but instead to "volver por mí misma" 'I come [...] but only for myself' (I. 185; I. 77), and assert her own agency and desire.

The speech is structured around three major topics. First, Marcela wittily asserts that her allegedly perfect beauty is precisely what frees her from having to accept any and all advances from so many lovers. In a line of reasoning that may refer implicitly to Grisóstomo, and which is certainly not meant to boost the present audience's confidence, Marcela wonders why a beautiful being who is loved is simply expected to love in return, even if the suitor is ugly and according to Neoplatonic theory, detestable: "Quiérote por hermosa; hasme de amar aunque sea feo" 'I love you for your beauty; you must therefore love me, even though I'm ugly' (I. 186; I. 77). She turns this Neoplatonic logic further against the addressees by reminding them that if she were unsightly, they would not love her nor would she expect them to love her: "Si no, decidme: si como el cielo me hizo hermosa me hiciera fea, ¿fuera justo que me quejara de vosotros porque no me amábades?" 'And tell me: if Heaven had made me ugly instead of beautiful, would it be right for me to complain about you, because you did not love me?' (I. 186; I. 77). Marcela's reasoning then takes another turn and argues for a disassociation between beauty and love, in what can be read as a statement against the platonic worldview. Even if both the body and the soul were equally beautiful, there is no requirement that can or should force amatory correspondence, "que no todas las hermosuras enamoran" 'for everything beautiful does not inspire love' (I. 186; I. 77). Marcela further exposes the impracticality of the Neoplatonic amatory fantasy when she makes the rational assumption that if every beauty was loved and in return loved each and every one of her suitors, "sería un andar las voluntades confusas y descaminadas [...] porque siendo infinitos los sujetos hermosos, infinitos habían de ser los deseos" 'desire would become confused and lose its way, [...] since an infinity of things beautiful makes for an infinity of desires' (I. 186; I. 77). As she makes clear in a beautifully constructed simile, physical beauty is an unsolicited gift from Nature that ironically performs as a serpent's venom; although it may sting and intoxicate, the "serpent" cannot be blamed for its effects: "[A]sí como la víbora no merece ser culpada por la ponzoña que tiene, puesto que con ella mata, por habérsela dado naturaleza, tampoco yo merezco ser reprehendida por ser hermosa" '[A]nd just as the viper should not be blamed for its venom, which has been given it by nature, even though it kills with that venom, so too I should not be reproached for my beauty' (I. 186; I. 77). Not to be outdone by Grisóstomo's legendary mastery of Platonic discourse, she turns around her own argument and manipulates to her advantage a strict correlation between inner and outer beauty and love: She who is beautiful should not be expected to love, for correspondence implies a loss of chastity, which in turn would make the soul, and as a result her whole being ugly.

> La honra y las virtudes son adornos del alma, sin las cuales el cuerpo, aunque lo sea, no debe de parecer hermoso. Pues si la honestidad es una de las virtudes que al cuerpo y alma más adornan y hermosean, ¿por qué la ha de perder la que es amada por hermosa, por corresponder a la intención de aquel que, por sólo su gusto, con todas sus fuerzas e industrias procura que la pierda? (I. 186)

> Honor and indeed all the virtues grace the soul and, whatever else the body may be, without them it cannot claim to be beautiful. And if modesty is one of the virtues that most adorn both body and soul, why does she who is loved for her beauty have to lose her modesty, in order to reward the desire of a man who, just for his own pleasure, strives as hard and as forcefully as he can to make her lose it? (I. 77-8)

By exploiting the pastoral's dependence on Platonic discourse, Marcela legitimizes her flight and chosen solitude, blaming Grisóstomo and his companions for wanting her to become an unworthy being when they chastise her for rejecting their love.

Second, Marcela embarks on a compelling declaration of independence made manifest in her separate pastoral sojourn: "Yo nací libre, y para poder vivir libre escogí la soledad de los campos. Los árboles destas montañas son mi compañía, y las claras aguas destos arroyos mis espejos; con los árboles y con las aguas comunico mis pensamientos y hermosura" 'I was born free, and I chose the solitude of the fields so I could live free. I find my friends among the trees in these mountains; the clear waters of these streams are my mirrors; I share my thoughts with the trees and the streams, as I share my beauty with them' (I. 186; I. 78). Believing her autonomy to be her birthright, Marcela exercises her agency–despite all protestations and social expectations–by choosing to live alone in the countryside. This is a solitude that effectively sets her apart and frees her physically, economically, and psychologically from unwelcome male influence and control. Moreover, she inhabits a bower where she is at one with a welcoming and plentiful Nature. With no consideration for the prescriptions of silence imposed by society, she can speak her mind and cultivate her beauty, whether physical, intellectual, or spiritual. Furthermore, but seemingly no less important for Marcela, her freedom is nourished by the companionship of the shepherdesses who tend their flocks with her, subsidized by her own wealth: "La conversación honesta de las zagalas destas aldeas y el cuidado de *mis cabras* me entretiene" 'Chaste conversation with the shepherdesses I meet, and taking care of *my goats*, are all the diversions I need' (I. 188; I. 78-9, my emphasis). In a society where her material possessions had been as attractive as her beauty, Marcela willfully decides to bankroll her own independence. It is here, therefore, among mountains, trees, springs, her goats, and her fellow countrywomen where she can, without restraint, exercise her right to be her own self.

Third, Marcela forcefully defends her chosen independence by adopting a superior tone against the insulting complaints of her "lovers."²⁹ Like her weapons, the fire and the spear, she will hurt those who claim her. Notwithstanding her aversion to love, Marcela soundly puts the responsibility of pain and disillusionment on those who insist on pursuing her. Despite her honest and plainly stated desire to live and share her "fruit" solely with the earth ("vivir en perpetua soledad, y de que sola la tierra gozase el fruto de mi recogimiento y los despojos de mi hermosura" 'to live forever alone, and that only the earth would ever possess the fruits of either my mind or my body' [I. 187; I. 78]), Grisóstomo blindly persisted. And it is this hopeless chase which leads him to a destructive, and unwarranted, desperation:

> [E]n fin, de ninguno dellos, bien se puede decir que antes le mató su porfía que mi crueldad. [...] [Y] si él, con todo este desengaño, quiso porfiar contra la esperanza y navegar contra el viento, ¿qué mucho se anegase en la mitad del golfo de su desatino? Si yo le entretuviera, fuera falsa; si le contentara, hiciera contra mi mejor intención y prosupuesto. Porfió desengañado, desesperó sin ser aborrecido. (I. 187)

> [S]o you might better blame their stubbornness than any cruelty of mine for their deaths. [...] [S]o that if he, in spite of all this straightforward explanation, chose to insist, against all reasonable expectations, and to sail right against the wind, is there any wonder that he drowned out in the deepest waters of his own folly? Had I dallied with him, I'd have been a deceiver; had I made him happy, I'd have betrayed what I myself most wanted and strove for. I told him the truth, and he persisted; he fell into despair, but I never hated him. (I. 78)

Breaking with the conventional pastoral love lyric, Marcela defines the insistent forlorn lover not as noble and enlightened, but as a fool or "desatinado," whose complaints have no validity and whose sacrifice is worthless, unbecoming, and definitively not her responsibility. She insists on her right to decide her destiny and expects

---

²⁹ I am indebted to Montserrat Pérez Toribio's for her analysis of Marcela's speech as an example of a Butlerian "hate speech act."

her suitors to take her words seriously, respect her wishes, and not seek her company or expect her to comply with their requests. Heaven has not willed that she fall in love and, to any extent, this is a decision that is hers to make and no one else's. What is more, she mocks those who attack her by highlighting the inconsistency in professing love for a beloved whose character is so poorly considered: "El que me llama fiera y basilisco, déjeme como cosa perjudicial y mal; el que me llama ingrata, no me sirva; el que desconocida, no me conozca; quien cruel, no me siga; que esta fiera, este basilisco, esta ingrata, cruel y esta desconocida, ni los buscará, servirá, conocerá ni seguirá en ninguna manera" 'He who calls me savage, and a basilisk, should shun me as something dangerous and evil; he who calls me ungrateful should not woo me; if I'm fickle, stay away from me; if I'm cruel, don't come after me; because this savage beast, this stone monument, this ungrateful wretch, this cruel and fickle woman will neither seek them out, nor woo them, nor know them, nor chase after them in any way whatever' (I. 187; I. 78). Marcela's practical expectations as well as her lack of remorse for Grisóstomo's death or the suffering of her suitors, read as an antipastoral manifesto. Love for Marcela is only virtuous when both parts freely and equally comply. Otherwise, it is as I have alluded to in previous chapters, a narcissistic practice that feeds one side by obliterating the agency and particular desires of the other. By allowing Marcela's voice to so effectively unveil the repressive, inequitable, and pathetic nature of bucolic love, Cervantes's pastoral parody severely undercuts the thematic and rhetorical structures that support the pastoral fantasy. Moreover, it allows for the pastoral other to occupy center stage and deny the genre's symbolic ideality and patriarchal ideology to remain uncontested.

Marcela had started her speech declaring that she would be brief and asking the audience to pay close attention: "no será menester mucho tiempo ni gastar muchas palabras para persuadir una verdad a los discretos" 'it won't take long, nor will it waste many words, to convince wise men of the truth' (I. 185; I. 77). As innumerable texts of the period show, to be "discreto" ("discreet") is among the most desirable and admired of personal characteristics. Sebastián de Covarrubias defines the discreet man as, "el hombre cuerdo y de buen seso, que sabe ponderar las cosas y dar a cada una su lugar" 'a sane and intelligent man, who knows how to reflect upon things and give each its place' (found under "discernir," 475; my translation). What Marcela requires and expects from her audience is that it discerns the truth of her words. Primarily, it is fundamental that she shed the label of "pastora homicida" and not be held responsible for Grisóstomo's unprovoked death. More importantly, she demands that the *oyentes* accept her right to an alternative pastoral fantasy, one whose design and rules reject the narcissistic tendencies of its male counterpart. Marcela's hope is for the audience to give each "its place," accept her agency, and celebrate her chosen destiny.

Ironically, Marcela's speech seemingly has the exact opposite effect. Instead of exercising their discretion, many of the lovers are ready to follow her and pursue their own intentions. But unlike that of *La Diana* or *La Galatea*, *Don Quixote*'s narrative voice does not unilaterally sustain the shepherds' worldview. To the contrary, it directly points at their lack of discernment: "Y algunos dieron muestras [...] de quererla seguir, *sin aprovecharse del manifiesto desengaño que habían oído*" '–those [...]–showed signs of wanting to follow after her, *paying no attention to the plain truths they had heard*' (I. 188; I. 79, my emphasis). *Don Quixote* thus presents this community's pursuit of Marcela as an intellectual and moral failure, and Grisóstomo's death as a senseless and wasteful fiasco. Seen from this perspective, Ambrosio's epitaph for the dead shepherd echoes a hollow ring, and underscores the inability of pastoral discourse to recognize the voice and particular desires of the woman it purports to adore.

Don Quixote's reaction at the end of Marcela's speech has also been read as confirming Marcela's objectification.[30] Enthralled by her beauty and upset at her departure, the knight errant swears he will follow her into the countryside. Yet I believe that his reaction and its connection to his own imagined idyll are not coincidental. Marcela's interlude corresponds to and actualizes the Knight Errant's imaginary mythic past where beautiful, innocent women roamed: "andaban las hermosas y simples zagalejas de valle en valle y de otero en otero en trenza y en cabello" 'Simple, beautiful country damsels, their hair braided or worn round their heads, roamed

---

[30] For example, Jehenson interprets Don Quixote's reaction strictly within an objectifying mechanism. According to Jehenson, "Marcela has subverted the male view of her as a textual object, but she remains a sexual object. Everyone, including Don Quixote, wants to go after this beautiful object" (30-1).

from valley to valley, in that time, and from hill to hill' (I. 156; I. 59). If we take seriously Don Quixote's *raison d'être*, his protective attitude toward Marcela goes beyond simple objectification; he is seeking to guard a space where Marcela can live out her own feminine idyll as he imagined it in his Golden Age speech. Thinking back to the end of his speech, Don Quixote contrasts the Golden to the Iron Age:

> Las doncellas y la honestidad andaban, como tengo dicho, por dondequiera, sola y señora, sin temor que la ajena desenvoltura y lascivo intento le menoscabasen. [...]. Y agora, en estos nuestros detestables siglos, no está segura ninguna [...]. Para cuya seguridad, andando más los tiempos y creciendo más la malicia, se instituyó la orden de los caballeros andantes, para defender las doncellas, amparar las viudas y socorrer a los huérfanos y a los menesterosos. (I. 157)

> Damsels and decency both walked everywhere, as I have said, either alone or chaperoned, unafraid that impudence and lust might attempt to menace them; [...]. But now, in our era of abominations, none of them are safe [...]. And for their protection, as time went on and wickedness grew, the order of knights errant was established, to defend damsels, shelter widows, and succor orphans and those in need. (I. 60)

The purpose of knighthood is to protect women from the libidinal desire that constantly threatens them in the Iron Age. Don Quixote's insistence in following Marcela should therefore be interpreted as an attempt to keep out the encroachment of a world that would sully her willed chastity: "Ninguna persona, de cualquier estado y condición que sea, se atreva a seguir a la hermosa Marcela, so pena de caer en la furiosa indignación mía [...] en lugar de ser seguida y perseguida, sea honrada y estimada de todos los buenos del mundo, pues muestra que en él ella es sola la que con honesta intención vive" "'Let no one, no matter what his rank or state, dare to follow after the beautiful Marcela, under penalty of incurring my implacable wrath. [...] instead of being followed and persecuted, she be honored and appreciated by all good men in this world, having shown herself to be the only woman alive who can hold to such impeccable modesty'" (I. 188; I. 79). For Don Quixote Marcela embodies the seemingly lost Golden Age of women unfettered by the corrupting effects of love. Not without irony, it is Don Quixote who seems to be the most *discreto*. He has clearly understood the meaning of Marcela's words and honors her desire to remain alone in the countryside. For this reason he is willing to follow her and defend with his arms her choice and liberty.

In the end, Don Quixote's assumed role as knight is precisely what precludes him from entering a pastoral space he had imagined, and which Marcela brings into being and makes a reality. He is a man whose mission pertains to the Iron Age and his presence would only bring in elements foreign to Marcela's vision of a life free from male desire and objectification. Despite his best efforts, this female pastoral space proves to be elusive and ultimately inaccessible: "[É]l y su escudero se entraron por el mismo bosque donde vieron que se había entrado la pastora Marcela; y, habiendo andado más de dos horas por él, buscándola por todas partes sin poder hallarla, vinieron a parar en un prado lleno de fresca hierba [...]" '[H]e and his squire went into the same wood where, as they'd seen, the shepherdess Marcela had gone. After proceeding for more than two hours, searching everywhere but unable to find her, they stopped at a meadow full of fresh grass' (I. 190; I. 81). They have entered the *locus amoenus* but what emerges is Rocinante's libidinal desire for the *yangüeses'* mares, in what is obviously and hilariously characterized as a reflection of Don Quixote's own repressed sexual hunger. Plainly, Marcela's desire to live out her own pastoral fantasy—one which does not require the participation of men as lovers or as protectors—would be ruined by Don Quixote's presence. When looked at from this perspective, the episode's most subtle irony lies in how Don Quixote's speech and his vision of a female pastoral space per force make superfluous his own role as a lover and as a defender of Marcela's honor, thus rejecting the motivating forces behind his knight errancy. As envisioned in the Golden Age speech, Marcela and her *zagalejas* are entitled to and can alone sustain an unspoiled female pastoral space. This conclusion to the interlude masterfully contributes to the text's parodic effects. But again it is through parody and its dismantling of pastoral convention and ideology that Marcela can emerge and uphold a textual—and extra-textual—existence independent from the objectifying influence of both her pastoral suitors and this eager Knight.

Given the set of elements that come together in this pastoral interlude, both Quixote's vision of the Golden Age myth as well as a clear expression of female agency, we could well attribute to Marcela what George Mariscal has argued as the *Don Quixote* of 1605's "emergent individuality" (179). Mariscal does not speak directly to Marcela's significance in this text. Nevertheless, his description of the Knight's contradictory subjectivity applies just as well to the much maligned "pastora homicida":

> Don Quixote's charismatic authority originates in two distinct and seemingly antithetical ideological centers: first, the imaginary moment, now past [of the Golden Age], a utopian community founded on Christian virtues, and, second, the incipient figure of an autonomous subject (the individual) relatively free of the inherited determinants of blood and caste. [...] [D]espite the fact that one would seem to cancel out the other, their combined appeal is what makes Don Quixote such a formidable figure [...]. (187)

Mariscal goes on to lament what he views as Part II's movement away from the "extreme subjectivism of the original" (176-7). Don Quixote, vexed by the way in which the outside world appropriates his chivalric project and makes of it a source of otherness and spectacle, cannot sustain his radical and self-determined individuality. Marcela, in contrast, does triumph as an autonomous subject by claiming her pastoral dream as a reality that no one, not even Grisóstomo's lurking ghost, can diminish or destroy. She will go and live the rest of her life as a shepherdess tending her flock in the company of her friends, disengaged from any and all other expectations or requests. In other words, Marcela manages to realize the Quixotic project where Don Quixote ultimately fails. Her "mad" quest for a self-defined pastoral retreat prevails even if Don Quixote's chivalric quest ultimately fails.[31]

As in Marcela's case, Leandra's interlude has at its center a female protagonist whose staunch will and agency distinguish her from her pastoral predecessors. If, as Poggioli has pointed out, "the

---

[31] Sieber speaks to this idea when he states that "Marcela finishes her speech and disappears into "lo más cerrado de un monte que allí cerca estaba." The word *cerrado* also alludes to Marcela's closed mind and world, a world of madness characteristic of Foucault's "organisation singulière, abusive, dont la particularité obstinée fait la folie." Don Quijote protects her solitude and confirms her madness with his own" (194). I, as my analysis demonstrates, take a less severe stance of Marcela's "mad" flight into "lo más cerrado de un monte que allí cerca estaba."

pastoral insists on the preliminaries of love, rather than its final consummation" (54), Leandra's story introduces the disabling presence of a desiring female sexuality. Leandra never desires to be or pretends to be a shepherdess. Still, she is inadvertently chosen as the motivating force behind this second pastoral sojourn in *Don Quixote*. As I will demonstrate, her personal and sexual agency is thus integral to the explosion of yet another pastoral interlude in this Cervantine text.

Leandra, like Marcela before her, is known throughout as an incredibly beautiful girl, causing people to see her "como a imagen de milagros" 'like [...] some sacred miracle' (I. 591; I. 343). Also like Marcela, Leandra, the daughter of a rich peasant family, loses her mother at an early age. Attracted by her father's money, her beauty, and her youth, many suitors ask for her hand in marriage hoping to possess "tan rica joya" 'such a splendid jewel' (I. 591; I. 343). Leandra's father, unable to pick one among the many worthy suitors, offers his daughter the chance to choose for herself, "[que] era bien dejar a la voluntad de su querida hija el escoger a su gusto" 'she ought to be free to choose whoever she liked best' (I. 591; I. 343). To the apparent surprise of all involved, this is exactly what Leandra does. Contrary to Marcela, Leandra does not refuse love and escape to the solitude of the bucolic space. Instead, she executes her will and runs away with Vicente de la Rosa, a young brash soldier who has recently returned from Italy, and who evidently is not among those whom her father had in mind when he awarded her freedom of choice.

True to the literary stereotype of the Italianate soldier, Vicente is a poor country bumpkin who upon his return from his military adventures, is transformed into an extravagant and gender-bending figure: "[V]olvió el mozo [...] vestido a la soldadesca, pintado con mil colores, lleno de mil dijes de cristal y sutiles cadenas de acero. Hoy se ponía una gala y mañana otra; pero todas sutiles, pintadas, de poco peso y menos tomo" 'Vincente came back, decked out in all shorts of military finery, splashed with a thousand different colors, covered with a thousand crystal trinkets and hammered steel chains. He wore one uniform today and another tomorrow, but all fancy, gaudy, without much weight and worth even less' (I. 592; I. 343). The satirical effect of this type depends on the arrogance and feminized loquaciousness of the returning soldier. And Vicente does not disappoint. Constantly changing his dress in order to make it seem as if he had a great number of clothing and demonstrating equal inventiveness with the presentation of his lineage, his adventures, and musical and poetic talents, Vicente constructs an extraordinary mirage. Fascinated by the soldier's striking appearance, Leandra is unable to resist the temptation and enthusiastically falls in love:

> [E]ste Vicente de la Rosa, este bravo, este galán, este músico, este poeta fue visto y mirado muchas veces de Leandra [...]. Enamoróla el oropel de sus vistosos trajes; encantáronla sus romances, que de cada uno que componía daba veinte traslados, llegaron a sus oídos las hazañas que él de sí mismo había referido, y, finalmente, que así el diablo lo debía de tener ordenado, ella se vino a enamorar dél, antes que en él naciese presunción de solicitalla. (1. 593)
>
> [T]his Vincente de Rosa, this braggart, this ladies man, this musician, this poet, had lots of chances to see and be seen by Leandra, [...]. She fell in love with all the tinsel he wore; she was charmed by his poems (because he distributed twenty copies of every one he wrote); she heard about all the great and noble deeds he'd performed (as he himself had narrated them); and, in a word, as the devil must have arranged it, she fell in love with him even before he got the idea of trying to win her. (I. 344)

In Leandra's case her agency and particular desire is thus manifested in a radically different manner from Marcela. A damsel firmly grounded in the Iron Age, Leandra willfully chooses the "amorosa pestilencia" 'amorous plague' (I. 157; I. 60) and happily "[da] con todo su recogimiento al traste" 'achieve its object in spite of all our sheltering devices, fervent in its cursed busyness' (I. 157; I. 60)–as Don Quixote had described in his Golden Age speech–in her love for Vicente. Not only does she voluntarily give into her desire, but equally significant to our discussion, she pursues a man diametrically opposed to the figure of the noble, chaste, and unadorned shepherd-lover. Leandra's affection for Vicente is of a dangerous kind and disregards the boundaries of honor and decorum, as well as her father's and proper suitors interests.

Three days after her escape, "la antojadiza" 'tickle' Leandra is found betrayed by the soldier and robbed of all her material possessions, but with her virginity still intact: "[S]in quitalle su honor, le robó cuanto tenía, y la dejó en aquella cueva, y se fue" 'the soldier had robbed her of everything she had except her honor, then just left her in the cave and gone away' (I. 594; I. 345).[32] The father, thankful that his daughter's "most precious jewel" had not been robbed, sends her to a monastery in the hope that with time the villagers will forget his daughter's impropriety. But neither the villagers, her suitors, nor the text can erase or redeem Leandra's manifest desire. Her flight well establishes her unwillingness to comply with the patriarchal prescriptions that frame her life as a beautiful and wealthy *dama*. Furthermore, the consciously risqué nature of her escape greatly hampers her father's attempts to rehabilitate her now tarnished image, making clear the disruptive nature of feminine libidinal desire: "pero los que conocían su discreción y mucho entendimiento no atribuyeron a ignorancia su pecado, sino a su desenvoltura y a la natural inclinación de las mujeres que, por la mayor parte, suele ser desatinada y mal compuesta" 'but those who knew her better, and knew her good sense and her sharp mind, could not attribute her fall to ignorance but, rather, to boldness and to the natural tendencies of women in general, which are usually, for the most part, wild and unsettled' (I. 594; I. 345).

Sequestered and among nuns, Leandra's absence predictably promotes the mass exodus of her suitors to the countryside. Completely inaccessible, Leandra promises to be a perfect object for the narcissistic lover and his community. The male pastoral fantasy is thus once more set into motion in *Don Quixote*. Yet, in spite of these seemingly propitious conditions, the shepherd-lovers fail to expunge the memory of Leandra's sexual proclivity. It is evident that the shepherds would profit from fully repressing Leandra's agency through their lyrical expression, singing instead about their own constancy and nobility. Nonetheless, this pastoral community cannot come to terms with the beloved's troublesome conduct and drastically disagrees as to how to treat her resolve to flee with Vi-

---

[32] Robert L. Hathaway has explored "that nagging question" of whether Leandra did or did not have sexual relations with Vicente. In my opinion and as it regards my reading of the episode, this question is irrelevant. Leandra's flight with Vicente–regardless of the degree of intimacy they experienced–has a series of detrimental effects with her patriarchal society that include her father locking her away, her neighbors' public derision, and her pastoral lovers fighting over her proper objectification. And perhaps most importantly, as Don Quixote himself points out, she finds herself in a situation where she can hardly exercise her own will and where she most probably finds herself to be rather unhappy.

cente. After all, Leandra had publicly wielded her independence with the wrong man. She had fallen in love with Vicente, solicited his attention, gladly believed his false promises, and freely elected to escape her father's house in order to go to "la más rica y más viciosa ciudad que había en todo el universo mundo, que era Nápoles" 'the richest and most depraved city in the whole world, which of course was Naples' (I. 594; I. 344). In a move both parallel and opposite to Marcela, Leandra flees to the city to establish her autonomy. This type of self-indulgence was never available to the traditional female protagonists of the pastoral novel, and resists the pastoral community's obliterating idealization of the beloved. We can recall Montemayor's Diana or Cervantes's own Galatea, female pastoral protagonists who can hardly escape the disabling effects of amatory rhetoric, and whose fathers decide their choice of spouses. Leandra is far from mirroring this type of feminine pastoral model. It is true that Vicente's interest in her dress, rather than in her love, seemingly trivializes Leandra's act. Nonetheless, we should not loose sight that by choosing Vicente and voluntarily running off with him, Leandra impairs the proper function of the mechanisms upon which pastoral love and ideality depend.

Feeding into the dismantling of the pastoral dream in this episode, Eugenio–one of Leandra's shepherd-lovers–continuously proclaims his annoyance with Leandra's "perdition":

> Y como en los casos de amor no hay ninguno que con más facilidad se cumpla que aquel que tiene de su parte *el deseo de la dama,* con facilidad se concertaron Leandra y Vicente, y primero que alguno de sus muchos pretendientes cayesen en la cuenta de su deseo, ya ella le tenía cumplido, habiendo dejado la casa de su querido y amado padre, que madre no la tiene, y ausentándose de la aldea con el soldado [...]. (I. 593, my emphasis)

> And since no love affairs ever go smoother than those *the lady herself wants,* Leandra and Vincente had no trouble getting together, and before any of her many suitors knew which way she was leaning, she'd already fallen, having deserted her dear, beloved papa's house (for she had no mother) and gone off with the soldier [...]. (I. 344, my emphasis)

Notwithstanding her lovers' intent to imitate the tone and content of an idealizing amatory register, Leandra's manifest sexual desire frustrates a productive poetic practice. She is a broken mirror for a community of lovers in disarray. Pivotal to the episode's comedic effect, the shepherds' versions of Leandra as object clash at their most basic levels. While some choose to wholly ignore Leandra's sexuality, others fixate on the weakness of the female condition.

> Éste la maldice y la llama antojadiza, varia y deshonesta; aquél la condena por fácil y ligera; tal la absuelve y la perdona, y tal la justicia y vitupera; uno celebra su hermosura, otro reniega de su condición, y, en fin, todos la deshonran, y todos la adoran, y de todos se estiende a tanto la locura, que hay quien se queje de desdén sin haberla jamás hablado, y aun quien se lamente y sienta la rabiosa enfermedad de los celos, que ella jamás dio a nadie; porque, como ya tengo dicho, antes se supo su pecado que su deseo. (I. 595)

> In one place there'll be fiery curses mixed with wild passion and an outcry against her lewdness; in another, she'll be pardoned and absolved, and still elsewhere condemned and reviled; someone will sing praises to her beauty, someone else says she's worthless –and, to make a long story short, everyone loathes Leandra, and everyone adores Leandra, and everyone raves so wildly that we have men whining disdainfully about her who've never even spoken to her, and others mourning, insane with jealousy, whom she's never even met–because, as I said, everyone found out about her fall before they learned about her falling in love. (I. 345)

Even though each version could be said to erase Leandra's particular motivations and desires, it is important to stress that Anselmo and Eugenio, the two main lovers, are never able to reconcile their contrary accounts of the "beloved." More precisely, they fail to wholly objectify her into specular perfection and thus are unable to form a coherent ego boosting group. Instead their voices clash, making the bower a place of dissent and contrariness.[33] As Eugenio disappointedly admits:

> Entre estos disparatados, el que muestra que menos y más juicio tiene es mi competidor Anselmo, el cual teniendo tantas cosas de

---

[33] Finello states: "[The episode's] worn-out rhetoric is meant to demonstrate the ultimate bankruptcy of pastoral fetishism" (231). Finello's analysis of the pastoral elements in *Don Quixote* is detailed in his book *Pastoral Themes and Forms in Cervantes's Fiction*.

que quejarse, sólo se queja de su ausencia; [...]. Yo sigo otro camino más fácil, y a mi parecer el más acertado, que es decir mal de la ligereza de las mujeres, de su inconstancia, de su doble trato, de sus promesas muertas, de su fe rompida, y, finalmente, del poco discurso que tienen en saber colocar sus pensamientos e intenciones que tienen. (I. 595)

Of all these madmen, the one who displays both the most and the least good sense is my rival, Anselmo, because having so many more things to complain about than he ever so much as mention, all he complains about is being kept away from her, [...]. I've taken an easier road, which also seems to me better justified, and that is to criticize the fickleness of women, their inconstancy, their double-dealing, their broken promises, the good faith they can't and won't keep, and–to sum it all up–the lack of good sense they display in directing their thoughts and desires. (I. 345-6)

This is not to say that there are no cases in the *libros de pastores* where the male protagonists enact diverging viewpoints. Again, Montemayor's *La Diana* and Cervantes's *La Galatea* provide telling examples. Sylvano's position throughout the last five books as a *desamorado* vis-à-vis Sireno's continual dedication to love in *La Diana*, or the varied positions adopted by the participants of the Eclogue in *La Galatea* immediately come to mind. Still, as I demonstrated in Chapter Two, the male pastoral community always remains tightly knit and produces coherent amatory and poetic identities for the shepherds who through their *canto amebeo*, successfully uphold the male bonds central to the bucolic fantasy. In the case of Leandra, Eugenio mocks Anselmo and does not feel he can sing along with his competitor: "Yo sigo otro camino más fácil, y a mi parecer el más acertado." Strife and dissonance are thus this group's defining characteristics. The shepherd-lovers, instead of being sustained by the group's homogeneity, find themselves frustrated and angry, as Eugenio well demonstrates in his tirade against his goat, "la Manchada." Cervantes's use of parody in this episode depends on the comic effect produced by Leandra's suitors's pathetic attempt to reproduce an amatory idyll. Moreover, the episode marks the failure of the pastoral fantasy when faced with the persistent expression of feminine desire. Unable to transform Leandra into a proper specular object and repress her libidinal agency, the pastoral metaphor at the end of Part I is fundamentally endangered and its gender ideology put under great duress.

Don Quixote's own mixed reaction to Leandra's story is made evident in the response he offers to Eugenio's complaint. Although he, as a knight errant, is aware of his duty to uphold feminine honor and chastity, Don Quixote contradictorily wishes he could liberate Leandra from her present confinement. He wants to please the shepherd, but above all else recognizes Leandra's own desire and is sure of her unhappiness under the nuns' supervision: "que yo sacara del monasterio, donde, sin duda alguna, debe estar contra su voluntad, a Leandra" 'I'd rescue your Leandra from that convent, where she's plainly being held against her will' (I. 596; I. 346). This is the last mention of Leandra in the text and one that fittingly plays up her insistent agency and its role in upsetting the reproduction of pastoral ideology. By Eugenio's account, Leandra embodies all the deficiencies that make the female gender untrustworthy and inferior. Yet, if we follow Don Quixote's final word, Leandra's "voluntad" is what must be respected and protected despite her lover's protest.

The inability of the idyll to successfully assimilate the presence of a desiring female subject is again confirmed at the end of Part II of *Don Quixote* and the final pitch for a pastoral retreat. Tired, beaten, and with the fantasy of the "caballería andante" rapidly disintegrating, Don Quixote proposes an escape to the countryside. Accompanied by Sancho, the priest, the barber, and Sansón Carrasco, they would assume new identities as shepherds, take on new names, and sing poems in honor of their beloved ladies. Although there are many potential issues that underlie this particular pastoral's frustrated inception, it can be argued that the problem of female agency is pivotal and most disruptive to the Knight Errant's last chance for literary flight.

Sanchica, Sancho's pubescent daughter, is a female character whose association with the pastoral fantasy is made possible only through her own father's description of her as a "ninfa verde del bosque" 'nymph in the green wood' (II. 129; II. 423) and his musings about a pastoral escape at the end of Book II. Nonetheless, I would argue that Sanchica's appearance in *Don Quixote* is perhaps Cervantes's keenest dismantling of the pastoral amatory convention. Like Marcela and Leandra, Sanchica is defined throughout Book II in terms of her marriageability and the hazards associated with her sexuality. The exchanges between her parents consistently touch upon her future status as a wife, and at fourteen we are told that she is hurriedly saving for her dowry. The peril of her situation, although couched in her parents' comedic dialogue, is always at the forefront. For any young woman coming of age in Sanchica's class the question looms: Will she find a husband or will she be a loose woman? Aware of the danger, Teresa Panza pleads with her husband to secure their daughter's chances for a respectable marriage: "Mirad también que Mari Sancha, vuestra hija, no se morirá si la casamos; que me va dando barruntos que desea tanto tener marido como vos deseáis veros con gobierno; y, en fin, mejor parece la hija mal casada que bien abarraganada" 'And remember: Mari Sancha, your daughter, won't drop dead if we get her married, because I've got a hunch she's as anxious to have a husband as you are to have a governorship–and, to make a long story short, it's better to have a daughter badly married than living in sin' (II. 74; II. 385). Obviously in the midst of her social and sexual awakening, Sanchica mirrors her own father's staunch resolve to be governor of an *ínsula* in her own search for a mate. Except that in her case and as her mother well knows, Sanchica's prospective union is a matter that can be easily corrupted and go awry. While Teresa thinks of Sancho's governorship and its potential financial exploits as key to Sanchica's honorable marriage with a man of their own social class, Sancho views his daughter's future through rose-tinted glasses and deems her worthy of a nobleman. It is a classic moment of irony and comedy in the text, for while Teresa Panza is fully aware of her daughter's social place and libidinal potency, Sancho prefers to idealize his own daughter's desire, as well as her social and material circumstance, and predicts that "Sanchica ha de ser condesa, aunque tú más me digas" 'Sanchica's going to be a countess, no matter what you say' (II. 76; II. 386).

The tension between Sanchica's true state and her father idealized erasure of her sexuality is intensified and exposed in Sancho's conversation with the squire of the Knight of the Forest. In what constitutes one of Sancho's most comical interventions, he reconstructs his daughter's beauty and character through an absurd imitation of lyrical amatory language: "Dos tengo yo [hijos], que se pueden presentar al Papa en persona, especialmente una muchacha a quien crío para condesa, si Dios fuere servido, aunque a pesar de su madre [...]. Quince años ha, dos más o menos; pero es tan grande como una lanza, y tan fresca como una mañana de abril, y tiene una fuerza de un ganapán" '"I've got two [children]," said Sancho, "and they're good enough to present to the Pope Himself, especially the girl, because I'm raising her to be a countess, may it please Our Lord, in spite of her mother." [...] "Fifteen, give or take a couple of years," answered Sancho, "but she's as tall as a spear, as fresh as an April morning–and as strong as a longshoreman"' (II. 129; II. 423). Sancho intends to describe Sanchica as an object of great worth and beauty; however, he mixes into conventional idealization a description of his daughter's physique and strength that implicitly seems to point toward an aggressive sexual potency. This is a contradiction that is noted by the Knight of the Forest's squire who in his response, juxtaposes both the sublime and carnal aspects of Sanchica as a "condesa": "Partes son ésas no sólo para ser condesa, sino para ser ninfa verde del bosque. ¡Oh hideputa, puta, y qué rejo debe tener la bellaca!" '"Why, she could be a nymph in the green wood," said the Knight of the Wood's squire, "not just a countess. Oh, the little whore, I'll bet that little bitch is a strong one!"' (II. 129; II. 423). As a "ninfa verde del bosque" (and here we should not miss the connection that this fellow makes between Sancho's description and the pastoral fantasy) and a "puta," Sanchica embodies the double nature of feminine representation. The possible slippage from ideal object to whore is one that Sancho does not accept lightly but that he can only tenuously avoid: "Ni ella es puta, ni lo fue su madre, ni lo será ninguna de las dos, Dios quiriendo, mientras yo viviere" 'She's no whore, and neither is her mother, and neither of them are going to be, either, God willing, as long as I'm alive' (II. 129; II. 423). The twofold nature of Sanchica's identity as a virginal "mañana de abril" and "ninfa" and a "bellaca" cannot be repressed by Sancho's indignant rejoinder, and is bolstered by a gender ideology that limits his daughter's social existence to either being an honorable wife or a whore.

The conflict between Sanchica's idealization as a perfect object of desire and the imminence of her sexual initiation again surfaces in Teresa's letter to Sancho when he becomes governor of Barataria. Before mentioning Sanchica's good fortune at no longer having to save for her own dowry, Teresa tells Sancho of the latest news concerning the town's young women:

> Las nuevas de este lugar son que la Berrueca casó a su hija con un pintor de mala mano, que llegó a este pueblo a pintar lo que

saliese; mandóle el Concejo pintar las armas de su Majestad sobre las puertas del Ayuntamiento, pidió dos ducados, diéronselos adelantados, trabajó ocho días, al cabo de los cuales no pintó nada, y dijo que no acertaba a pintar tantas baratijas; volvió el dinero, y con todo eso, se casó a título de buen oficial; verdad es que ya ha dejado el pincel y tomado el azada, y va al campo como gentilhombre. El hijo de Pedro de Lobo se ha ordenado de grados y corona, con intención de hacerse clérigo; súpolo Minguilla, la nieta de Mingo Silvato, y hale puesto demanda de que la tiene dada palabra de casamiento; malas lenguas quieren decir que ha estado encinta dél, pero él lo niega a pies juntillas. (II. 438-9)

What's new here is that Old Lady Berrueca married her daughter to a worthless painter, who came here to paint whatever he could find; the town council hired him to paint His Majesty's coat of arms over the town hall doors, and he said it would cost two dollars, so they paid him in advance, and he worked for a whole week, but he hadn't painted anything the whole time and said he couldn't be bothered painting such a geegaws and knicknacks, so he gave them back the money and, somehow or other, he's still gotten the reputation of a reliable workman; anyway, I admit he's put down his paint brush and picked up a shovel, and now he works in the fields like a gentleman. Pedro de Lobo's son has taken minor orders, and his head's been clipped, and he means to become a priest; Minguilla, Mingo Silvato's granddaughter, found out about it, and she's hauled him into court on a breach of promise charge; there are wicked tongues saying he's gotten her pregnant, but he denies the whole thing. (II. 639)

Teresa's account is formidable in that it touches upon issues of politics, religion, and class. Nonetheless, the motivating force behind this gossip is Teresa's (and Sancho's) concern with Sanchica and their efforts to keep her within the boundaries of honor and respectability. If she were to follow her neighbors' example, Sanchica's future does not seem promising. Chances are she will either end up with a questionable choice for husband (as Berrueca's daughter) or end up tricked and pregnant (as Minguilla). In either case, it is the management of Sanchica's impending sexual initiation that is seen as the determining factor of her personal and social well-being.

This concern with Sanchica's sexuality is carried through to the end of the novel in Don Quixote and Sancho's last return to their village. No longer a governor, Sancho cannot easily or substantially provide for his daughter's dowry and has resigned himself to cast his lot once more with Don Quixote and his uncertain adventures. When the promise of a pastoral sojourn is offered by the Knight, Sancho momentarily regains his naive hope of securing for his wife and daughter both material goods and social respectability. Sancho savors the delights offered by a pastoral topography: "Qué de migas, qué de natas, qué de guirnaldas y qué de zarandajas pastoriles" 'What nice fried breadcrumbs, what good rich cream, what garlands, what little pastoral thises and thats!' (II. 550; II. 716). To Teresa, or his *pastora* Teresona, he will sing chastely, "celebrándola yo en mis versos vengo a descubrir mis castos deseos, pues no ando a buscar pan de trastrigo por las casas ajenas" 'so when I sing songs about her, and get to talking about my chaste desires, it won't look as if I'm hunting for better bread in other people's houses' (II. 549; II. 715). Sanchica, in turn, could roam freely through the countryside and provide for Sancho's most basic need, food: "Sanchica mi hija nos llevará la comida al hato" 'My daughter Sanchica will bring our meals to our shepherds' hut' (II. 550; II. 716). In this vision of idyllic wholeness, mother, daughter, and Sancho would all feast together in the plenitude of the countryside, unfettered by economic or personal adversity. In fact, the pastoral retreat initially seems to be a much more suitable ideal world for Sancho than that of chivalry. There his family and Don Quixote could be together, Sancho would not have to endure any type of physical hardship, he would always have plenty to eat, and his class status and questionable social graces would be considered largely irrelevant. In turn, Sanchica would be able to realize her potential as a "ninfa del bosque."

Yet, despite what seems to be a perfect situation for all, Sancho ultimately cannot let himself be fully taken in by the pastoral fantasy. He thinks through his daughter's situation and is unable on this occasion to erase her emerging sexuality. He then quickly retracts his initial enthusiasm for the pastoral sojourn:

> Pero, ¡guarda!, que es de buen parecer, y hay pastores más maliciosos que simples, y no querría que fuese por lana y volviese trasquilada; y también suelen andar los amores y los no buenos deseos por los campos como por las ciudades, y por las pastorales chozas como por los reales palacios, y quitada la causa se quita el pecado; y ojos que no veen, corazón que no quiebra; y más vale salto de mata que ruego de hombres buenos. (II. 550)

> But wait a minute! She's good looking, and there are shepherds who are sly and wicked, rather than innocent, and I don't want her to come for wool but go back shorn, because there are just as many lovers, and there's just as much lust, out in the fields as in the cities, and there's no difference between shepherds' huts and royal palaces, and if you take away the cause you stop the sin, and when the eyes don't see anything, the hearts don't break, and you're better off getting away from good men than asking them for help. (II. 716)

Unlike Don Quixote, Sancho is aware of the nature of all men and the danger that sexual desire poses in the countryside as in the city. In other words, Sancho understands the pastoral fantasy as a failed symbolic act or metaphor: it intends to cover over but cannot eliminate or resolve the contestatory libidinal desires that persist in the real world. He, therefore, waivers when faced with the possibility of Sanchica's becoming a desiring and desirable woman in the loose confines of a fluid bucolic geography, and is ultimately unable to fully objectify and idealize his own daughter's libidinal agency. It is true that Sancho foresees Sanchica's sexual activity as something that is going to be done to her: "no querría que fuese por lana y volviese trasquilada." Nonetheless, as the Knight Errant had warned in his Golden Age speech, even in the bower sexual exploration is a matter of choice. Despite her father's paternalistic view of the world, we can assume that Sanchica (as Leandra before her) can and will fall in love and gladly indulge her own satisfaction. Her potential presence as a desiring subject effectively invalidates Don Quixote and Sancho's pastoral fantasy and its repression of feminine desire. As in the case of Marcela and Leandra, Sanchica's irrepressible agency annuls an idealizing erasure and objectification in favor of an active position as agent of her own destiny.

In *Don Quixote* female agency veritably nullifies the possibility of the traditional pastoral. Cervantes was most certainly exploiting the pathetic and comic ironies of the male pastoral fantasy, taking to its limit the pastoral paradox of love as impossibility and hyperbolizing its effects. Nevertheless, the text opens through opposition a space where woman, as irreducible presence, is crucial and insistent. In *Don Quixote* the male pastoral fantasy collapses when confronted with Marcela, Leandra, and Sanchica as agents of their own desire. When we consider the precursory pastoral models, which include Cervantes's own *La Galatea*, we cannot ignore *Don Quixote*'s undoing of the pastoral metaphor and its ideological suppositions. It marks the progressive dismantling of the genre in the late Renaissance and the Baroque as well as Cervantes's unwillingness to be held back by the genre's formal, thematic, or symbolic parameters. Through parody Cervantes questions the fundamental suppositions of the pastoral literary vision and regenerates the mode by legitimizing and giving voice to those elements that had been repressed or ignored in the patriarchal and aristocratic conception of the bucolic fantasy. Unlike its source texts, *Don Quixote* allows full participation of woman as subject and explodes the genre's ideological prescriptions from within. Cervantes's novel brings to full view the possibility of a multiplicity of alternative pastoral spaces that challenges the homogeneous ideality of its predecessors. Even more meaningfully, it portrays psychologically complex female characters who serve as models for readers and promotes a literary milieu where writers such as María de Zayas y Sotomayor and Ana Caro can thrive.[34] In short, Cervantes's pastoral parody displaces the symbolic referent of the pastoral and offers a renewed bucolic space where the female Other, desirous and wonderfully imperfect, takes on center stage.

---

[34] For an analysis of Cervantes's influence upon María de Zayas see Hernández-Pecoraro's "*La fuerza del amor* or the Power of Self-Love: Zayas's response to Cervantes's *La fuerza de la sangre*."

WORKS CITED

Alpers, Paul J. *What is Pastoral?* Chicago: U of Chicago P, 1996.
Althusser, Louis. "Ideology and Ideological State Apparatuses." *Lenin and Philosophy and Other Essays. Part 2.* Trans. Ben Brewster. New York: Monthly Review Press, 1971. 127-186.
Anderson, James A. *Encina and Virgil.* Mississippi: Romance Monographs Inc. U of Mississippi, 1974.
Anes Álvarez, Gonzalo et al. *La economía agraria en la historia de España.* Madrid: Ediciones Alfaguara, 1978.
———. "The Agrarian 'depression' in Castile in the Seventeenth Century." *The Castilian Crisis of the Seventeenth Century. New Perspectives on the Economic and Social History of Seventeenth-Century Spain.* Ed. I.A.A. Thompson and Bartolomé Yun Casalilla. Cambridge: Cambridge UP, 1994. 60-76.
Armas, Frederick A. de. "Cervantes and the Italian Renaissance." *The Cambridge Companion to Cervantes.* Ed. Anthony J. Cascardi. Cambridge: Cambridge UP, 2002. 32-57.
———. "Ekphrasis and Eros in Cervantes' *La Galatea*: The Case of the Blushing Nymphs." *Cervantes for the 21st Century. Studies in Honor of Edward Dudley.* Ed. Francisco La Rubia Prado. Newark: Juan de la Cuesta, 2000. 33-47.
Armas Wilson, Diana de. *Allegories of Love: Cervantes's Persiles and Sigismunda.* Princeton: Princeton UP, 1991.
———. *Cervantes, the Novel, and the New World.* Oxford: Oxford UP, 2000.
Avalle Arce, Juan Bautista, ed. "Introducción." *La Diana.* Barcelona: Crítica, 1996.
———. *La novela pastoril española.* 2nd ed. Madrid: Istmo, 1974.
Azáceta, José María. *Poesía cancioneril.* Barcelona: Plaza y Janés, 1984.
Azar, Inés. *Discurso retórico y mundo pastoral en la "Égloga segunda" de Garcilaso.* Purdue University Monographs in Romance Languages Vol. 5. Amsterdam: J. Benjamins B.V., 1981.
Baena, Julio. "Poesía como mercancía en Montemayor." *Calíope* 9, no. 2 (2003): 75-91.
Bauer, Dale M. *Feminist Dialogics: a Theory of Failed Community.* Albany: State U of New York P, 1988.
Bellamy, Elizabeth Jane. "Desires and Disavowal: Speculations on the Aftermath of Stephen Greenblatt's 'Psychoanalysis and Renaissance Culture'." *CLIO* 34, no. 3 (2005): 297-315..
Bilbao, L.M. and E. Fernández de Pinedo. "Wool Exports, Transhumance and Land Use in Castile in the Sixteenth, Seventeenth and Eighteenth Centuries." *The*

Castilian Crisis of the Seventeenth Century. New Perspectives on the Economic and Social History of Seventeenth-Century Spain. Ed. I.A.A. Thompson and Bartolomé Yun Casalilla. Cambridge: Cambridge UP, 1994. 101-114.

Blecua, José Manuel, ed. *Poesía de la Edad de Oro.* 2 vols. Madrid: Castalia, 1982.

Boase, Roger. "Courtly Love in Spanish Literature: A Continuing Debate." *Journal of Hispanic Philology* 9, no. 1 (1984): 67-73.

———. "The Meaning of the Crow-Hunting Episode in Garcilaso's *Égloga segunda* (II. 260-95)." *Journal of Hispanic Philology* 13, no. 1 (1988): 41-48.

———. *The Origin and Meaning of Courtlly Love: A Critical Study of European Scholarship.* Manchester: Manchester UP, 1977.

Borrero Fernández, Mercedes. "Peasant and Aristocratic Women: their Role in the Rural Economy of Seville at the End of the Middle Ages." *Women at Work in Spain.* Ed. Marilyn Stone and Carmen Benito-Vessels. New York: Peter Lang, 1988. 11-29.

Bromberg, Rachel. *The Pastoral Novels.* Brooklyn: Postar, 1970.

Butler, Judith. *Bodies that Matter. On the Discursive Limits of 'Sex.'* New York: Routledge, 1993.

———. *Gender Trouble: Feminism and the Subversion of Identity.* New York: Routledge, 1990.

Canavaggio, Jean. *Cervantès dramaturge: un théâtre à naître.* Paris: Presses Universitaires de France, 1977.

Casalduero, Joaquín. "La bucólica, la pastoril y el amor." *Estudios de Literatura Española.* Madrid: Gredos, 1967. 64-9.

Casey, James. *Early Modern Spain. A Social History.* New York: Routledge, 1999.

Cervantes Saavedra, Miguel de. *El ingenioso hidalgo Don Quijote de la Mancha.* Ed. Luis Andrés Murillo. 2 vols. Madrid: Castalia, 1978.

———. *Don Quijote.* Trans. Burton Raffel. Ed. Diana de Armas Wilson. New York: Norton, 1999.

———. *La casa de los celos. Obras Completas, Vol. 3.* Ed. Florencio Sevilla Arroyo and Antonio Rey Hazas. Alcalá de Henares: Centro de Estudios Cervantinos, 1995. 139-237.

———. *La Galatea.* Ed. Francisco López Estrada and María Teresa López García-Berdoy. Madrid: Cátedra, 1995.

———. *Galatea. The Complete Works of Miguel de Cervantes Saavedra, Vol. II.* Trans. H. Oelsner and A. B. Welford. Ed. James Fitzmaurice-Kelly. Glasgow: Cowans and Gray, 1903.

Chevalier, Maxime. "La antigua enfadosa suegra." *"La Galatea" de Cervantes: cuatrocientos años después: Cervantes y lo pastoril.* Ed. Juan Bautista Avalle-Arce. Newark: Juan de la Cuesta, 1985. 103-9.

Cody, Richard. *The Landscape of the Mind: Pastoralism and Platonic Theory in Tasso's Aminta and Shakespeare's Early Comedies.* Oxford: Clarendon Press, 1969.

Cooper, Helen. *Pastoral. Medieval into Renaissance.* New Jersey: Rowman and Littlefield, 1977.

Covarrubias Orozco, Sebastián de. *Tesoro de la lengua castellana o española.* Ed. Felipe C. R. Maldonado and Manuel Camarero. Madrid: Castalia, 1995.

Crawford, J.P. Wickersham. *Spanish Drama before Lope de Vega.* Philadelphia: U of Pennsylvania P, 1937.

Creel, Bryant L. "Aesthetics of Change in Renaissance Pastoral: New Ideals of Moral Culture in Montemayor's *Diana.*" *Hispanófila* 99, no. 3 (1990): 3-27.

Cruz, Anne J. "Arms versus Letters: The Poetics of War and the Career of the Poet in Early Modern Spain." *European Literary Careers. The Author From Antiquity to the Renaissance.* Ed. Patrick Cheney and Frederick A. de Armas. Toronto: U of Toronto P, 2002. 186-205.

Cruz, Anne J. "Challenging Lives: Gender and Class as Categories in Early Modern Spanish Biographies." *Disciplines on the Line: Feminist Research on Spanish, Latin American, and U. S. Latina Women*. Ed. Anne J. Cruz, Rosilie Hernández-Pecoraro, and Joyce Tolliver. Newark: Juan de la Cuesta, 2003. 103-123.

———. *Discourses of Poverty: Social Reform and the Picaresque Novel in Early Modern Spain*. Toronto: U of Toronto P, 1999.

———. "Luisa de Carvajal y Mendoza y su conexión jesuita." *La mujer y su representación en las literaturas hispánicas*. Ed. Juan Villegas. Irvine: Asociación Internacional de Hispanistas, 1994. 97-104.

———. "Mirroring Others: A Lacanian Reading of the Letrados in Don Quixote." *Quixotic Desire: Psychoanalytic Perspectives on Cervantes*. Ed. Ruth Anthony El Saffar and Diana de Armas Wilson. Ithaca: Cornell UP, 1993. 93-116.

———. "Self-Fashioning in Spain: Garcilaso de la Vega." *Romanic Review* 83, no. 4 (1992): 517-38.

———. "Transgendering the Mystical Voice: Angela de Foligno, San Juan, Santa Teresa, Luisa de Carvajal." *Echoes and Inscriptions: Comparative Approaches to Early Modern Spanish Literatures*. Ed. Barbara Simerka and Christopher B. Weimer. Lewisburg, PA.: Bucknell UP, 2000. 127-41.

Cull, John T. "Another Look at Love in *La Galatea*." *Cervantes and the Pastoral. Proceedings*. Ed. José Labrador Herraiz and Juan Fernández Jiménez. Erie: Behrend College, Penn State U; Cleveland: Cleveland State U, 1986. 63-80.

Damiani, Bruno Mario. "Death in Cervantes' *Galatea*." *Cervantes: Bulletin of the Cervantes Society of America* 4, no. 1 (1984): 53-78.

———. "Didacticism in Cervantes's *Galatea*." *Diakonia: Studies in Honor of Robert T. Meyer*. Ed. Thomas Halton and Joseph P. Williman. Washington D.C.: The Catholic U of America P, 1986. 185-90.

———. *La Diana of Montemayor as Social and Religious Teaching*. Kentucky: UP of Kentucky, 1983.

Damiani, Bruno Mario and Barbara Louise Mujica. *Et in Arcadia Ego: Essays on Death in the Pastoral Novel*. Lanham: UP of America, 1990.

Darst, David H. "Techniques of Evasion in Montemayor's *Diana*." *Symposium* 43, no. 3 (1989): 184-193.

Davies, Tony. *Humanism*. London: Routledge, 1997.

Deveny, Thomas. "The Pastoral and the Epithalamium of the Spanish Golden Age." *Cervantes and the Pastoral: Proceedings*. Ed. José Labrador Herraiz and Juan Fernández Jiménez. Erie: Behrend College, Penn State U; Cleveland: Cleveland State U, 1986. 81-99.

Diego Vila, Juan. "Gelasia, Anaxárate y la flor de Gnido: Ejemplaridad mítica y reminiscencias garcilasianas en el final de *La Galatea*." *Actas del II congreso internacional de la asociación de cervantistas*. Ed. Giuseppe Grilli. Napoli: Istituto Universitario Orientale, 1995. 243-58.

Domínguez Ortiz, Antonio. *Estudios de historia económica y social de España*. Granada: Universidad de Granada, 1987.

Dudley, Edward. "The Lady is Out of this World." *Negotiating Past and Present: Studies in Spanish Literature for Javier Herrero*. Ed. David Thatcher Gies and Javier Herrero. Charlottesville: Rockwood, 1997. 176-93.

Durling, Robert M. *Petrarch's Lyric Poems*. Cambridge: Harvard UP, 1976.

Egido, Aurora. "Las dos Rosauras de *La Galatea* a *La vida es sueño*." *Atti delle Giornate Cervantine*. Ed. Carlos Romero Muñoz, Donatella Pini Moro, and Antonella Cancellier. Padua: Unipress, 1995. 39-53.

Elliot, John H. *Imperial Spain 1469-1716*. London: Penguin, 1990.

———. *The Old World and the New 1492-1650*. Cambridge: Cambridge UP, 1970.

El Saffar, Ruth Anthony. *Beyond Fiction: the Recovery of the Feminine in the Novels of Cervantes*. Berkeley: U of California P, 1984.

El Saffar, Ruth Anthony. "In Marcela's Case." *Quixotic Desire: Psychoanalytic Perspectives on Cervantes*. Ed. Ruth Anthony El Saffar and Diana de Armas. Ithaca: Cornell UP, 1993. 157-78.

Empson, William. *Some Versions of Pastoral*. Norfolk: New Directions, 1950.

Fernández-Cañadas de Greenwood, Pilar. "Las mujeres en la semántica de *La Galatea*". *Cervantes and the Pastoral: Proceedings*. Ed. José Labrador Herraiz and Juan Fernández Jiménez. Erie: Behrend College, Penn State U; Cleveland: Cleveland State U, 1986. 51-61.

———. *Pastoral Poetics; the Uses of Conventions in Renaissance Pastoral Romances: "Arcadia," "La Diana," "La Galatea," "L'Astrée."* Madrid: Studia humanitatis, 1983.

Fernández de Retana, Luis. *Doña Juana de Austria: gobernadora de España, hermana de Felipe II, madre de don Sebastián el Africano, Rey de Portugal, fundadora de las Descalzas Reales de Madrid, 1535-1573*. Madrid: Editorial El Perpetuo Socorro, 1995.

Feros, Antonio. *Kingship and Favoritism in the Spain of Philip III, 1598-1621*. Cambridge: Cambridge UP, 2000.

Ferrer Valls, Teresa. *Nobleza y Espectáculo Teatral (1535-1622)*. Valencia: UNED, 1993.

Ficino, Marsilio. *Commentary on Plato's Symposium on Love*. Trans. and ed. by Sears Jayne. Dallas: Spring Publications, 1985.

Finello, Dominick L. *Pastoral Themes and Forms in Cervantes's Fiction*. Lewisburg: Bucknell University Press; London: Associated UP, 1994.

Forcione, Alban. "Cervantes en busca de una pastoral auténtica." *Nueva Revista de Filología Hispánica* 36, no. 2 (1988): 1011-43.

———. "Marcela and Grisóstomo and the Consummation of *La Galatea*." *On Cervantes: Essays for L. A. Murillo*. Ed. James A. Parr. Newark: Juan de la Cuesta, 1991. 47-62.

Frenk, Margit. "Transculturación de la voz popular femenina en la lírica renacentista." *Images de la femme en Espagne aux XVIe et XVIIe siècles: Des traditions aux renouvellements et à l'emergence d'images nouvelles*. Ed. Augustin Redondo. Paris: Presses de la Sorbonne Nouvelle, 1994. 91-102.

Freud, Sigmund. "Civilization and its Discontents." *The Standard Edition of the Complete Psychological Works of Sigmund Freud*. Trans. and ed. James Strachey. Vol. 21. London: Hogarth, 1962.

———. "A Difficulty in the Path of Psycho-Analysis." *The Standard Edition of the Complete Psychological Works of Sigmund Freud*. Trans. and ed. James Strachey. Vol. 17. London: Hogarth, 1962.

———. "Group Psychology and the Analysis of the Ego." *The Standard Edition of the Complete Psychological Works of Sigmund Freud*. Trans. and ed. James Strachey. Vol. 18. London: Hogarth, 1962.

———. "Mourning and Melancholia." *The Standard Edition of the Complete Psychological Works of Sigmund Freud*. Trans. and ed. James Strachey. Vol. 17. London: Hogarth, 1962.

———. "On Narcissism: An Introduction." *The Standard Edition of the Complete Psychological Works of Sigmund Freud*. Trans. and ed. James Strachey. Vol. 14. London: Hogarth, 1962.

Friedman, Edward H. *The Unifying Concept: Approaches to the Structure of Cervantes' Comedias*. South Carolina: Spanish Literature Publications Co., 1981.

García García, Bernardo J. *La Nueva Babilonia de España*. Madrid: Akal, S.A., 2000.

García Martín, Pedro. *La Mesta*. Madrid: Historia 16, 1989.

Gaylord, Mary. "Cervantes' other fiction." *The Cambridge Companion to Cervantes*. Ed. Anthony J. Cascardi. Cambridge: Cambridge UP, 2002. 100-30.

Gaylord, Mary. "The Language of Limits and the Limits of Language: The Crisis of Poetry in *La Galatea*." *Modern Language Notes* 97 (1982): 254-71.
Gelabert, Juan E. "Urbanisation and Deurbanisation in Castille, 1500-1800." *The Castilian Crisis of the Seventeenth Century. New Perspectives on the Economic and Social History of Seventeenth-Century Spain*. Ed. I.A.A. Thompson and Bartolomé Yun Casalilla. Cambridge: Cambridge UP, 1994. 182-205.
Gicovate, Bernard. *Garcilaso de la Vega*. Boston: Twayne, 1975.
Gifford, Terry. *Pastoral*. London: Routledge, 1999.
Goldberg, Jonathan. *Desiring Women Writing: English Renaissance Examples*. Stanford: Stanford UP, 1997.
Grant, Michael and Hazel, John. *Who's Who in Classical Mythology*. Oxford: Oxford UP, 1993.
Graves, Robert. *The Greek Myths: 1*. London: Penguin, 1960.
Greenblatt, Stephen. "Psychoanalysis and Renaissance Culture." *Literary Theory/ Renaissance Texts*. Ed. Patricia Parker and David Quint. Baltimore: Johns Hopkins UP, 1986. 210-224.
Grosz, Elizabeth. *Jacques Lacan: A Feminist Introduction*. Sydney: Allen and Unwin, 1990.
Guevara, Antonio de. *Menosprecio de corte y alabanza de aldea*. Ed. Asunción Rallo Gruss. Madrid: Cátedra, 1984.
Haber, Judith D. *Pastoral and the Poetics of Self-Contradiction*. Cambridge: Cambridge UP, 1994.
Hanke, Lewis. *All Mankind is One; a Study of the Disputation between Bartolomé de Las Casas and Juan Ginés de Sepúlveda in 1550 on the Intellectual and Religious Capacity of the American Indians*. DeKalb: Northern Illinois UP, 1974.
Hathaway, Robert L. "Leandra and that Nagging Question." *Cervantes: Bulletin of the Cervantes Society of America* 15, no. 2 (1995): 58-74.
Hebreo, León. *Diálogos de Amor*. Trans. Inca Garcilaso de la Vega. Buenos Aires: Espasa-Calpe, 1947.
Hernández-Pecoraro, Rosilie. "'Busco la muerte en mi daño, que ella es vida a mi dolencia': diversas manifestaciones de la muerte en *La Galatea*." *Estas primicias del ingenio. Jóvenes cervantistas en Chicago*. Ed. Francisco Caudet and Kerry Wilks. Madrid: Castalia, 2003. 113-34.

———. "*La fuerza del amor* or the Power of Self-Love: Zayas's response to Cervantes's *La fuerza de la sangre*." *Hispanic Review* 70 (2002): 39-57.
Hutchinson, Steven. "Desire Mobilized in Cervantes' Novels." *Journal of Hispanic Philology* 14, no. 2 (1990): 159-74.
Izquierdo Izquierdo, José Antonio. *Diego López o el virgilianismo español en la escuela del Brocense*. Cáceres: Institución Cultural El Brocense, 1989.
Jakobson, Roman. "Two Aspects of Language and Two Types of Aphasic Disturbances." *Fundamentals of Language*. 4th ed. The Hague: Mouton, 1980. 69-96.
Jameson, Fredric. *The Political Unconscious. Narrative as a Socially Symbolic Act*. Ithaca, NY: Cornell UP, 1981.

———. "The Cultural Logic of Late Capitalism." *Postmodernism, or, The Cultural Logic of Late Capitalism*. Durham: Duke UP, 1991. 1-54.
Jehenson, Yvonne. "The Pastoral Episode in Cervantes' *Don Quijote*: Marcela Once Again." *Cervantes* 20, no. 2 (1991): 15-35.
Johnson, Carroll B. "'Amor-Aliqua Vincit': Erotismo y Amor en la *Diana*." *Erotismo en las letras hispánicas: Aspectos, modos y fronteras*. Ed. Luce López-Baralt and Francisco Márquez Villanueva. México: El Colegio de México, 1995. 165-81.

———. *Cervantes and the Material World*. Urbana and Chicago: U of Illinois P, 2000.

Johnson, Carroll B. "Cervantes' *Galatea*: The Portuguese Connection, I." *Iberoromania: Zeitschrift für die Iberoromanischen Sprachen und Literaturen in Europa and Amerika/ Revista Dedica* 23 (1986): 91-105.

———. "Montemayor's *Diana*: A Novel Pastoral." *Bulletin of Hispanic Studies* 48, no. 1 (1971): 20-35.

Kagan, Richard. *Lucrecia's Dreams: Politics and Prophecy in Sixteenth-Century Spain.* Berkeley: U of California P, 1990.

Kamen, Henry. *Crisis and Change in Early Modern Spain.* Brookfield: Variorum, 1993.

———. "Golden Age, Iron Age: A Conflict of Concepts in the Renaissance." *Journal of Medieval and Renaissance Studies* 4 (1974): 135-155.

Klein, Julius. *La Mesta.* Trans. C. Muñoz. Madrid: Alianza Editorial, 1936, 1979.

Lacan, Jacques. *Le Séminaire. Livre IV. La relation d'objet, 1956-57.* Ed. Jacques-Alain Miller. Paris: Seuil, 1994.

———. "Some Reflections on the Ego." *International Journal of Psychoanalysis* 34 (1953): 11-17.

———. "The Mirror Stage as Formative of the Function of the I." *Écrits. A Selection.* Trans. Alan Sheridan. New York: Norton, 1977. 1-7.

———. *The Seminar. Book I. Freud's Papers on Technique, 1953-1954.* Trans. John Forrester. New York: Norton, 1988.

———. *The Seminar. Book II. The Ego in Freud's Theory and in the Technique of Psychoanalysis.* Trans. Sylvia Tomaselli. New York: Norton, 1988.

———. "The Split Between the Eye and the Gaze." *The Four Fundamental Concepts of Psycho-Analysis.* Trans. Alan Sheridan. New York: Norton, 1981. 67-78.

Lapesa, Rafael. *La trayectoria poética de Garcilaso.* Madrid: Revista de Occidente, 1948.

León, Fray Luis de. *La perfecta casada.* Mexico: Editorial Porrúa, 1999.

———. *The Perfect Wife.* Trans. Alice Philena Hubbard. Denton: College Press, T.S.C. W., 1943.

López Estrada, Francisco. "Introducción." *Los siete libros de la Diana.* 3rd ed. Ed. Francisco López Estrada. Madrid: Espasa-Calpe, 1962.

———. *Los libros de pastores en la literatura española.* Madrid: Gredos, 1974.

López Estrada, Francisco, Javier Huerta Calvo, and Víctor Infantes de Miguel. *Bibliografía de los Libros de Pastores en la Literatura Española.* Cuadernos de Filología Hispánica. Madrid: Universidad Complutense de Madrid, 1984.

López-Salazar Pérez, J. *Mesta, pastos y conflictos en el campo de Calatrava durante el siglo XVI.* Madrid: Centro de Estudios Históricos, 1987.

Lorraine, Tamsin E. *Gender, Identity, and the Production of Meaning.* Boulder: Westview, 1990.

Losada, Ángel. "The controversy between Sepúlveda and Las Casas in the junta of Valladolid." *Bartolomé de las Casas in History: Toward an Understanding of the Man and his Work.* Ed. Juan Friede and Benjamin Keen. DeKalb: Northern Illinois UP, 1971. 279-308.

Maravall, José Antonio. *Carlos V y el pensamiento político del Renacimiento.* Madrid: Instituto de Estudios Políticos, 1960.

———. *Utopia and Counterutopia in the "Quixote."* Trans. Robert W. Felkel. Detroit: Wayne State UP, 1991.

Marinelli, Peter V. *Pastoral.* Critical Idiom, no. 15. London: Methuen, 1971.

Mariscal, George. *Contradictory Subjects: Quevedo, Cervantes, and Seventeenth-Century Spanish Culture.* Ithaca, NY: Cornell UP, 1991.

Marks, Morley Hawk. "Deformación de la tradición pastoril en *La casa de los celos* de Miguel de Cervantes." *Cervantes and the Pastoral: Proceedings.* Ed. José Labrador Herraiz and Juan Fernández Jiménez. Erie: Behrend College, Penn State U; Cleveland: Cleveland State U, 1986. 129-38.

Márquez Villanueva, Francisco. "Los joyeles de Felismena." *Revue de Littérature Comparée* 52 (1978): 157-178.
Martin, Adrienne L. "Apuntes en torno a 'mito' y deseo homosexual en *La Diana* de Montemayor." *Lecturas críticas de textos hispánicos. Estudios de literatura española. Siglos de Oro*. Ed. Florencio Calvo and Melchora Romanos. Vol. 2. Buenos Aires: Universidad de Buenos Aires, 2000. 99-106.
———. *Cervantes and the Burlesque Sonnet*. Berkeley: U of California P, 1991.
Mazzio, Carla and Douglas Trevor, ed. *Historicism, Psychoanalysis, and Early Modern Culture*. New York: Routledge, 2000.
Menéndez Pelayo, Marcelino. *Orígenes de la novela*. 2nd ed. Ed. Enrique Sánchez. Vol. 1. Madrid: CSIC, 1961.
Montemayor, Jorge de. *La Diana*. 3rd ed. Ed. Asunción Rallo. Madrid: Cátedra, 1999.
———. *The Diana*. Trans. RoseAnna M. Mueller. Lewiston: Edwin Mellen, 1989.
Montero, Juan. "¿Mató Montemayor a Celia? La historia de Felismena a la luz de sus fuentes." *Hommage à Robert Jammes*. Ed. Francis Cerdan. Vol. 3. Toulouse: Presses Universitaires du Mirail, 1994. 865-74.
Montrose, Louis Adrian. "The Elizabethan Subject and the Spenserian Text." *Literary Theory/Renaissance Texts*. Ed. Patricia Parker and David Quint. Baltimore: Johns Hopkins UP, 1986. 303-40.
Morgan, Thaïs E. *Men Writing the Feminine Literature, Theory, and the Question of Genders*. Ed. Thaïs E. Morgan. Albany: State U of New York P, 1994.
Mujica, Barbara. *Iberian Pastoral Characters*. Washington, D.C.: Scripta Humanistica, 1986.
Nader, Helen, ed. *Power and Gender in Renaissance Spain. Eight Women of the Mendoza Family, 1450-1650*. Urbana and Chicago: U of Illinois P, 2004.
Nalle, Sara T. "Literacy and Culture in Early Modern Castile." *Past and Present* 125 (1989): 65-96.
Olivares, Julián and Elizabeth S. Boyce. *Tras el espejo la musa escribe: Lírica femenina de los Siglos de Oro*. Madrid: Siglo Veintiuno, 1993.
Ovid. *Metamorphoses*. Trans. and ed. Charles Martin. New York: Norton, 2004.
Paiewonsky-Conde, Edgar. "Cervantes y la teoría renacentista del deseo." *Anales Cervantinos* 23 (1985): 71-81.
Patterson, Annabel M. *Pastoral and Ideology: Virgil to Valéry*. Berkeley and Los Angeles: U of California P, 1987.
Pérez, José C. "El amor en la *Diana* de Montemayor." *Explicación de textos literarios* 19, no. 2 (1990-91): 60-66.
Pérez Toribio, Montserrat. "Boquitas pintadas: supervivencia lingüística en los discursos subversivos de los personajes femeninos cervantinos." Annual Cervantes Symposium. The Newberry Library, Chicago, IL. April 2002.
Perry, Mary Elizabeth. *Gender and Disorder in Early Modern Seville*. Princeton: Princeton UP, 1990.
Perry, T. Anthony. "Ideal Love and Human Reality in Montemayor's *La Diana*." *PMLA* 84 (1969): 227-34.
Poggioli, Renato. *The Oaten Flute*. Cambridge: Harvard UP, 1975.
Rabasa, José. *Inventing America. Spanish Historiography and the Formation of Eurocentrism*. Norman: U of Oklahoma P, 1993.
Rhodes, Elizabeth. "Skirting the Men: Gender Roles in Sixteenth-Century Pastoral Books." *Journal of Hispanic Philology* 11, no. 2 (1987): 131-49.
———. *The Unrecognized Precursors of Montemayor's "Diana."* Columbia: University of Missouri Press, 1992.
Ringhofer, Kelly Rae. "Portuguese Influences on the Court of Juana of Austria, Princess of Portugal: The Regency in Spain, 1554-1559." Renaissance Society of America Annual Meeting. New York City, NY. April 2004.

Rivers, Elias L. *Garcilaso de la Vega: Poems, a Critical Guide.* London: Grant and Cutler, 1980.

———. "Pastoral, Feminism, and Dialogue in Cervantes." *La Galatea de Cervantes: cuatrocientos años después.* Ed. Juan Bautista Avalle-Arce. Newark: Juan de la Cuesta, 1985. 7-15.

Rosenmeyer, Thomas G. *The Green Cabinet: Theocritus and the European Pastoral Lyric.* Berkeley: University of California Press, 1969.

Ruiz Martín, Felipe. "Pastos y ganaderos en Castilla: La Mesta, 1450-1600." *Mesta, transhumancia y lana en la España moderna.* Ed. Felipe Ruiz Martín and Ángel García Sanz. Barcelona: Crítica/Fundación Duques de Soria, 1998. 42-64.

Ruiz Martín, Felipe and Ángel García Sanz, ed. *Mesta, transhumancia y lana en la España moderna.* Barcelona: Crítica/Fundación Duques de Soria, 1998.

Sánchez, Alberto. "Los sonetos de *La Galatea.*" *La Galatea de Cervantes-cuatrocientos años después: Cervantes y lo pastoril.* Ed. Juan Bautista Avalle-Arce. Newark: Juan de la Cuesta, 1985. 17-36.

Sánchez, Magdalena S. *The Empress, the Queen, and the Nun: Women and Power at the Court of Philip III of Spain.* Baltimore: Johns Hopkins UP, 1998.

Sannazaro, Jacobo. *Opere Volgari.* Gimmi: Gius, Laterza & Figli, 1961.

———. *Arcadia & Piscatorial Eclogue.* Trans. Ralph Nash. Detroit: Wayne State University Press, 1966.

Sieber, Harry. "The Marcela-Grisóstomo Episode of Don Quijote." *Estudios Literarios de Hispanistas Norteamericanos dedicados a Helmut Hatzfeld con motivo de su 80 aniversario.* Ed. Josep M. Sola-Solé, Alessandro Crisafulli, and Bruno Damiani. Barcelona: Ediciones Hispam, 1974. 185-94.

Solé-Leris, Amadeu. *The Spanish Pastoral Novel.* Boston: Twayne, 1980.

Souviron López, Begoña. *La mujer en la ficción arcádica: aproximación a la novela pastoril española.* Frankfurt: Vervuert; Madrid: Iberoamericana, 1997.

Stagg, Geoffrey L. "The Composition and Revision of La Galatea." *Cervantes: Bulletin of the Cervantes Society of America* 14, no. 2 (1994): 9-25.

Subirats, J. "La *Diane* de Montemayor, roman à clef?" *Etudes Ibériques et Latino-Américaines, IVe congrès des hispanistes français (Poitiers, 18-20 mars 1967).* Paris: Presses Universitaires de France, 1968. 105-18.

Surtz, Ronald. *The Birth of a Theater: Dramatic Convention in the Spanish Theater from Juan del Encina to Lope de Vega.* Princeton: Publicaciones del Departamento de Lenguas y Literaturas Románicas de la Universidad de Princeton; Madrid: Castalia, 1979.

Thompson, Earl. "Shepherds as Spanish Society: Cervantes's View in One Comedia." *Varia hispanica: Homenaje a Alberto Porqueras Mayo.* Ed. Joseph L. Laurenti and Vern G. Williamsen. Kassel: Edition Reichenberger, 1989. 7-15.

Trambaioli, Marcella. "Notas sobre el papel de Lenio en *La Galatea:* ¿gracioso o 'pastor fino'?" *Romance Notes* 35, no. 1 (1994): 45-51.

Tresidder, Jack. *Dictionary of Symbols; an Illustrated Guide to Traditional Images, Icons, and Emblems.* San Francisco: Chronicle Books, 1997.

Valdés, Alfonso de. *Diálogo de las cosas acaecidas en Roma.* Ed. Rosa Navarro Durán. Madrid: Cátedra, 1992.

———. *Diálogo de Mercurio y Carón.* Ed. Rosa Navarro Durán. Madrid: Cátedra, 1999.

Vann, Richard T. *Century of Genius: European Thought, 1600-1700.* Englewood Cliffs: Prentice, 1967.

———. "Toward a New Lifestyle: Women in Preindustrial Capitalism." *Becoming Visible: Women in European History.* Ed. Renate Bridenthal and Claudia Koonz. Boston: Houghton, 1977. 192-216.

Vega, Garcilaso de la. *Poesías Castellanas Completas.* Ed. Elias L. Rivers. Madrid: Castalia, 1989.

Vega, Garcilaso de la. "Eclogue II." *The Works of Garcilaso de la Vega*. Ed. and trans. J.H. Wiffen. London: Hurst, Robinson, and Co., 1823. 198-265.
Vigil, Mariló. *La vida de las mujeres en los siglos XVI y XVII*. 2nd ed. Madrid: Siglo Veintiuno Editores, 1994.
Vives, Juan Luis. *Instrucción de la mujer cristiana*. 1524. Ed. Juan Justiniano and Elizabeth Teresa Howe. Madrid: Fundación Universitaria. Universidad Pontificia de Salamanca, 1995.
Vossler, Karl. *La poesía de la soledad en España*. Trans. Ramón de la Serna y Espina. Buenos Aires: Editorial Losada, 1946.
Wardropper, Bruce W. "The *Diana*: Revaluation and Interpretation." *Studies in Philology* 48 (1951): 126-44.
Weber, Alison. *Teresa of Avila and the Rhetoric of Femininity*. Princeton: Princeton UP, 1990.
Whinnom, Keith. "The Problem of the 'Best-Seller' in Spanish Golden-Age Literature." *Bulletin of Hispanic Studies* 57 (1980): 189-98.
White, Hayden. "The Noble Savage Theme as Fetish." *First images of America: the Impact of the New World on the Old*. Ed. Fredi Chiappelli, Michael J. B. Allen, and Robert Louis Benson. Vol. 1. Berkeley and Los Angeles: U of California P, 1976. 121-35.
Williams, Raymond. *Problems in Materialism and Culture: Selected Essays*. London: Verso, 1980, 1982.
——. *The Country and the City*. New York: Oxford UP, 1973.
Zamora, Margarita. *Reading Columbus*. Berkeley: U of California P, 1993.

INDEX

Alanio, 160, 162-64
Alba, Fernando de, 137-38
Albanio, 133-37, 139, 142
Alcalá Galán, Mercedes, 180n27
aldea (village), 35, 45, 46, 47, 48, 52, 100, 114, 125, 139, 163, 174, 178, 220, 227, 237. *See also corte;* Spain, and city/country dichotomy; pastoral literature, city/country dichotomy
Alfeo, 147
Alfonso X, 34
Alpers, Paul, 16, 17n4, 45n27, 82
Althusser, Louis, 26, 27n12, 39
Ambrosio, 222, 225, 230
Andresa, 154, 155, 156
anecdote, use of, 13
Angélica, 202, 204n10
Aphrodite, 92, 92n12
Ares, 55, 55n43
Ariosto, Ludovico, 202
Armas Wilson, Diana de, 23, 23n10, 201
Armia, 154, 155, 168
Arsenio, 144-45, 145n10, 147, 148n12
Arsileo, 111, 144-48, 145n10
Arsindo, 107
Artandro, 177-78
Artidoro, 174-77, 177n25, 190
Aurelio, 120
Avalle-Arce, Juan Bautista, 19, 25, 25n11, 158, 198n3, 222n27
Azáceta, José María, 81n4
Azar, Inés, 132-33, 133n4, 137-38, 137n8

Bacchus, 205
Baena, Julio, 23
Baroque, 197, 198, 198n3, 246

Bauer, Dale, 131, 131n1, 143
Belisa (*La Diana*), 88-89, 105n23, 144-48, 145n10, 148n12, 172, 176, 183, 192
Belisa (*La Galatea*), 193
Bellamy, Elizabeth Jane, 78n1
Bible, the, 80
Binche, palace of, 49, 51, 71
Blanca, 112, 179n26, 183, 184n31, 190, 191
Blecua, José Manuel, 180n27
Boccaccio, Giovanni, 80, 81
Boiardo, Matteo, 202
Boscán, Juan, 124n41
Boyce, Elizabeth, 180
Broeucq, Jacques de, 49
Bromberg, Rachel, 27n13
Burke, Kenneth, 16
Butler, Judith, 181n28, 182, 185, 195, 228n29

Calíope, 183n30
Camila, 133-36
cancioneros (songbooks), 81, 124n41
Capellanus, Andreas, 80
Carino (*Arcadia*), 84n8
Carino (*La Galatea*), 54, 108
Caro, Ana, 246
Carpio, Bernardo del, 51
Carrasco, Sansón, 240
Carvajal, Luisa de, 61
casa de los celos y selvas de Ardenia, La, 15, 26, 28, 132, 200-3, 202n8, 202n9, 205n11, 207, 207n13, 208. *See also* Angélica; Cervantes, Miguel de; Clori; Corinto; Reinaldo; Roldán; Rústico

Casalduero, Joaquín, 92n13
Casey, James, 34n8, 61n52
Catholicism. *See* religion
Celestina, La, 13
Celia, 158, 164-68, 167n21
Cervantes, Miguel de, 11, 15, 20, 22, 23-26, 23n10, 28, 44, 45, 47n30, 52-53, 57, 78, 89, 91, 98, 99, 104, 107, 111, 112n51, 115, 119, 120, 126, 131, 132, 142, 171n24, 175, 180, 180n27, 182n29, 183, 185n33, 187n35, 194, 195n36, 196, 197n2, 200-203, 201n6, 205n11, 206n12, 207n13, 208, 213-15, 219, 223n28, 225, 229, 237, 239, 240, 245-46, 246n34. *See also casa de los celos y selvas de Ardenia, La; Don Quixote; Galatea, La; Novelas Ejemplares; Persiles*
Chaide, Malón de, 67-68
chaos, theme of, 28, 37, 46, 113, 221
Charles V, 31-32, 31n4, 33n6, 49, 54n39, 70-71, 73, 141
Charles VIII, 21
Christianity. *See* religion
Cid, the, 51
Clori, 203-10, 210n17
Cody, Richard, 16
conduct manuals, 14, 64-65
Cooper, Helen, 81
Corinto, 203-9, 204n10
corte (urban court), 45, 46-48, 52-53, 138, 165, 200, 208, 220. *See also aldea;* pastoral literature, city/country dichotomy; Spain, and city/country dichotomy
court, and courtiers' standards of behavior, 14, 41, 45, 50, 70, 80n2, 81, 96, 178, 184; and culture of, 13, 14, 20-23, 28n14, 46-47, 49, 49n33, 54, 56, 61, 65, 70, 110, 137-39, 208, 211; and theater, 14, 20, 24. *See also* love, courtly
Covarrubias Orozco, Sebastián de, 54n39, 218n24, 229
Crawford, J. P. Wickersham, 21
Creel, Bryant, 92n13
Crisio, 107, 124-25
Cronos, 55, 55n42
Cruz, Anne, 36n12, 37n13, 61n48, 63, 96, 140-41, 214n22
Cruz, Magdalena de la, 64
Cull, Jonathan, 112, 112n31, 122
Cupid, 91n11, 117, 186, 207, 207n14, 208n15

Damiani, Bruno, 22, 23
Damón, 124, 125
Danae, 208n16
Dante Alighieri, 80, 80n3
Danteo, 88, 105-6, 154-57, 168
Daranio, 112-13, 125, 155
Darst, David H., 153n15
Davies, Tony, 96
death, topic of, 22, 23, 28, 38, 73, 107, 139, 141-42, 167, 168, 216-17, 221, 223
Delio, 56, 56n44, 111
Diana (character), 22, 56-57, 86-89, 103-4, 106, 106n24, 111-13, 113n35, 114, 115, 123-24, 128, 130, 143, 148n13, 150-55, 153n15, 161, 194, 237
Diana (goddess), 70, 98
Diana, La, 13-15, 19, 22-28, 27n13, 44-48, 50-54, 56, 58, 65-68, 65n56, 66n60, 68n61, 70, 74, 76, 85-88, 92, 92n13, 97, 103, 105, 109-10, 111n30, 113, 123, 126-32, 142-44, 147-48, 150, 150n14, 154, 156-59, 168-70, 170n22, 172, 176, 196-98, 202, 211, 214, 216, 217, 219, 224, 230, 239. *See also* Alanio; Alfeo; Andresa; Armia; Arsileo; Belisa; Celia; Danteo; Diana; Duarda; Fabio; Felicia; Felis; Felismena; Montemayor, Jorge de; Selvagia; Sireno; Sylvano; Ysmenia
Diego Vila, Juan, 195n36
Domínguez Ortiz, Antonio, 60, 61n49
Don Quixote (book), 15, 20, 22, 26, 28, 47n30, 132, 142, 194, 200-202, 210-12, 216, 219, 224, 230, 233-34, 240, 245-46. *See also* Carrasco, Sansón; Cervantes, Miguel de; Don Quixote (character); Eugenio; Grisóstomo; Guillermo; Leandra; Marcela; Panza, Teresa; Pedro; Rosa, Vicente de la; Sanchica; Sancho
Don Quixote (character), 210-16, 212n20, 214n22, 215n23, 221, 230-32, 235, 236, 240, 243, 244, 245
Duarda, 88n10, 106, 154-57, 168
Dudley, Edward, 198n3
Durling, Robert M., 80n3

Egido, Aurora, 188
El Saffar, Ruth, 22, 212
Elicio, 57-58, 89, 90-92, 97, 98-100, 99n18, 104, 106, 108-10, 124-26, 128, 172-73, 186, 186n34, 214, 223n28
Elisa, 25

Elliott, John, 31, 34n8, 38, 198
Elpino, 84
Empson, William, 16, 17n4
Encina, Juan del, 20, 31
Enríquez, María, 140
epithalamia, 112
Erasmus, 30
Erastro, 57-58, 89-92, 99-100, 99n18, 104, 110, 118, 120, 124-25, 173, 186, 207n13, 214
Ergasto, 82
Eugenio, 210, 237-40
Extremadura, 34

Fabio, 166n20
Felicia, 47-52, 47n30, 54, 70, 76, 97, 98, 111n30, 113, 113n35, 115, 122, 123, 146, 151, 157, 164, 172
Felis, 55, 164-67, 166n20, 169
Felismena, 49-50, 52, 54-56, 105n23, 155, 158, 164-69, 164n19, 172; and role as Valerio, 164-69, 166n20
Ferdinand I, 31
Fernández Cañadas-Greenwood, Pilar, 23, 171, 182n29
Feros, Antonio, 199, 200n5
Ferrer Valls, Teresa, 20, 21
Ficino, Marsilio, 101; and *Commentary*, 159; and *Symposium on Love*, 101
Filis, 108
fin' amours. See love, courtly
Finello, Dominick, 206n12, 238n33
Florisa, 52, 91-92, 173-74, 176-78, 179n 26, 183-86, 188, 195
Fonseca, Antonio de, 51
Forcione, Alban, 112n32, 113n33, 117n36, 172, 219
Frenk, Margit, 182, 183, 188
Freud, Sigmund, 93-94, 94n14, 96, 97, 109, 109n26, 109n27, 109n28, 110, 110n29, 127, 127n43. See also narcissism; psychoanalysis
Friedman, Edward, 202-3

Galatea (character), 24-25, 52, 57-58, 68n61, 89-92, 97-99, 99n18, 104-7, 116, 120, 128, 130, 172-74, 176-79, 183-88, 183n30, 186n34
Galatea, La, 15, 19, 22-28, 44-45, 47n30, 52-54, 56-67, 74, 92, 97, 100, 103-4, 106-7, 109-13, 115, 120, 122, 124-32, 127n42, 143, 170-74, 170n22, 179-80, 179n26, 180n27, 182-83. See also Ar-

sindo; Artandro; Artidoro; Aurelio; Blanca; Cervantes, Miguel de; Crisio; Damón; Daranio; Elicio; Erastro; Filis; Florisa; Galercio; Gelasia; Grisaldo; Lauso; Lenio; Leonarda; Lisandro; Marsilio; Maurisa; Mierno; Nísida; Orfenio; Orompo; Polydora; Rosaura; Silerio; Silveria; Teolinda; Thyrsis; Timbrio
Galercio, 108, 177n25
Galicio, 83
Garber, Marjorie, 78n1
Gaylord, Mary, 24, 107n25, 112, 121
Gelasia, 116, 118, 179n26, 183, 194-95, 195n36, 219
Gicovate, Bernard, 132-33, 132n2, 135
Gifford, Terry, 17, 17n4, 18n5, 20
Ginés de Sepúlveda, 38, 39n17, 141
Goldberg, Jonathan, 78n1, 181, 183
Golden Age, 13n1, 14, 20, 30, 31, 32, 38, 39, 40, 51, 55, 55n42, 65, 180, 180n27, 200, 211, 212, 212n20, 213-16, 214n22, 215n23, 231-33, 235, 245. See also utopian view
González, Fernán, 51
Graces, Three, 91-92, 92n12
Greenblatt, Stephen, 78
Grisaldo, 112, 177-79
Grisóstomo, 216-17, 219-22, 222n27, 225-30, 233
Grosz, Elizabeth, 94n15, 145n11, 170n 23
Guevara, Antonio de, 30, 32, 46
Guillermo, 217
Guzmán de Alfarache, 13

Haber, Judith, 18
hagiographies, 15
Hapsburg dynasty, 31, 41, 54, 54n39, 55-56, 71, 73
Hathaway, Robert, 236n32
Hebreo, León, 101, 101n21
Hephaestus, 159n18
Herrera, Martín de, 21
hidalgo class, 25, 218
Horace, 46
humanism, 66n59
Hutchinson, Steven, 95n16, 130

Irigaray, Luce, 170n22
Iris, 90-91
Iron Age, 38, 202, 204, 212, 216, 231-32, 235

irony, 47n30, 68, 97, 135, 198, 201, 207, 218, 232, 241
Isabel Clara Eugenia, 61
Isabel of Portugal, 61
Isabel I, 31

Jakobson, Roman, 41-42
Jameson, Fredric, 24, 39, 39n18, 40, 40n19, 42-44, 43n25, 59n47, 78, 170. See also Golden Age
Jehenson, Yvonne, 223, 224, 230n30
Johnson, Carroll, 23, 88n10, 143, 147, 153n15, 163, 168, 211n19
Jones, Ann, 78n1
Jove, 208n16
Juana of Portugal, 46, 46n29, 49, 61, 71-73, 71n63

Kamen, Henry, 33n7

Lacan, Jacques, 40, 40n19, 40n20, 93, 94, 122n40, 126, 181
Lapesa, Rafael, 132n2
Las Casas, Bartolomé de, 38
Lauso, 23n10, 115-16, 119-20, 203-9
Leandra, 216, 233-40, 236n32, 245
Lenio, 115, 116-20, 120n37, 127n42
León, Fray Luis de, 46, 62
León, Lucrecia de, 64
Leonarda, 175, 177, 177n25, 179n26
Lerma, Duke of, 199
libros de caballería. See literature, Spanish
libros de entretenimiento. See literature, Spanish
libros de pastores. See pastoral literature
Lisandro, 108-9, 128
literature, Spanish, 21, 29, 143; *amor cortés* literature, 80, 80n2; devotional literature, 13n1, 15; *libros de caballería* (books of chivalry), 15, 48, 50n33, 67; *libros de entretenimiento* (entertainment books), 13; *novelas cortesanas* (court novels), 20. See also novel, chivalric; pastoral literature
locus amoenus, 25, 47, 52, 58, 76, 82, 85, 86, 122, 134, 138, 139, 195, 215n23, 232. See also pastoral literature, bower; pastoral literature, city/ country dichotomy; Spain, and city/country dichotomy
Logisto, 84

Longus, 81
Lope de Vega, Félix, 25
López Estrada, Francisco, 14, 19, 28n 14, 91n11, 158
lords, feudal, 35
Lorraine, Tamsin, 169-70, 170n22, 179
Louis of Hungary and Bohemia, 70n62
love, courtly, 15, 67, 80
love, pastoral, 14, 58, 70, 79, 93, 106n24, 116, 121, 150, 153n15, 157, 164, 169, 185, 228, 237; and arranged marriage, 106, 112, 120, 173, 188, 223n28; and chastity, 58, 64, 66, 69, 80n2, 90, 97, 98, 99, 112, 118, 148, 176, 184, 204, 213, 215, 219, 226, 231, 240; and *desamorado*, 113, 114, 115, 116, 119, 123, 127n42, 151, 239; and *enamorada*, 76, 176, 184, 193; and *enamorado*, 111, 114, 115, 116, 119, 120, 123, 127n42, 172, 194; and marriage, 56, 68n61, 93, 99, 111-13, 111n30, 113n33, 175, 189, 201, 218, 240, 241; and suffering, 45, 77, 80, 80n2, 84-85, 97-98, 103, 105-8, 107n25, 110, 111, 113n33, 117, 118, 123, 125, 126, 148, 161, 163, 164, 187, 191, 193, 214, 216, 229; and wedding, 112, 112n31, 113n33, 175

Madrid, 71, 73
Madrid, Francisco de, 21
Maravall, José Antonio, 30, 32, 32n5, 33n6, 38n16, 85, 201, 201n6, 213, 213n21
Marcela, 194, 216-37, 218n25, 221n26, 223n28, 228n29, 233n31, 240, 245
March, Ausias, 80
Margaret of Austria, 61
Margaret of the Cross, 61
María Manuela of Portugal, 71
María of Hungary, 49
Mariscal, George, 233
Márquez Villanueva, Francisco, 55
Mars, 51, 55, 139, 164
Marsilio, 101, 107, 124-25, 193
Martin, Adrienne, 158, 180n27
Marxism, 40
masques. See court, and theater
Maurisa, 107
Mazzio, Carla, 78n1
Menéndez Pelayo, Marcelino, 19, 158
Mendoza women's clan, 61

Mesta, The, 34, 34n8
Minerva, 159, 159n18, 163
Montemayor, Jorge de, 13, 23-25, 44-49, 46n29, 52, 55, 56, 70-71, 73, 78, 85, 86, 97, 98, 103, 105, 106n24, 111, 122, 132, 142-44, 147-48, 162, 197n2, 210, 214, 237, 239. *See also Diana, La*
Moors, 37
Morgan, Thaïs, 181, 183
Mother Nature, 212-14
Mujica, Barbara, 22, 215n23

Nalle, Sara T., 13n1, 50n33
narcissism, 78, 93-95, 94n14, 95n16, 100, 102, 109-10, 113, 116, 120, 122-23, 122n40, 136, 143-44, 150, 153, 169-70, 170n22, 170n23, 173, 185, 195n36, 203-4, 210, 215, 216, 219, 224, 229, 230, 236
Narcissus, 94-95
Nemoroso, 25, 136-38, 137n8, 142
Neoplatonism, 15, 16, 101, 126, 159, 225, 226
Neptune, 159n18
New World, the, 23, 38, 61
Nísida, 53, 107n25, 112, 179n26, 183, 183n30, 184n31, 190-93
novel, chivalric. *See* literature, Spanish
novelas cortesanas. *See* literature, Spanish
Novelas Ejemplares, 20

Olivares, Julián, 180, 200
Orfenio, 107, 125
Orompo, 107
ouroboros, 55
Ovid, 30, 205n11, 213; and *Ars Amatoria*, 80; and *Metamorphoses*, 212, 213

Pallas, 55, 55n41, 164n19
Panza, Teresa, 241
Paris, Gaston, 80, 80n2
parody, 22, 26, 28, 132, 142, 198, 201, 219, 224, 229, 232, 239, 246
pastoral literature:
  as entertainment, 15, 16, 22, 39
  bower, 22, 25, 27, 41, 45, 47, 49, 50, 52, 53, 59, 67, 68, 70, 79, 90, 101, 107, 108, 112, 121, 128, 130, 132, 133, 134, 144, 147, 164, 165, 172, 175, 178, 179, 184, 188, 196, 202, 211, 213, 214, 219, 227, 238, 245

city/country dichotomy, 18, 46, 48-49, 53, 245
class distinctions in, 14, 25, 27, 40, 41, 42, 50, 51, 56, 57, 62, 91, 104, 110, 128, 144, 203, 206, 241, 243, 244
early modern, 16, 17, 20, 22, 24, 26, 28, 29-30, 40-42, 76, 78, 85, 95, 97, 110, 128, 160, 197
gender distinctions. *See* pastoral literature, portrayal of shepherds; pastoral literature, portrayal of women
homoerotic desire, 158-59, 164-70
idealization of nature, 16, 18, 29, 44-45, 46n28, 52, 77, 81-82, 135, 195
love. *See* love, pastoral
narrative voice, 28, 88-89, 91, 112, 143, 152, 157, 172, 230
Pérez de Herrera, Cristóbal, 63
portrayal of shepherds:
  characteristics of, 19, 24, 27, 29, 32, 45, 46, 47, 52, 56n44, 57-59, 67, 76, 77, 79, 81, 85, 92n13, 93, 95, 97, 98, 102, 112, 113, 121-24, 127, 150, 153, 169, 187, 202, 210, 213, 216, 217, 220, 221n26, 230, 239. *See also* narcissism
  and homogenous community, 27, 78, 79, 85, 103-5, 110-11, 120, 124, 179, 215, 218, 239
  and use of poetry, 82, 84, 103, 123, 126, 214, 239
portrayal of women, 25, 28, 29, 53, 58, 59, 65-70, 72-75, 77, 80n2, 82, 86, 88-89, 92n13, 128-32, 148-150, 170-72, 170n22, 184, 185, 188, 190, 191, 193-96, 203, 210, 213-15, 215n23, 216, 219, 222, 223, 225, 227-28, 230, 232-33, 236-40, 245-46
  and *esquiva*, 172, 174, 184, 185, 186n34, 193, 194, 222, 223
  and female community, 105n23, 171-74, 177, 179, 179n26, 180, 183-84, 192
  and physical beauty, 52, 58, 65, 66, 69, 71, 73-74, 77, 82, 85, 86, 88-89, 92, 99, 101, 106-7, 107n25, 118, 140, 145, 165, 213-14, 216, 218, 225-27, 230, 234, 236, 238, 241, 242

and subversive behavior, 143-44, 146, 148, 148n13, 156, 234
and use of poetry, 180-84, 180n27, 188-90, 192, 194-96
as object of man's desire, 85, 86, 89, 92, 92n13, 94-95, 97-98, 99, 106n24, 109n27, 113, 115, 117, 120, 144, 145-48, 145n31, 150-52, 153n15, 157, 164, 169, 185, 208, 215n23, 216, 220, 223, 223n28, 225, 230n30, 236, 238, 239, 242
See also pastoral literature, homoerotic desire; subjectivity, and female
reader of, 41, 47-48, 51, 55, 56, 74, 77, 79, 97, 102, 106, 113, 120, 127, 128, 138, 139, 153, 157, 159, 160, 163, 167, 187n35, 202, 203, 221n26
religious values in, 23, 39, 40, 59, 80n2, 144, 243
sexual desire in, 27, 54, 59, 77-78, 99, 99n18, 133, 135-36, 137, 144, 145n31, 146-48, 158-64, 166-70, 176-77, 179, 232, 237, 239-42, 245. *See also* pastoral literature, homoerotic desire
See also locus amoenus; pastoral tradition, Italian; topography, pastoral
pastoral tradition, Italian, 81, 84, 186, 197n2
patriarchal values, 25, 26, 27, 28, 41, 59, 62, 64-67, 70, 77, 110, 128, 131, 152, 153, 168, 170n22, 181, 181n28, 188, 193, 196, 223, 224, 225, 229, 236, 236n32, 246
Patterson, Annabel, 17
Pedro, 217-18
Pérez, José, 88n9, 111, 153n15
Pérez Toribio, Montserrat, 228n29
Perry, Mary Elizabeth, 61n49
Perry, T. Anthony, 98, 100, 153n15
Perseus, 208n16
Persiles, 201
Petrarch, 25, 80, 80n3, 81, 82, 84, 180, 186, 193; and *Bucolicum Carmen*, 81; and *Rime Sparse*, 80, 80n3, 124n41
Philip I, 32, 71, 199
Philip III, 199-200, 200n5
Philip IV, 200
Phoebus, 139

Poggioli, Renato, 16, 113n34, 221n26, 222, 233
Polydora, 122
Portugal, 23, 46, 46n29, 71, 71n63, 72, 73
Pradilla, Bachiller de la (Hernando de la), 21
psychoanalysis, 78-79, 78n1, 95-96, 100, 145n11
psychology, group, 78, 109, 109n26, 110n29, 120

Rallo, Asunción, 13n2, 14
Reinaldos, 202, 204n10
religion, 23, 37, 39, 40, 59-61, 63-64, 66n59, 71, 73, 81, 96, 110, 128, 144, 199, 200n5; and Catholicism, 37, 51; and Catholic monarchy, 20, 31, 41, 51; and Christianity, 32, 37-38, 54, 63-64, 76, 119, 159, 178, 233; and church doctrine, 64, 68-69, 109n26, 159, 199; and Jews, 37. *See also* pastoral literature, religious values in
Renaissance, 21, 24, 25, 29, 30, 38, 46, 66, 78, 81, 121, 132, 143, 183, 197, 198, 199, 201, 246
Rentana, Fernández de, 71
Rhodes, Elizabeth, 23, 66, 66n58, 66n59, 66n60, 107n25, 168
Rivers, Elias, 114, 132n3
Roldán, 202, 204n10
Rosa, Vicente de la, 234-35
Rosaura, 112, 177-79
Rosenmeyer, Thomas, 16
Ruiz Martín, Felipe, 34, 34n8
Rústico, 203-10, 207n14

Salicio, 25, 135-37, 139, 142
Sánchez, Alberto, 180n27
Sanchica, 216, 240-45
Sancho, 210-12, 240-45
Sannazaro, Jacobo, 82, 85; and *Arcadia*, 80, 81, 83-84, 134, 136. *See also* Elpino; Ergasto; Galicio; Logisto
Sant Jordi, Jordi de, 80
Saturn, 29, 55, 55n42
Selvagia, 105n23, 106n24, 113n35, 114, 123, 130, 143, 148-52, 148n13, 158-65, 159n18, 169, 172
Severo, 137-38, 137n8, 142
Sieber, Harry, 24, 221, 221n26, 233n31
Silerio, 53, 107, 107n25, 112, 190-91

Silveria, 112, 113n33, 125
Sireno, 45, 56, 86-88, 88n10, 97-98, 103-6, 106n24, 111-15, 123-24, 128, 143, 146, 148, 148n13, 150-152, 155, 157, 160, 163, 214, 239
Solé-Leris, Amadeu, 81
song, amoebaean, 82, 104, 105, 24
Souviron López, Begoña, 185n33
Spain, 15, 21, 24, 28-33, 33n7, 37-38, 40-41, 46-47, 51, 53, 58, 76, 81, 197, 200; and city/country dichotomy, 29, 36; and religion, *see* religion; and women's role in society, 60-67, 61n49, 66n59, 70-74
Stagg, Geoffrey, 23
Stallybrass, Peter, 78n1
subjectivity, 76-78, 95, 100, 102, 126, 170n22, 204; and female, 27, 79, 88, 92, 131, 144, 145n11, 170, 180, 201, 208, 210, 224, 225; and male, 74, 95, 99, 124, 130, 196, 233
Surtz, Ronald, 21
Sylvano, 56, 56n44, 85-88, 88n10, 98, 103-6, 106n24, 110-15, 113n35, 123-24, 128, 143, 146, 148, 148n13, 150-51, 153n15, 160, 163-64, 214, 239

Tagus, River, 24, 25, 52, 106, 107, 200n4
Teolinda, 130, 174-78, 177n25, 180n27, 183, 188-90
Teresa of Ávila, St., 61, 64
theater. *See* court, and theater
Theocritus, 16, 45n27
Thompson, Earl, 202
Thyrsis, 120, 125, 126
Timbrio, 53, 112, 190, 191, 193
Tirsi, 99-101, 100n20, 108, 117, 119-20, 125, 126, 127n42

Tolliver, Joyce, 131n1
topography, pastoral, 14-16, 21, 25, 26, 43, 46, 49, 51, 79, 85, 86, 132, 139, 154, 200, 203, 210, 212, 214, 223n28, 244
Torquemada, Tomás de, 30
Trambaioli, Marcella, 120n37, 171n24
Trevor, Douglas, 78n1

utopian view, 22, 31, 32, 42, 43, 43n25, 170, 172, 203, 210, 233. *See also* Golden Age; Jameson, Frederic

Valdés, Alfonso de, 32, 32n5
Valencia de Don Juan, Dukes of, 46
Vega, Garcilaso de la, 25, 38n16, 85, 96, 101n21, 132, 188, 197, 198n3; and *Elegía II*, 25, 27, 132-33, 132n3, 133n4, 135, 137-42. *See also* Albanio; Camila; Enriquez, María; Nemoroso; Salicio; Severo
Venus, 55, 160, 164, 164n19
Vespucci, Amerigo, 38
Vigil, Mariló, 13n3, 64, 67, 69
Vilanova family, 51
Virgil, 16, 24, 31, 44, 46, 46n28, 57, 79, 81, 85
Vives, Juan Luis, 30, 63, 64
Vossler, Karl, 102n22

Wardropper, Bruce, 66, 143, 158
Whinnom, Keith, 13n1, 65n56
Williams, Raymond, 17, 17n4, 18n5, 19, 42

Ynduráin, Francisco, 180n27
Ysmenia, 159-65

Zayas, María de, 246, 246n34

NORTH CAROLINA STUDIES IN THE ROMANCE LANGUAGES AND LITERATURES

I.S.B.N. Prefix 0-8078-

Recent Titles

PUERTO RICAN CULTURAL IDENTITY AND THE WORK OF LUIS RAFAEL SÁNCHEZ, by John Dimitri Perivolaris. 2000. (No. 268). *-9272-6.*
MANNERISM AND BAROQUE IN SEVENTEENTH-CENTURY FRENCH POETRY: THE EXAMPLE OF TRISTAN L'HERMITE, by James Crenshaw Shepard. 2001. (No: 269). *-9273-4.*
RECLAIMING THE BODY: MARÍA DE ZAYA'S EARLY MODERN FEMINISM, by Lisa Vollendorf. 2001. (No. 270). *-9274-2.*
FORGED GENEALOGIES: SAINT-JOHN PERSE'S CONVERSATIONS WITH CULTURE, by Carol Rigolot. 2001. (No. 271). *-9275-0.*
VISIONES DE ESTEREOSCOPIO (PARADIGMA DE HIBRIDACIÓN EN EL ARTE Y LA NARRATIVA DE LA VANGUARDIA ESPAÑOLA), por María Soledad Fernández Utrera. 2001. (No. 272). *-9276-9.*
TRANSPOSING ART INTO TEXTS IN FRENCH ROMANTIC LITERATURE, by Henry F. Majewski. 2002. (No. 273). *-9277-7.*
IMAGES IN MIND: LOVESICKNESS, SPANISH SENTIMENTAL FICTION AND *DON QUIJOTE*, by Robert Folger. 2002. (No. 274). *-9278-5.*
INDISCERNIBLE COUNTERPARTS: THE INVENTION OF THE TEXT IN FRENCH CLASSICAL DRAMA, by Christopher Braider. 2002. (No. 275). *-9279-3.*
SAVAGE SIGHT/CONSTRUCTED NOISE. POETIC ADAPTATIONS OF PAINTERLY TECHNIQUES IN THE FRENCH AND AMERICAN AVANT-GARDES, by David LeHardy Sweet. 2003. (No. 276). *-9281-5.*
AN EARLY BOURGEOIS LITERATURE IN GOLDEN AGE SPAIN. *LAZARILLO DE TORMES, GUZMÁN DE ALFARACHE* AND BALTASAR GRACIÁN, by Francisco J. Sánchez. 2003. (No. 277). *-9280-7.*
METAFACT: ESSAYISTIC SCIENCE IN EIGHTEENTH-CENTURY FRANCE, by Lars O. Erickson. 2004. (No. 278). *-9282-3.*
THE INVENTION OF THE EYEWITNESS. A HISTORY OF TESTIMONY IN FRANCE, by Andrea Frisch. 2004. (No. 279). *-9283-1.*
SUBJECT TO CHANGE: THE LESSONS OF LATIN AMERICAN WOMEN'S *TESTIMONIO* FOR TRUTH, FICTION, AND THEORY, by Joanna R. Bartow. 2005. (No. 280). *-9284-X.*
QUESTIONING RACINIAN TRAGEDY, by John Campbell. 2005. (No. 281). *-9285-8.*
THE POLITICS OF FARCE IN CONTEMPORARY SPANISH AMERICAN THEATRE, by Priscilla Meléndez. 2006. (No. 282). *-9286-6.*
MODERATING MASCULINITY IN EARLY MODERN CULTURE, by Todd W. Reeser. 2006. (No. 283). *-9287-4.*
PORNOBOSCODIDASCALUS LATINUS (1624). KASPAR BARTH'S NEO-LATIN TRANSLATION OF *CELESTINA*, by Enrique Fernández. 2006. (No. 284). *-9288-2.*
JACQUES ROUBAUD AND THE INVENTION OF MEMORY, by Jean-Jacques F. Poucel. 2006. (No. 285). *-9289-0.*
THE "I" OF HISTORY. SELF-FASHIONING AND NATIONAL CONSCIOUSNESS IN JULES MICHELET, by Vivian Kogan. 2006. (No. 286). *-9290-4.*
BUCOLIC METAPHORS: HISTORY, SUBJECTIVITY, AND GENDER IN THE EARLY MODERN SPANISH PASTORAL, by Rosilie Hernández-Pecoraro. 2006. (No. 287). *-9291-2.*

When ordering please cite the *ISBN Prefix* plus the last four digits for each title.

Send orders to: University of North Carolina Press
P.O. Box 2288
Chapel Hill, NC 27515-2288
U.S.A.
www.uncpress.unc.edu
FAX: 919 966-3829

The Department of Romance Studies Digital Arts and Collaboration Lab at the University of North Carolina at Chapel Hill is proud to support the digitization of the North Carolina Studies in the Romance Languages and Literatures series.

www.ingramcontent.com/pod-product-compliance
Lightning Source LLC
Chambersburg PA
CBHW030616230426
43661CB00053B/2017